Practical Cookery

Fish & Seafood

Fish & Seafood

p

This is a Parragon Publishing Book
First published in 2000

Parragon Publishing
Queen Street House
4 Queen Street
Bath BA1 1HE, UK

ISBN: 0-75253-966-3

Printed in Indonesia

NOTE
Unless otherwise stated, milk is assumed to be whole fat, eggs are large, and pepper
is freshly ground black pepper.

Recipes using uncooked eggs should be
avoided by infants, the elderly, pregnant women, and anyone
suffering from an illness.

Contents

Introduction 8

Soups

Snacks, Light Meals, and Salads

Pasta & Noodles

Rice, Legumes, & Grains

Low Fat Dishes

Oriental Dishes

Mediterranean Dishes

Introduction

Seafood rightly deserves its image as a healthy food. It is high in protein and with the added bonus of oily fish, such as mackerel and herring, being high in polyunsaturated fat—this is the one that helps reduce cholesterol levels.

White fish are a good source of minerals as well as being low in fat, especially if poached, steamed, or lightly grilled. Although shellfish have been linked with high cholesterol, they are also low in saturated fats and are therefore fine eaten in moderation. The sheer variety of fish and shellfish is staggering. If you decided to eat seafood just once a week, you could go for a whole year without eating the same dish twice. Seafood is also quick and easy to prepare, making it an attractive ingredient to the busy cook. Often sold ready-to-cook fish can be prepared in minutes and most shellfish is sold already cooked, needing even less preparation.

Fish is also very good value for money compared to meat, as there is much less waste and no fat or gristle to contend with. Therefore making fish a regular part of your diet makes a lot of sense.

Buying Fish and Shellfish

Wherever you are shopping for fish, at your local trusted fish store or supermarket, the guidelines are the same:

- The eyes of the fish should be clear, bright, and moist. Fish with dull, grey, or cloudy eyes should be avoided.
- The gills of the fish should be bright red or pink, not dull and grey.
- The fish should smell of the sea and nothing else.
- If you press the fish lightly with your thumb, the flesh should spring back, leaving little or no imprint.
- The shells of hinged shellfish, such as oysters, mussels, and clams, should be tightly closed prior to cooking. If they are slightly open, tap them sharply. If they do not close, discard them.
- Cooked shellfish should smell fresh, with no hint of ammonia. If available, check the use-by-date.

Storing

As you never know how long ago the fish was caught, especially in a supermarket, it is best to buy fish and cook it on the same day. Unfortunately, modern refrigerators are not ideal places to store fish as they tend to have a temperature of about 38°F and fish is best kept at

Introduction

32°F. If you have to keep fish, do not keep it for more than one or two days. Put the fish into a plastic container and scatter over some ice. Cover with plastic wrap and keep in the coldest part of the refrigerator.

Firmer fleshed fish, such as turbot, Dover sole, and angler fish, freeze better than less firm-fleshed fish like bass, lemon sole and plaice

but all will deteriorate over a relatively short period. Oily fish is the least successful when frozen. However, if you have to keep your fish for more than a day or two, then freezing is the best option. Ensure that you thaw fish thoroughly and slowly before cooking.

Preparation

How much preparation your fish needs depends on where you buy it. Supermarkets may have a wet fish counter with a trained fish store on hand while others sell their fish vacuum-packed. Many fish are sold already scaled and gutted, and are often available either whole or filleted. It is usually cheaper, however, to buy a whole fish and prepare it yourself. A fish store will usually do this job for you for the price of a whole fish. However, it is not difficult to do yourself and only

takes some practice.

Equipment

Although, in general, you do not need a great deal of specialist equipment, there are a few items you might consider if you plan on cooking a lot of fish. If, for example, you are planning on poaching whole fish, then a wise investment would be a fish kettle. This is an oblong stainless steel pan with a lifter and lid. They usually come in several sizes.

A wok or large, heavy-bottomed skillet is useful for frying and stir-frying. If you like to steam fish you might like to consider a double boiler, bamboo steamer, or electric steamer. A thermometer is useful for deep-frying as is a deep-frying basket and large pan.

If you intend cleaning your own fish, a good filleting knife is a must. Tweezers are also useful for removing

Introduction

small bones. Different fish suit different cooking methods but, as a general rule, poaching, steaming, and stewing tend to produce moister results than broiling, baking, or grilling. Drying out can be minimized, however, if the latter three methods are used at sufficiently high temperatures to reduce moisture loss by cooking the fish very quickly.

Poaching

the fish is immersed in a poaching liquid, which might be a court-bouillon, fish stock, milk, beer, or

cider. Bring the liquid to a boil and as soon as it boils, remove the pan from the heat, and leave the fish to finish cooking in the residual heat. This method helps to prevent overcooking and is also excellent if you want to serve the fish cold.

Steaming

Both fish and shellfish benefit from being steamed. Again, a flavored liquid can be used for the steaming, which will impart some of its flavor to the fish as it is being cooked. This method is especially good for keeping the fish moist and the flavor delicate. Steaming can be done in a fish kettle, double boiler, or steamer inserted over a pan of boiling water.

Stewing

Either whole fish or smaller pieces can be cooked in liquid along with other ingredients, such as

vegetables, as a stew. The fish flavors the liquid as it cooks, giving a distinctive flavor.

Broiling

This is one of the quickest and easiest cooking methods for fish. Cook either whole fish, steaks, or fillets. Shellfish can also be broiled, but may need halving lengthways first. Whatever you are cooking, ensure that the broiler is on its highest setting and that the fish is cooked as close to the heat source as possible. A grill is also a very useful tool for broiling fish. Brush the fish with butter, oil, or a marinade before and during cooking to ensure that the flesh remains moist.

Baking and Roasting

This covers all methods of cooking in the oven, including open roasting, casseroling, or en papillote. This is a

Introduction

good method to choose for entertaining because, once the dish is in the oven, you are free to attend to other things.

Deep-Frying

The fish is either coated in batter, flour, or bread crumbs and deep fried in oil. You need a large, heavy-bottemed saucepan or a deep fat fryer. Large pieces of fish in batter are best cooked at a lower temperature of 350°F which allows the fish to cook without burning the batter. Smaller pieces of fish, like goujons

in breadcrumbs, should be cooked at a higher temperature of 375°F. Drain deep-fried items well on paper towels to ensure that they remain crisp.

Shallow or Pan-Frying

This is a quick method for cooking fish and shellfish and can take as little as 3–4 minutes. A shallow layer of oil or butter and oil is heated in a skillet, the fish added, and cooked until just tender, and lightly browned. A good non-stick skillet is an essential piece

of equipment. The argument for increasing the amount of fish and seafood in our diets is compelling. Fish and seafood can provide variety, versatility, creativity, and luxury as well as being much more healthy than meat. Why not give it a try?

Fresh Fish Stock

MAKES 7½ CUPS

1 head of a cod or salmon, etc, plus the trimmings, skin, and bones or just the trimmings, skin, and bones

1-2 onions, sliced

1 carrot, sliced

1-2 celery stalks, sliced

good squeeze of lemon juice

1 Bouquet Garni or 2 fresh or dried bay leaves

1 Wash the fish head and trimmings and place in a saucepan. Cover with water and bring to a boil.

2 Remove any scum with a draining spoon, then add the remaining ingredients. Cover and simmer for about 30 minutes.

3 Strain and cool. Store in the refrigerator and use within 2 days.

How to Use This Book

Each recipe contains a wealth of useful information, including a breakdown of nutritional quantites, preparation, and cooking times, and level of difficulty. All of this information is explained in detail below.

The nutritional information provided for each recipe is per serving or per portion. Optional ingredients, variations, or serving suggestions have not been included in the calculations.

The number of chef's hats represents the difficulty of each recipe, ranging from easy (1 chef's hat) to difficult (5 chef's hats).

This amount of time represents the preparation of ingredients, including cooling, chiling, and soaking times.

This represents the cooking time.

The ingredients for each recipe are listed in the order that they are used.

158 Practical Fish and Seafood

Baked Trout Mexican-Style

Make this dish as hot or as mild as you like by adjusting the amount of red chilli. The green chillies are milder and add a pungency to the dish.

NUTRITIONAL INFORMATION

Calories . . . . .329 Sugars 5g
Protein . . . . .53g Fat 10g
Carbohydrate . . . .6g Saturates 2g

10 MINS   30 MINS

SERVES 4

INGREDIENTS

4 trout, 225 g/8 oz each

1 small bunch fresh coriander (cilantro)

4 shallots, shredded finely

1 small yellow (bell) pepper, deseeded and very finely chopped

1 small red (bell) pepper, deseeded and very finely chopped

2 green chillies, deseeded and finely chopped

1–2 red chillies, deseeded and finely chopped

1 tbsp lemon juice

½ tbsp white wine vinegar

2 tsp caster (superfine) sugar

salt and pepper

fresh coriander (cilantro), to garnish

salad leaves, to serve

COOK'S TIP

For the chilli bean rice, cook 225 g/8 oz/1¼ cup long-grain white rice. Drain and rinse a 400 g/14 oz can kidney beans and stir into the rice with 1 tsp each of ground cumin and coriander Stir in 4 tbsp chopped fresh coriander (cilantro) and season.

1 Preheat the oven to 190°C/250°F/Gas Mark 4. Wash the trout and pat dry with kitchen paper (paper towels). Season and stuff with coriander (cilantro) leaves.

2 Place the fish side by side in a shallow ovenproof dish. Sprinkle over the shallots, (bell) pepper and chillies.

3 Mix together the lemon juice, vinegar and sugar in a bowl. Spoon over the trout and season with salt and pepper. Cover the dish and bake for 30 minutes or until the fish is tender and the flesh is opaque.

4 Remove the the fish with a fish slice and drain. Transfer to warm serving plates and spoon the cooking juices over the fish. Garnish with fresh coriander (cilantro) and serve with salad and chilli bean rice (see Cook's Tip).

The method is clearly explained with step-by-step instructions that are easy to follow.

A full-color photograph of the finished dish.

The method is illustrated with step-by-step photographs, making the recipe easy to follow.

Cook's tips and variations provide useful information regarding ingredients or cooking techiques.

Soups

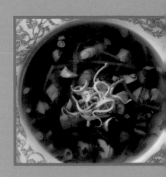

Using fish and seafood in soups makes wonderful sense. It doesn't require much cooking, making it ideal as a basis for a mid-week supper, and it combines well with an enormous variety of flavors. Oriental cooks make frequent excellent use of shellfish in quick, easy, and very tasty piquant soups, while the Italians incorporate fish into

thick, stew-like, nourishing soups. Even though there are many different types of fish available to us, it seems that fish is undervalued as a foodstuff in the English-speaking world. Other parts of the world use fish as a staple part of their diet and this chapter includes many dishes from a variety of places.

Italian Seafood Soup

This colorful mixed seafood soup would be superbly complemented by a dry white wine.

NUTRITIONAL INFORMATION

Calories 668   Sugars 3g
Protein ....48g   Fat 43g
Carbohydrate ...21g   Saturates 25g

5 MINS   55 MINS

SERVES 4

I N G R E D I E N T S

4 tbsp butter

1 lb assorted fish fillets, such as red
   mullet and snapper

1 lb prepared seafood, such as squid
and shrimp

8 oz fresh crabmeat

1 large onion, sliced

¼ cup all-purpose flour

5 cups fish stock

¾ cup dried pasta shapes,
   such as ditalini or elbow macaroni

1 tbsp anchovy extract

grated rind and juice of 1 orange

¼ cup dry sherry

1 ¼ cups heavy cream

salt and pepper

crusty brown bread, to serve

1 Melt the butter in a large saucepan, add the fish fillets, seafood, crabmeat, and onion and cook gently over a low heat for 6 minutes.

2 Add the flour to the seafood mixture, stirring thoroughly to avoid any lumps from forming.

3 Gradually add the stock, stirring, until the soup comes to a boil. Reduce the heat and simmer for 30 minutes.

4 Add the pasta to the pan and cook for a further 10 minutes.

5 Stir in the anchovy essence, orange rind, orange juice, sherry, and heavy cream. Season to taste with salt and pepper.

6 Heat the soup until completely warmed through.

7 Transfer the soup to a tureen or to warm soup bowls and serve with crusty brown bread.

Potato & Mixed Fish Soup

Any mixture of fish is suitable for this recipe, from simple smoked and white fish to salmon or mussels, depending on the occasion.

NUTRITIONAL INFORMATION

Calories	458	Sugar	.........5g
Protein	........28g	Fats	.........25g
Carbohydrates	...22g	Saturates	.....12g

 10 MINS   35 MINS

SERVES 4

INGREDIENTS

2 tbsp vegetable oil

1 lb small new potatoes, halved

1 bunch scallions, sliced

1 yellow bell pepper, sliced

2 garlic cloves, crushed

1 cup dry white wine

2½ cups fish stock

8 oz white fish fillet, skinned and cubed

8 oz smoked cod fillet, skinned and cubed

2 tomatoes, peeled, seeded and chopped

3½ oz peeled cooked shrimp

⅔ cup heavy cream

2 tbsp shredded fresh basil

1 Heat the vegetable oil in a large saucepan and add the halved potatoes, sliced scallions, bell pepper, and the garlic. Stir-fry gently for 3 minutes, stirring constantly.

2 Add the white wine and fish stock to the saucepan and bring to a boil. Reduce the heat and simmer for 10-15 minutes.

3 Add the cubed fish fillets and the tomatoes to the soup and continue to cook for 10 minutes or until the fish is cooked through.

4 Stir in the shrimp, cream, and shredded basil and cook for 2-3 minutes. Pour the soup into warmed bowls and serve immediately.

COOK'S TIP

For a soup which is slightly less rich, omit the wine and stir unsweetened yogurt into the soup instead of the heavy cream.

Mediterranean Fish Soup

Juicy chunks of fish and sumptuous shellfish are cooked in a flavorsome stock. Serve with toasted bread rubbed with garlic.

NUTRITIONAL INFORMATION

Calories	.316	Sugar	.4g
Protein	.53g	Fats	.7g
Carbohydrates	.5g	Saturates	.1g

1 HOUR   15 MINS

SERVES 4

INGREDIENTS

1 tbsp olive oil

1 large onion, chopped

2 garlic cloves, finely chopped

1¾ cups fresh fish stock (see page 14)

⅔ cup dry white wine

1 bay leaf

1 sprig each fresh thyme, rosemary, and oregano

1 lb firm white fish fillets (such as cod, monkfish, or halibut), skinned and cut into 1 inch cubes

1 lb fresh mussels, prepared

14 oz can chopped tomatoes

8 oz peeled shrimp, thawed if frozen

salt and pepper

sprigs of thyme, to garnish

TO SERVE

lemon wedges

4 slices toasted French bread, rubbed with cut garlic clove

1 Heat the olive oil in a large saucepan and gently fry the onion and garlic for 2–3 minutes until just softened.

2 Pour in the stock and wine and bring to a boil.

3 Tie the bay leaf and herbs together with clean string and add to the saucepan together with the fish and mussels. Stir well, cover, and simmer for 5 minutes.

4 Stir in the tomatoes and shrimp and continue to cook for a further 3–4 minutes until very hot and the fish is cooked through.

5 Discard the herbs and any mussels that have not opened. Season to taste, then ladle into warm bowls.

6 Garnish with sprigs of fresh thyme and serve with lemon wedges and toasted bread.

Chili Fish Soup

Chinese mushrooms add an intense flavor to this soup which is unique.
If they are unavailable, use open-cap mushrooms, sliced.

NUTRITIONAL INFORMATION

Calories 166	Sugars 1g
Protein 23g	Fat 7g
Carbohydrate 4g	Saturates 1g

15 MINS   15 MINS

SERVES 4

INGREDIENTS

½ oz Chinese dried mushrooms

2 tbsp sunflower oil

1 onion, sliced

1½ cups snow peas

1½ cups bamboo shoots

3 tbsp sweet chili sauce

5 cups fish or vegetable stock

3 tbsp light soy sauce

2 tbsp fresh cilantro, plus extra to garnish

1 lb cod fillet, skinned and cubed

COOK'S TIP

Cod is used in this recipe as it is a meaty white fish. For real luxury, use monkfish tail instead.

There are many different varieties of dried mushrooms, but shiitake are best. They are not cheap, but a small amount will go a long way.

1 Place the mushrooms in a large bowl. Pour over enough boiling water to cover and leave to stand for 5 minutes. Drain the mushrooms thoroughly in a colander. Using a sharp knife, roughly chop the mushrooms.

2 Heat the sunflower oil in a preheated wok or large skillet. Add the sliced onion to the wok and stir-fry for 5 minutes, or until softened.

3 Add the snow peas, bamboo shoots, chili sauce, stock, and soy sauce to the wok and bring to a boil.

4 Add the cilantro and cod and leave to simmer for 5 minutes or until the fish is cooked through.

5 Transfer the soup to warm bowls, garnish with extra cilantro, if wished, and serve hot.

Fish & Vegetable Soup

A chunky fish soup with strips of vegetables, all flavored with ginger and lemon, makes a meal in itself.

NUTRITIONAL INFORMATION

Calories 88   Sugars 1g
Protein ....12g   Fat 3g
Carbohydrate ....3g   Saturates 0.5g

  40 MINS   20 MINS

SERVES 4

I N G R E D I E N T S

9 oz white fish fillets (cod, halibut, haddock, sole, and so on)

½ tsp ground ginger

½ tsp salt

1 small leek, trimmed

2-4 crab sticks, defrosted if frozen (optional)

1 tbsp sunflower oil

1 large carrot, cut into julienne strips

8 canned water chestnuts, thinly sliced

5 cups fish or vegetable stock

1 tbsp lemon juice

1 tbsp light soy sauce

1 large zucchini, cut into julienne strips

black pepper

1 Remove any skin from the fish and cut into cubes, about 1 inch. Combine the ground ginger and salt and use to rub into the pieces of fish. Leave to marinate for at least 30 minutes.

2 Meanwhile, divide the green and white parts of the leek. Cut each part into 1 inch pieces and then into julienne strips down the length of each piece, keeping the two parts separate. Slice the crab sticks into ½-inch pieces.

3 Heat the oil in the wok, swirling it around so it is really hot. Add the white part of the leek and stir-fry for a couple of minutes, then add the carrots and water chestnuts, and continue to cook for 1-2 minutes, stirring thoroughly.

4 Add the stock and bring to a boil, then add the lemon juice and soy sauce and simmer for 2 minutes.

5 Add the fish and continue to cook for about 5 minutes until the fish begins to break up a little, then add the green part of the leek and the zucchini and simmer for about 1 minute. Add the sliced crab sticks, if using, and season to taste with black pepper. Simmer for a further minute or so and serve very hot.

COOK'S TIP

To skin fish, place the fillet skin-side down and insert a sharp, flexible knife at one end between the flesh and the skin. Hold the skin tightly at the end and push the knife along, keeping the blade flat against the skin.

Oriental Fish Soup

This is a deliciously different fish soup which can be made quickly and easily in a microwave.

NUTRITIONAL INFORMATION

Calories	105	Sugars	.........1g
Protein	........13g	Fat	...........5g
Carbohydrate	....1g	Saturates	.......1g

 20 MINS   10 MINS

SERVES 4

I N G R E D I E N T S

1 egg

1 tsp sesame seeds, toasted

1 celery stalk, chopped

1 carrot, cut into julienne strips

4 scallions, sliced on the diagonal

1 tbsp oil

1½ cups fresh spinach

3½ cups hot vegetable stock

4 tsp light soy sauce

9 oz haddock, skinned and cut into small chunks

salt and pepper

VARIATION

Instead of topping the soup with omelet shreds, you could pour the beaten egg, without the sesame seeds, into the hot stock at the end of the cooking time. The egg will set in pretty strands to give a flowery look.

1 Beat the egg with the sesame seeds and seasoning. Lightly oil a plate and pour on the egg mixture. Cook on HIGH power for 1½ minutes until just setting in the center. Leave to stand for a few minutes then remove from the plate. Roll up the egg and shred thinly.

2 Mix together the celery, carrot, scallions, and oil. Cover and cook on HIGH power for 3 minutes.

3 Wash the spinach thoroughly under cold, running water. Cut off and discard any long stalks and drain well. Shred the spinach finely.

4 Add the hot stock, soy sauce, haddock, and spinach to the vegetable mixture. Cover and cook on HIGH power for 5 minutes. Stir the soup and season to taste. Serve in warmed bowls with the

Fish Soup with Wontons

This soup is topped with small wontons filled with shrimp, making it both very tasty and satisfying.

NUTRITIONAL INFORMATION

Calories 115	Sugars 0g	
Protein 16g	Fat 5g	
Carbohydrate 1g	Saturates 1g	

 10 MINS   ⊙ 15 MINS

SERVES 4

I N G R E D I E N T S

4½ oz large, cooked, peeled shrimp

1 tsp chopped chives

1 small garlic clove, finely chopped

1 tbsp vegetable oil

12 wonton wrappers

1 small egg, beaten

3¾ cups fish stock

6 oz white fish fillet, diced

dash of chili sauce

sliced fresh red chili and chives, to garnish

1 Roughly chop a quarter of the shrimp and mix together with the chopped chives and garlic.

2 Heat the oil in a preheated wok or large skillet until it is really hot.

3 Stir-fry the shrimp mixture for 1–2 minutes. Remove from the heat and set aside to cool completely.

4 Spread out the wonton wrappers on a work counter. Spoon a little of the shrimp filling into the center of each wrapper. Brush the edges of the wrappers with beaten egg and press the edges together, scrunching them to form a "moneybag" shape. Set aside while you are preparing the soup.

5 Pour the fish stock into a large saucepan and bring to a boil. Add the diced white fish and the remaining shrimp and cook for 5 minutes.

6 Season to taste with the chili sauce. Add the wontons and cook for a further 5 minutes.

7 Spoon into warmed serving bowls, garnish with sliced red chili and chives, and serve immediately.

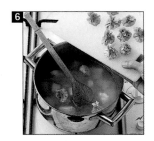

VARIATION

Replace the shrimp with cooked crabmeat for an alternative flavor.

Mussel & Potato Soup

This quick and easy soup would make a delicious summer lunch, served with fresh crusty bread.

NUTRITIONAL INFORMATION

Calories 804   Sugars 3g
Protein . . . . .17g   Fat 68g
Carbohydrate . . .32g   Saturates 38g

 10 MINS   35 MINS

SERVES 4

INGREDIENTS

1 lb 10 oz mussels

2 tbsp olive oil

7 tbsp unsalted butter

2 slices rindless fatty bacon, chopped

1 onion, chopped

2 garlic cloves, minced

½ cup all-purpose flour

1 lb potatoes, thinly sliced

¾ cup dried conchigliette

1 ¼ cups heavy cream

1 tbsp lemon juice

2 egg yolks

salt and pepper

TO GARNISH

2 tbsp finely chopped fresh parsley

lemon wedges

1 Debeard the mussels and scrub them under cold water for 5 minutes. Discard any mussels that do not close immediately when sharply tapped.

2 Bring a large pan of water to a boil, add the mussels, oil, and a little pepper. Cook until the mussels open. (discard any mussels that remain closed).

3 Drain the mussels, reserving the cooking liquid. Remove the mussels from their shells.

4 Melt the butter in a large saucepan, add the bacon, onion, and garlic and cook for 4 minutes. Carefully stir in the flour. Measure 5 cups of the reserved cooking liquid and stir it into the pan.

5 Add the potatoes to the pan and simmer for 5 minutes. Add the conchigliette and simmer for a further 10 minutes.

6 Add the cream and lemon juice, season to taste with salt and pepper, and add the mussels to the pan.

7 Blend the egg yolks with 1-2 tbsp of the remaining cooking liquid, stir into the pan and cook for 4 minutes.

8 Ladle the soup into 4 warm individual soup bowls, garnish with the chopped fresh parsley and lemon wedges, and serve immediately.

Salmon Bisque

A filling soup which is ideal for all types of occasion, from an elegant dinner to a picnic. For a touch of luxury, garnish with smoked salmon.

NUTRITIONAL INFORMATION

Calories 272	Sugars 1g	
Protein 17g	Fat 19g	
Carbohydrate 5g	Saturates 8g	

5 MINS   40 MINS

SERVES 4-6

INGREDIENTS

1–2 salmon heads (depending on size) or a tail piece of salmon weighing about 1 lb 2 oz

3½ cups water

1 fresh or dried bay leaf

1 lemon, sliced

a few black peppercorns

2 tbsp butter or margarine

2 tbsp finely chopped onion or scallions

¼ cup all-purpose flour

⅔ cup dry white wine or fish stock (see page 14)

⅔ cup light cream

1 tbsp chopped fresh fennel or dill

2–3 tsp lemon or lime juice

salt and pepper

TO GARNISH

1–1½ oz smoked salmon pieces, chopped (optional)

sprigs of fresh fennel or dill

1 Put the salmon, water, bay leaf, lemon, and peppercorns into a saucepan. Bring to a boil, remove any scum from the surface, cover the pan, and simmer gently for 20 minutes until the fish is cooked through.

2 Remove from the heat, strain the stock, and reserve 2½ cups. Remove and discard all the skin and bones from the salmon and flake the flesh, removing all the pieces from the head, if using.

3 Melt the butter or margarine in a saucepan and fry the onion or scallions gently for about 5 minutes until soft. Stir in the flour and cook for 1 minute then stir in the reserved stock and wine or fish stock. Bring to a boil, stirring. Add the salmon, season well, then simmer gently for about 5 minutes.

4 Add the cream and the chopped fennel or dill and reheat gently, but do not boil. Sharpen to taste with lemon or lime juice and season again. Serve hot or chilled, garnished with smoked salmon (if using) and sprigs of fennel or dill.

Smoked Haddock Soup

Smoked haddock gives this soup a wonderfully rich flavor, while the mashed potatoes and cream thicken and enrich the stock.

NUTRITIONAL INFORMATION

Calories 169	Sugars 8g
Protein 16g	Fat 5g
Carbohydrate ...16g	Saturates 3g

 25 MINS   40 MINS

SERVES 4–6

I N G R E D I E N T S

8 oz smoked haddock fillet

1 onion, chopped finely

1 garlic clove, minced

2½ cups water

2½ cups skimmed milk

1–1½ cups hot mashed potatoes

2 tbsp butter

about 1 tbsp lemon juice

6 tbsp low-fat natural fromage blanc

4 tbsp fresh parsley, chopped

salt and pepper

1 Put the fish, onion, garlic, and water into a saucepan. Bring to a boil, cover and simmer for 15–20 minutes.

2 Remove the fish from the pan, strip off the skin, and remove all the bones. Flake the flesh finely.

3 Return the skin and bones to the cooking liquor and simmer for 10 minutes. Strain, discarding the skin and bone. Pour the liquor into a clean pan.

4 Add the milk, flaked fish, and seasoning to the pan, bring to a boil and simmer for about 3 minutes.

5 Gradually whisk in sufficient mashed potato to give a fairly thick soup, stir in the butter, and sharpen to taste with lemon juice.

6 Add the fromage blanc and 3 tablespoons of the chopped parsley. Reheat gently and adjust the seasoning. Sprinkle with the remaining parsley and serve immediately.

COOK'S TIP

Undyed smoked haddock may be used in place of the bright yellow fish; it will give a paler color but just as much flavor. Alternatively, use smoked cod or smoked whiting.

Partan Bree

This traditional Scottish soup is thickened with a purée of rice and crabmeat cooked in milk. Add soured cream, if liked, at the end of cooking.

NUTRITIONAL INFORMATION

Calories	.112	Sugars	.5g
Protein	.7g	Fat	.2g
Carbohydrate	.18g	Saturates	.0.3g

1 HOUR   35 MINS

SERVES 6

INGREDIENTS

1 medium-sized boiled crab

scant ½ cup long-grain rice

2½ cups skimmed milk

2½ cups fish stock (see page 14)

1 tbsp anchovy paste

2 tsp lime or lemon juice

1 tbsp chopped fresh parsley or I tsp chopped fresh thyme

3–4 tbsp soured cream (optional)

salt and pepper

snipped chives, to garnish

1 Remove and reserve all the brown and white meat from the crab, then crack the claws and remove and chop that meat; reserve the claw meat.

COOK'S TIP

If you are unable to buy a whole crab, use about 6 oz frozen crabmeat and thaw thoroughly before use; or a 6 oz can of crabmeat which just needs thorough draining.

2 Put the rice and milk into a saucepan and bring slowly to a boil. Cover and simmer gently for about 20 minutes.

3 Add the reserved white and brown crabmeat and seasoning and simmer for a further 5 minutes.

4 Cool a little, then press through a strainer or blend in a food processor or blender until smooth.

5 Pour the soup into a clean saucepan and add the fish stock and the reserved claw meat. Bring slowly to a boil, then add the anchovy paste and lime or lemon juice, and adjust the seasoning.

6 Simmer for a further 2–3 minutes. Stir in the parsley or thyme and then swirl soured cream (if using) through each serving. Garnish with snipped chives.

Coconut & Crab Soup

Thai red curry paste is quite fiery, but adds a superb flavor to this dish. It is available in jars or packets from supermarkets.

NUTRITIONAL INFORMATION

Calories	122	Sugar	.........9g
Protein	........11g	Fats	...........4g
Carbohydrates	...11g	Saturates	......1g

 5 MINS   10 MINS

SERVES 4

INGREDIENTS

1 tbsp groundnut oil

2 tbsp Thai red curry paste

1 red bell pepper, seeded and sliced

2½ cups coconut milk

2½ cups fish stock

2 tbsp fish sauce

8 oz canned or fresh white crabmeat

8 oz fresh or frozen crab claws

2 tbsp chopped fresh cilantro

3 scallions, trimmed and sliced

1 Heat the oil in a large preheated wok.

2 Add the red curry paste and red bell pepper to the wok and stir-fry for 1 minute.

3 Add the coconut milk, fish stock, and fish sauce and bring to a boil.

4 Add the crabmeat, crab claws, cilantro, and scallions to the wok.

5 Stir the mixture well and heat thoroughly for 2–3 minutes or until everything is warmed through.

6 Transfer the soup to warm bowls and serve hot.

COOK'S TIP

Clean the wok after use by washing it with water, using a mild detergent if necessary, and a soft cloth or brush. Do not scrub or use any abrasive cleaner as this will scratch the surface. Dry thoroughly and then wipe the surface all over with a little oil to protect the surface.

Fish & Crab Chowder

Packed full of flavor, this delicious fish dish is a meal in itself, but it is ideal accompanied with a crisp side salad.

NUTRITIONAL INFORMATION

Calories	440	Sugars	........10g
Protein	........49g	Fat	..........7g
Carbohydrate	...43g	Saturates	......1g

1¼ HOURS   25 MINS

SERVES 4

INGREDIENTS

1 large onion, chopped finely

2 celery sticks, chopped finely

⅔ cup dry white wine

2½ cups fresh fish stock (see page 14)

2½ cups skimmed milk

1 dried bay leaf

1½ cups smoked cod fillets, skinned and cut into 1 inch cubes

8 oz undyed smoked haddock fillets, skinned and cut into 1 inch cubes

2 x 6 oz cans crabmeat, drained

8 oz blanched green beans, sliced into 1 inch pieces

1½ cups cooked brown rice

4 tsp cornstarch mixed with 4 tablespoons cold water

salt and pepper

chopped fresh parsley to garnish

mixed green salad, to serve

 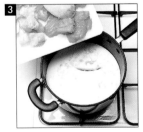 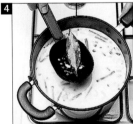

1 Place the onion, celery, and wine in a large non-stick saucepan. Bring to a boil, cover, and cook for 5 minutes.

2 Uncover and cook for 5 minutes until the liquid has evaporated.

3 Pour in the stock and milk and add the bay leaf. Bring to a simmer and stir in the cod and haddock. Simmer gently, uncovered, for 5 minutes.

4 Add the crabmeat, green beans, and rice and cook gently for 2–3 minutes until heated through. Remove the bay leaf from the soup with a draining spoon.

5 Stir in the cornstarch mixture until thickened slightly. Season to taste and ladle into 4 warmed soup bowls. Garnish with chopped parsley and serve with a mixed salad.

Crab & Ginger Soup

Two classic ingredients in Chinese cooking are blended together in this recipe for a special soup.

NUTRITIONAL INFORMATION

Calories . . . . .32 Sugars 1g
Protein . . . . .6g Fat 0.4g
Carbohydrate . . . .1g Saturates 0g

10 MINS   25 MINS

SERVES 4

I N G R E D I E N T S

1 carrot

1 leek

1 bay leaf

3¾ cups fish stock

2 medium-sized cooked crabs

1-inch piece fresh root gingerroot, grated

1 tsp light soy sauce

½ tsp ground star anise

salt and pepper

1 Using a sharp knife, chop the carrot and leek into small pieces, and place in a large saucepan with the bay leaf and fish stock.

2 Bring the mixture in the saucepan to a boil.

3 Reduce the heat, cover, and leave to simmer for about 10 minutes, or until the vegetables are nearly tender.

4 Remove all of the meat from the cooked crabs. Break off and reserve the claws, break the joints, and remove the meat, using a fork or skewer.

5 Add the crabmeat to the pan of fish stock, together with the ginger, soy sauce, and star anise and bring to a boil. Leave to simmer for about 10 minutes, or until the vegetables are tender and the crab is heated through.

6 Season the soup then ladle into a warmed soup tureen or individual serving bowls and garnish with crab claws. Serve immediately.

VARIATION

If fresh crabmeat is unavailable, use drained canned crabmeat or thawed frozen crabmeat instead.

Corn & Crab Soup

Be sure to use proper creamed corn for this soup. It has a slightly mushy consistency making a deliciously thick, creamy soup.

NUTRITIONAL INFORMATION

Calories	133	Sugars	.........6g
Protein	........10g	Fat	..........3g
Carbohydrate	...19g	Saturates	.....0.4g

3½ HOURS   10 MINS

SERVES 4

I N G R E D I E N T S

4½ oz crabmeat (or 1 chicken breast)

¼ tsp finely chopped gingerroot

2 egg whites

2 tbsp milk

1 tbsp cornstarch paste

2½ cups Chinese stock

9 oz can creamed corn

salt and pepper

finely chopped scallions, to garnish

1 In a small bowl, flake the crabmeat. Add the chopped ginger root and mix well. If using chicken breast, coarsely chop and mix with the ginger.

2 Beat the egg whites until frothy, add the milk and cornstarch paste, and beat again until smooth.

3 Blend the crabmeat or chicken into the egg-white mixture.

4 In a wok or large frying pan, bring the stock to a boil, add the sweetcorn and bring to a boil, stirring gently.

5 Stir in the crabmeat or chicken pieces and egg-white mixture.

6 Add salt and pepper to taste and stir the soup gently until the mixture is well blended.

7 Pour the soup into a warm tureen or serving bowls, garnish with chopped spring onions, and serve immediately.

COOK'S TIP

Always obtain the freshest possible crab, although frozen or canned will work in this recipe. The delicate, sweet flavor of crab diminishes very quickly which is why Chinese chefs tend to buy live crabs.

Crab & Corn Soup

Crab and corn are classic ingredients in Chinese cookery. Here egg noodles are added for a filling dish.

NUTRITIONAL INFORMATION

Calories	324	Sugars	.........6g
Protein	........27g	Fat	...........8g
Carbohydrate	...39g	Saturates	.......2g

 5 MINS   20 MINS

SERVES 4

I N G R E D I E N T S

1 tbsp sunflower oil

1 tsp Chinese five-spice powder

8 oz carrots, cut into sticks

½ cup canned or frozen corn-on-the-cobs

¼ cup peas

6 scallions, trimmed and sliced

1 red chili, seeded and very thinly sliced

2 x 7 oz can white crabmeat

6 oz egg noodles

7½ cups fish stock

3 tbsp soy sauce

1 Heat the sunflower oil in a large preheated wok or heavy-based skillet.

2 Add the Chinese five-spice powder, carrots, sweetcorn, peas, scallions, and red chili to the wok and cook for about 5 minutes, stirring constantly.

3 Add the crabmeat to the wok and stir-fry the mixture for 1 minute, distributing the crabmeat evenly.

4 Roughly break up the egg noodles and add to the wok.

5 Pour the fish stock and soy sauce into the mixture in the wok and bring to a boil.

6 Cover the wok or skillet and leave the soup to simmer for 5 minutes.

7 Stir once more, then transfer the soup to a warm soup tureen or individual serving bowls, and serve at once.

COOK'S TIP

Chinese five-spice powder is a mixture of star anise, fennel, cloves, cinnamon, and Szechuan pepper. It has an unmistakeable flavor. Use it sparingly, as it is very pungent.

Louisiana Seafood Gumbo

Gumbo is a hearty, thick soup, almost a stew. This New Orleans classic must be served with a scoop of hot, fluffy, cooked rice.

NUTRITIONAL INFORMATION

Calories 267	Sugars 6g	
Protein 27g	Fat 8g	
Carbohydrate . . .24g	Saturates 1g	

 5 MINS | 35 MINS

SERVES 4

INGREDIENTS

1 tbsp all-purpose flour

1 tsp paprika

12 oz angler fish fillets, cut into chunks

2 tbsp olive oil

1 onion, chopped

1 green bell pepper, cored, seeded, and chopped

3 celery stalks, finely chopped

2 garlic cloves, minced

6 oz okra, sliced

2½ cups vegetable stock

15 oz can chopped tomatoes

1 bouquet garni

4½ oz peeled shrimp

juice of 1 lemon

dash of Tabasco

2 tsp Worcestershire sauce

generous 1 cup cooked long-grain rice

1 Mix the flour with the paprika. Add the angler fish chunks and toss to coat well with the flour.

2 Heat the olive oil in a large, heavy-bottomed pan. Add the angler fish pieces and fry until browned. Remove with a draining spoon and set aside.

3 Add the onion, green bell pepper, celery, garlic, and okra and fry gently for 5 minutes until softened.

4 Add the stock, tomatoes, and bouquet garni. Bring to a boil, reduce the heat, and simmer for 15 minutes.

5 Return the angler fish to the pan with the shrimp, lemon juice, Tabasco, and Worcestershire sauces. Simmer for a further 5 minutes.

6 To serve, place a mound of cooked rice in each warmed, serving bowl, then ladle over the seafood gumbo.

Spicy Shrimp Soup

Lime leaves are used as a flavoring in this soup to add tartness.

NUTRITIONAL INFORMATION

Calories 217   Sugars 16g
Protein . . . . .16g   Fat 4g
Carbohydrate . . .31g   Saturates 1g

 10 MINS   20 MINS

SERVES 4

I N G R E D I E N T S

2 tbsp tamarind paste

4 red chilies, very finely chopped

2 cloves garlic, minced

1 inch piece Thai ginger, peeled and very finely chopped

4 tbsp fish sauce

2 tbsp palm sugar or superfine sugar

5 cups fish stock

8 lime leaves

3½ oz carrots, very thinly sliced

12 oz sweet potato, diced

1 cup baby corn-on-the-cobs, halved

3 tbsp fresh cilantro, roughly chopped

3½ oz cherry tomatoes, halved

8 oz fan-tail shrimp

1 Place the tamarind paste, red chilies, garlic, ginger, fish sauce, sugar, and fish stock in a preheated wok or large, heavy skillet. Roughly tear the lime leaves and add to the wok. Bring to a boil, stirring constantly to blend the flavors.

2 Reduce the heat and add the carrot, sweet potato, and baby corn-on-the-cobs to the mixture in the wok.

3 Leave the soup to simmer, uncovered, for about 10 minutes, or until the vegetables are just tender.

4 Stir the cilantro, cherry tomatoes, and shrimp into the soup and heat through for 5 minutes.

5 Transfer the soup to a warm soup tureen or individual serving bowls and serve hot.

COOK'S TIP

Thai ginger or galangal is a member of the ginger family, but it is yellow in color with pink sprouts. The flavor is aromatic and less pungent than ginger.

Shrimp Dumpling Soup

These small dumplings filled with shrimp and pork may be made slightly larger and served as dim sum on their own, if you prefer.

NUTRITIONAL INFORMATION

Calories 311	Sugars 2g	
Protein 18g	Fat 8g	
Carbohydrate . . .41g	Saturates 2g	

20 MINS   10 MINS

SERVES 4

I N G R E D I E N T S

DUMPLINGS

1⅝ cups all-purpose flour

¼ cup boiling water

⅛ cup cold water

1½ tsp vegetable oil

FILLING

4½ oz ground pork

4½ oz cooked peeled shrimp, chopped

1¾ oz canned water chestnuts, drained, rinsed, and chopped

1 celery stalk, chopped

1 tsp cornstarch

1 tbsp sesame oil

1 tbsp light soy sauce

SOUP

3¾ cups fish stock

1¾ oz cellophane noodles

1 tbsp dry sherry

chopped chives, to garnish

1 To make the dumplings, mix together the flour, boiling water, cold water, and oil in a bowl until a pliable dough is formed.

2 Knead the dough on a lightly floured counter for 5 minutes. Cut the dough into 16 equal sized pieces.

3 Roll the dough pieces into rounds about 3 inches in diameter.

4 Mix the filling ingredients together in a large bowl.

5 Spoon a little of the filling mixture into the center of each round. Bring the edges of the dough together, scrunching them up to form a "moneybag" shape. Twist the gathered edges to seal.

6 Pour the fish stock into a large saucepan and bring to a boil.

7 Add the cellophane noodles, dumplings, and dry sherry to the pan and cook for 4–5 minutes, until the noodles and dumplings are tender. Garnish with chopped chives and serve immediately.

Shrimp Soup

This soup is an interesting mix of colors and textures. The egg may be made into a flat omelet and added as thin strips if preferred.

NUTRITIONAL INFORMATION

Calories	123	Sugars	.......0.2g
Protein	........13g	Fat	...........8g
Carbohydrate	....1g	Saturates	.......1g

5 MINS   20 MINS

SERVES 4

I N G R E D I E N T S

2 tbsp sunflower oil

2 scallions, thinly sliced diagonally

1 carrot, coarsely grated

4½ oz large closed cap mushrooms, thinly sliced

4 cups fish or vegetable stock

½ tsp Chinese five-spice powder

1 tbsp light soy sauce

4½ oz large peeled shrimp or peeled jumbor shrimp, defrosted if frozen

½ bunch watercress, trimmed and roughly chopped

1 egg, well beaten

salt and pepper

4 large shrimp in shells, to garnish (optional)

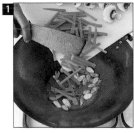  

1 Heat the oil in a wok, swirling it around until really hot. Add the scallions and stir-fry for a minute, add the carrots and mushrooms, and continue to cook for about 2 minutes.

2 Add the stock and bring to a boil, season to taste with salt and pepper, five-spice powder, and soy sauce, and simmer for 5 minutes.

3 If the shrimp are really large, cut them in half before adding to the wok and simmer for 3-4 minutes.

4 Add the watercress to the wok and mix well, then slowly pour in the beaten egg in a circular movement so that it cooks in threads in the soup. Adjust the seasoning and serve each portion topped with a whole shrimp.

COOK'S TIP

The large open mushrooms with black gills give the best flavor but they tend to spoil the color of the soup, making it very dark. Oyster mushrooms can also be used.

Shrimp Gumbo

This soup is thick with onions, red bell peppers, rice, shrimp, and okra, which both adds flavor and acts as a thickening agent.

NUTRITIONAL INFORMATION

Calories	177	Sugar	.........5g
Protein	........12g	Fats	..........8g
Carbohydrates	...15g	Saturates	......1g

1 HOUR   45 MINS

SERVES 4–6

I N G R E D I E N T S

1 large onion, chopped finely

2 slices lean bacon, chopped finely (optional)

1–2 garlic cloves, minced

2 tbsp olive oil

1 large or 2 small red bell peppers, chopped finely or minced coarsely

3½ cups fish or vegetable stock (see page 14)

1 fresh or dried bay leaf

1 blade mace

good pinch of ground allspice

3 tbsp long-grain rice

1 tbsp white wine vinegar

4½–6 oz okra, trimmed and sliced very thinly

½–⅔ cup peeled shrimp

1 tbsp anchovy paste

2 tsp tomato paste

1–2 tbsp chopped fresh parsley

salt and pepper

TO GARNISH

whole shrimp

sprigs of fresh parsley

1 Gently fry the onion, bacon (if using), and garlic in the oil in a large saucepan for 4–5 minutes until soft. Add the bell peppers to the pan and continue to fry gently for a couple of minutes.

2 Add the stock, bay leaf, mace, allspice, rice, vinegar, and seasoning and bring to a boil. Cover and simmer gently for about 20 minutes, giving an occasional stir, until the rice is just tender.

3 Add the okra, shrimp, anchovy paste, and tomato paste, cover, and simmer gently for about 15 minutes until the okra is tender and the mixture slightly thickened.

4 Discard the bay leaf and mace from the soup and adjust the seasoning. Stir in the parsley and serve each portion garnished with a whole shrimp and parsley sprigs.

Three-Flavor Soup

Ideally, use raw shrimp in this soup. If that is not possible, add ready-cooked ones at the very last stage.

NUTRITIONAL INFORMATION

Calories 117	Sugars 0g	
Protein 20g	Fat 3g	
Carbohydrate 2g	Saturates 1g	

3¹/₂ HOURS   10 MINS

SERVES 4

I N G R E D I E N T S

4½ oz skinned, boned chicken breast

4½ oz raw peeled shrimp

salt

½ egg white, lightly beaten

2 tsp cornstarch paste

4½ oz honey-roast ham

3 cups Chinese stock or water

finely chopped scallions, to garnish

1 Using a sharp knife or meat cleaver, thinly slice the chicken into small shreds. If the shrimp are large, cut each in half lengthways, otherwise leave them whole.

2 Place the chicken and shrimp in a bowl and mix with a pinch of salt, the egg white and cornstarch paste until well coated. Set aside until required.

3 Cut the honey-roast ham into small thin slices roughly the same size as the chicken pieces.

4 In a preheated wok or large, heavy skillet, bring the Chinese stock or water to a rolling boil, and add the chicken, the raw shrimp and the ham.

5 Bring the soup back to a boil, and simmer for 1 minute.

6 Adjust the seasoning to taste, pour the soup into four warmed individual serving bowls, garnish with the scallions, and serve immediately.

COOK'S TIP

Soups such as this are improved enormously in flavor if you use a well-flavored stock. Either use a bouillon cube, or find time to make Chinese stock. Better still, make double quantities and freeze some for future use.

Snacks, Light Meals, & Salads

The dishes in this chapter are designed to either whet the appetite for the main course to come, without being filling, or to be used as nibbles to serve with drinks before

supper. Fish and seafood make excellent appetizers as they are full of flavor and can be turned into a variety of delicious dishes. Fish is also much lighter than meat and therefore won't be too filling. Fish cooks quickly, making it ideal for entertaining, and – even better – any of the dishes in this chapter can be prepared well in advance if you are entertaining at home and either served cold or simply reheated.

Sesame Shrimp Toasts

These are one of the most recognized and popular starters in Chinese restaurants in the Western world. They are also quick and easy to make.

NUTRITIONAL INFORMATION

Calories 237	Sugars 1g
Protein 18g	Fat 12g
Carbohydrate ...15g	Saturates 2g

🔔 5 MINS   🕐 10 MINS

SERVES 4

INGREDIENTS

4 slices medium, thick-sliced white bread

8 oz cooked peeled shrimp

1 tbsp soy sauce

2 cloves garlic, crushed

1 tbsp sesame oil

1 egg

2 tbsp sesame seeds

oil, for deep-frying

sweet chili sauce, to serve

1 Remove the crusts from the bread, if desired, then set aside until required.

2 Place the peeled shrimp, soy sauce, crushed garlic, sesame oil, and egg into a food processor and blend until a smooth paste has formed.

3 Spread the shrimp paste evenly over the 4 slices of bread. Sprinkle the sesame seeds over the top of the shrimp mixture and press the seeds down with your hands so that they stick to the mixture. Cut each slice in half and in half again to form 4 triangles.

4 Heat the oil in a large wok or skillet and deep-fry the toasts, sesame seed-side up, for 4-5 minutes, or until golden .

5 Remove the toasts with a draining spoon, transfer to absorbent paper towels, and leave to drain thoroughly.

6 Serve the sesame shrimp toasts warm with sweet chili sauce for dipping.

VARIATION

Add 2 chopped scallions to the mixture in step 2 for added flavor and crunch.

Spicy Salt & Pepper Prawns

For best results, use raw jumbo shrimp in their shells. They are 3-4 inches long, and you should get 18-20 per 1lb.

NUTRITIONAL INFORMATION

Calories	160	Sugars	.......0.2g
Protein	........17g	Fat	..........10g
Carbohydrate	...0.5g	Saturates	.......1g

 35 MINS   20 MINS

SERVES 4

I N G R E D I E N T S

9-10½ oz raw prawns shrimp in their shells, defrosted if frozen

1 tbsp light soy sauce

1 tsp Chinese rice wine or dry sherry

2 tsp cornstarch

vegetable oil, for deep-frying

2-3 scallions, to garnish

SPICY SALT AND PEPPER

1 tbsp salt

1 tsp ground Szechuan peppercorns

1 tsp five-spice powder

1 Pull the soft legs off the shrimp, but keep the body shell on. Dry well on absorbent paper towels.

2 Place the shrimp in a bowl with the soy sauce, rice wine or sherry and cornstarch. Turn the shrimp to coat thoroughly in the mixture and leave to marinate for about 25-30 minutes.

3 To make the Spicy Salt and Pepper, mix the salt, ground Szechuan peppercorns and five-spice powder together. Place in a dry skillet and stir-fry for about 3-4 minutes over a low heat, stirring constantly to prevent the spices burning on the bottom of the pan. Remove from the heat and allow to cool.

4 Heat the vegetable oil in a preheated wok or large skillet until smoking, then deep-fry the shrimp in batches until golden brown. Remove the shrimp from the wok with a slotted spoon and drain on paper towels.

5 Place the scallions in a bowl, pour on 1 tablespoon of the hot oil and leave for 30 seconds. Serve the shrimp garnished with the scallions, and with the Spicy Salt and Pepper as a dip.

COOK'S TIP

The roasted spice mixture made with Szechuan peppercorns is used throughout China as a dip for deep-fried food. The peppercorns are sometimes roasted first and then ground. Dry-frying is a way of releasing the flavors of the spices.

Chili & Peanut Shrimp

Peanut flavors are widely used in Far East and South East Asian cooking and complement many ingredients.

NUTRITIONAL INFORMATION

Calories 478	Sugars 2g	
Protein 32g	Fat 30g	
Carbohydrate ...19g	Saturates 11g	

🍤 15 MINS   🕐 10 MINS

SERVES 4

I N G R E D I E N T S

1 lb jumbo shrimp, peeled apart from tail end

3 tbsp crunchy peanut butter

1 tbsp chili sauce

10 sheets phyllo pastry

1 oz butter, melted

1¾ oz fine egg noodles

oil, for frying

1 Using a sharp knife, make a small horizontal slit across the back of each shrimp. Press down on the shrimp so that they lie flat.

2 Mix together the peanut butter and chili sauce in a small bowl until well blended. Using a pastry brush, spread a little of the sauce onto each shrimp so they are evenly coated.

3 Cut each cookie sheet in half and brush with melted butter.

4 Wrap each shrimp in a piece of pastry, tucking the edges under to fully enclose the shrimp.

5 Place the fine egg noodles in a bowl, pour over enough boiling water to cover, and leave to stand for 5 minutes. Drain the noodles thoroughly. Use 2–3 cooked noodles to tie around each shrimp packet.

6 Heat the oil in a preheated wok. Cook the shrimp for 3–4 minutes, or until golden and crispy.

7 Remove the shrimp with a draining spoon, transfer to absorbent paper towels and leave to drain. Transfer to serving plates and serve warm.

COOK'S TIP

When using phyllo pastry, keep any unused pastry covered to prevent it drying out and becoming brittle.

Butterfly Shrimp

Use unpeeled, raw king or jumbo shrimp which are about
3-4 inches long.

NUTRITIONAL INFORMATION

Calories	157	Sugars	.......0.3g
Protein	.........8g	Fat	...........9g
Carbohydrate	....11g	Saturates	.......2g

🍤 25 MINS   🕐 10 MINS

SERVES 4

INGREDIENTS

12 raw jumbo shrimp in their shells

2 tbsp light soy sauce

1 tbsp Chinese rice wine or dry sherry

1 tbsp cornstarch

vegetable oil, for deep-frying

2 eggs, lightly beaten

8-10 tbsp bread crumbs

salt and pepper

shredded lettuce leaves, to serve

chopped scallions, either raw or soaked for
about 30 seconds in hot oil, to garnish

1 Shell and devein the shrimp leaving the tails on. Split them in half from the underbelly about halfway along, leaving the tails still firmly attached. Mix together the salt, pepper, soy sauce, wine, and cornstarch, add the shrimp and turn to coat. Leave to marinate for 10-15 minutes.

2 Heat the oil in a preheated wok. Pick up each shrimp by the tail, dip it in the beaten egg, and roll it in the bread crumbs to coat well.

3 Deep-fry the shrimp in batches until golden brown. Remove them with a draining spoon and drain on paper towels.

4 To serve, arrange the shrimp neatly on a bed of lettuce leaves and garnish with scallions.

COOK'S TIP

To devein shrimp, first
remove the shell. Make a
shallow cut about three-quarters
of the way along the back of each
shrimp, then pull out and discard
the black intestinal vein.

Salt & Pepper Shrimp

Szechuan peppercorns are very hot, adding heat and a red color to the shrimp. They are effectively offset by the sugar in this recipe.

NUTRITIONAL INFORMATION

Calories ....174 Sugars 1g
Protein ....25g Fat 8g
Carbohydrate ....1g Saturates 1g

  5 MINS   10 MINS

SERVES 4

I N G R E D I E N T S

2 tsp salt

1 tsp black pepper

2 tsp Szechuan peppercorns

1 tsp sugar

1 lb peeled raw jumbo shrimp

2 tbsp groundnut oil

1 red chili, seeded and finely chopped

1 tsp freshly grated gingerroot

3 cloves garlic, minced

scallions, sliced, to garnish

shrimp crackers, to serve

1 Grind the salt, black pepper, and Szechuan peppercorns using a pestle and mortar.

2 Mix the salt and pepper mixture with the sugar and set aside until required.

3 Rinse the jumbo shrimp under cold running water and pat dry with absorbent paper towels.

4 Heat the oil in a preheated wok or large skillet.

5 Add the shrimp, chopped red chili, ginger, and garlic to the wok or skillet and stir-fry for 4–5 minutes, or until the shrimp are cooked through.

6 Add the salt and pepper mixture to the wok and stir-fry for 1 minute, stirring constantly so it does not burn on the base of the wok.

7 Transfer the shrimp to warm serving bowls and garnish with scallions. Serve hot with shrimp crackers.

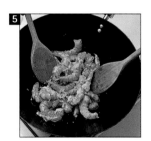

COOK'S TIP

Jumbo shrimp are widely available and have a lovely meaty texture. If using cooked jumbo shrimp, add them with the salt and pepper mixture in step 5 – if the cooked shrimp are added any earlier they will toughen up and be inedible.

Shrimp Packets

These small shrimp bites are packed with the flavor of lime and cilantro for a quick and tasty starter.

NUTRITIONAL INFORMATION

Calories ....305 Sugars 2g
Protein ....15g Fat 21g
Carbohydrate ...14g Saturates 8g

15 MINS   20 MINS

SERVES 4

INGREDIENTS

1 tbsp sunflower oil

1 red bell pepper, seeded and very thinly sliced

¾ cup beansprouts

finely grated zest and juice of 1 lime

1 red chili, seeded and very finely chopped

½ inch piece of gingerroot, peeled and grated

8 oz peeled shrimp

1 tbsp fish sauce

½ tsp arrowroot

2 tbsp chopped fresh cilantro

8 sheets phyllo pastry

2 tbsp butter

2 tsp sesame oil

oil, for frying

scallion tassels, to garnish

chili sauce, to serve

1 Heat the sunflower oil in a large preheated wok. Add the red bell pepper and beansprouts and stir-fry for 2 minutes, or until the vegetables have softened.

2 Remove the wok from the heat and toss in the lime zest and juice, red chili, ginger, and shrimp, stirring well.

3 Mix the fish sauce with the arrowroot and stir the mixture into the wok juices. Return the wok to the heat and cook, stirring, for 2 minutes, or until the juices thicken. Toss in the cilantro and mix well.

4 Lay the sheets of phyllo pastry out on a board. Melt the butter and sesame oil and brush each cookie sheet with the mixture.

5 Spoon a little of the shrimp filling onto the top of each sheet, fold over each end, and roll up to enclose the filling.

6 Heat the oil in a large wok. Cook the packets, in batches, for 2–3 minutes, or until crisp and golden. Garnish with scallion tassels and serve hot with a chili dipping sauce.

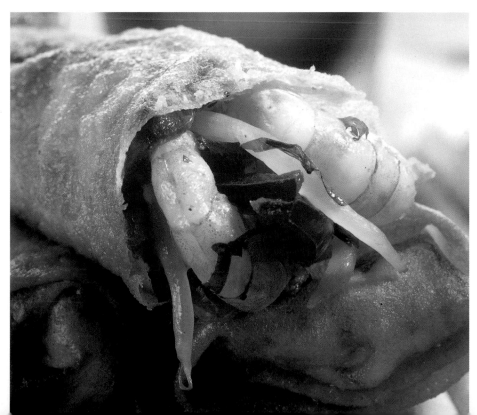

COOK'S TIP

If using cooked shrimp, cook for 1 minute only, otherwise the shrimp will toughen.

Sweet & Sour Shrimp

Shrimp are marinated in a soy sauce mixture then coated in a light batter, fried, and served with a delicious sweet-and-sour dip.

NUTRITIONAL INFORMATION

Calories 294	Sugars 11g	
Protein 14g	Fat 12g	
Carbohydrate ...34g	Saturates 2g	

  40 MINS   20 MINS

SERVES 4

INGREDIENTS

16 large raw shrimp, peeled

1 tsp grated fresh gingerroot

1 garlic clove, minced

2 scallions, sliced

2 tbsp dry sherry

2 tsp sesame oil

1 tbsp light soy sauce

vegetable oil, for deep-frying

shredded scallion, to garnish

BATTER

4 egg whites

4 tbsp cornstarch

2 tbsp all-purpose flour

SAUCE

2 tbsp tomato paste

3 tbsp white wine vinegar

4 tsp light soy sauce

2 tbsp lemon juice

3 tbsp light brown sugar

1 green bell pepper, seeded and cut into thin matchsticks

½ tsp chili sauce

1¼ cups vegetable stock

2 tsp cornstarch

1 Using tweezers, devein the shrimp, then flatten them with a large knife.

2 Place the shrimp in a dish and add the ginger, garlic, scallions, dry sherry, sesame oil, and soy sauce. Cover with plastic wrap and leave to marinate for 30 minutes.

3 Make the batter by beating the egg whites until thick. Fold in the cornstarch and all-purpose flour to form a light batter.

4 Place all of the sauce ingredients in a saucepan and bring to a boil. Reduce the heat and leave to simmer for 10 minutes.

5 Remove the shrimp from the marinade and dip them into the batter to coat.

6 Heat the vegetable oil in a preheated wok or large skillet until almost smoking. Reduce the heat and fry the shrimp for 3–4 minutes, until crisp and golden brown.

7 Garnish the shrimp with shredded scallion and serve with the sauce.

Shrimp Omelet

This is called *Fu-Yung* in China and is a classic dish which may be flavored with any ingredients you have to hand.

NUTRITIONAL INFORMATION

Calories	320	Sugars	.........1g
Protein	........31g	Fat	..........18g
Carbohydrate	....8g	Saturates	.......4g

🍲 5 MINS   🕐 10 MINS

SERVES 4

INGREDIENTS

3 tbsp sunflower oil

2 leeks, trimmed and sliced

12 oz raw jumbo shrimp

4 tbsp cornstarch

1 tsp salt

6 oz mushrooms, sliced

1½ cups beansprouts

6 eggs

deep-fried leeks, to garnish (optional)

1 Heat the sunflower oil in a preheated wok or large skillet. Add the sliced leeks and stir-fry for 3 minutes.

2 Rinse the shrimp under cold running water and then pat dry with paper towels.

3 Mix together the cornstarch and salt in a large bowl.

4 Add the shrimp to the cornstarch and salt mixture and toss to coat all over.

5 Add the shrimp to the wok or skillet and stir-fry for 2 minutes, or until the shrimp are almost cooked through.

6 Add the mushrooms and beansprouts to the wok and stir-fry for 2 minutes.

7 Beat the eggs with 3 tablespoons of cold water. Pour the egg mixture into the wok and cook until the egg sets, carefully turning over once. Turn the omelet out onto a clean board, divide into 4, and serve hot, garnished with deep-fried leeks (if using).

VARIATION
If liked, divide the mixture into 4 once the initial cooking has taken place in step 6 and cook 4 individual omelettes.

Chinese Omelet

This is a fairly filling omelet, as it contains chicken and shrimp. It is cooked as a whole omelet and then sliced for serving.

NUTRITIONAL INFORMATION

Calories	309	Sugars	.........0g
Protein	........34g	Fat	..........19g
Carbohydrate	...0.2g	Saturates	.......5g

 5 MINS   5 MINS

SERVES 4

INGREDIENTS

8 eggs

2 cups cooked chicken, shredded

12 jumbo shrimp, peeled and deveined

2 tbsp chopped chives

2 tsp light soy sauce

dash of chili sauce

2 tbsp vegetable oil

1 Lightly beat the eggs in a large mixing bowl.

2 Add the shredded chicken and jumbo shrimp to the eggs, mixing well.

3 Stir in the chopped chives, light soy sauce, and chili sauce, mixing well to combine all the ingredients.

4 Heat the vegetable oil in a large preheated skillet over a medium heat.

5 Add the egg mixture to the skillet, tilting the pan to coat the base completely.

6 Cook over a medium heat, gently stirring the omelet with a fork, until the surface is just set and the underside is a golden brown color.

7 When the omelet is set, slide it out of the pan, with the aid of a spatula.

8 Cut the Chinese omelet into squares or slices and serve immediately. Alternatively, serve the omelet as a main course for two people.

VARIATION

You could add extra flavor to the omelet by stirring in 3 tablespoons of finely chopped fresh cilantro or 1 teaspoon of sesame seeds with the chives in step 3.

Chili Fish Cakes

These small fish cakes are quick to make and are delicious served with a chili dip.

NUTRITIONAL INFORMATION

Calories	164	Sugars	.........1g
Protein	........23g	Fat	..........6g
Carbohydrate	....6g	Saturates	.......1g

5 MINS   40 MINS

SERVES 4

INGREDIENTS

1 lb cod fillets, skinned

2 tbsp fish sauce

2 red chilies, seeded and very finely chopped

2 cloves garlic, minced

10 lime leaves, very finely chopped

2 tbsp fresh cilantro, chopped

1 large egg

¼ cup all-purpose flour

3½ oz fine green beans, very finely sliced

peanut oil, for frying

chili dip, to serve

VARIATION

Almost any kind of fish fillets and seafood can used in this recipe, try haddock, crabmeat, or lobster.

1 Using a sharp knife, roughly cut the cod fillets into bite-sized pieces.

2 Place the cod in a food processor together with the fish sauce, chilies, garlic, lime leaves, cilantro, egg, and flour. Process until finely chopped and turn out into a large mixing bowl.

3 Add the green beans to the cod mixture and combine.

4 Divide the mixture into small balls. Flatten the balls between the palms of your hands to form circles.

5 Heat a little oil in a preheated wok or large skillet. Fry the fish cakes on both sides until brown and crispy on the outside.

6 Transfer the fish cakes to serving plates and serve hot with a chili dip.

Red Curry Fishcakes

You can use almost any kind of fish fillets or seafood for these delicious fishcakes which can be eaten as an appetizer or a light meal.

NUTRITIONAL INFORMATION

Calories	203	Sugars	.........1g
Protein	........32g	Fat	..........8g
Carbohydrate	....1g	Saturates	.......1g

 🍳 🍳 🍳

 15 MINS   🕐 15 MINS

SERVES 6

I N G R E D I E N T S

2 lb 4 oz fish fillets or prepared seafood, such as cod, haddock, shrimp, crabmeat, or lobster

1 egg, beaten

2 tbsp chopped fresh cilantro

red curry paste (store bought)

1 bunch scallions, finely chopped

vegetable oil, for deep-frying

chili flowers, to garnish

C U C U M B E R   S A L A D

1 large cucumber, peeled and grated

2 shallots, peeled and grated

2 red chilies, seeded and very finely chopped

2 tbsp fish sauce

2 tbsp dried powdered shrimps

1½-2 tbsp lime juice

COOK'S TIP

To save time, red curry paste can be bought ready-made in jars from Chinese grocery stores or large supermarkets.

1 Place the fish in a blender or food processor with the egg, cilantro, and curry paste and purée until smooth and well blended.

2 Turn the mixture into a bowl, add the scallions and mix well to combine.

3 Taking 2 tablespoons of the fish mixture at a time, shape into balls, then flatten them slightly with your fingers to make fishcakes.

4 Heat the vegetable oil in a preheated wok or skillet until hot.

5 Add a few of the fishcakes to the wok or pan and deep-fry for a few minutes until brown and cooked through. Remove with a draining spoon and drain on paper towels. Keep warm while cooking the remaining fishcakes.

6 Meanwhile, to make the cucumber salad, mix the cucumber with the shallots, chilies, fish sauce, dried shrimp, and lime juice.

7 Serve the cucumber salad immediately, with the warm fishcakes.

Crispy Crab Wontons

These delicious wontons are a superb appetizer. Deep-fried until crisp and golden, they are delicious with a chili dipping sauce.

NUTRITIONAL INFORMATION

Calories	266	Sugars	.......0.4g
Protein	........10g	Fat	..........17g
Carbohydrate	...18g	Saturates	.......5g

 10 MINS   15 MINS

SERVES 4

I N G R E D I E N T S

6 oz white crabmeat, flaked

1¾ oz canned water chestnuts, drained, rinsed, and chopped

1 small fresh red chili, chopped

1 scallion, chopped

1 tbsp cornstarch

1 tsp dry sherry

1 tsp light soy sauce

½ tsp lime juice

24 wonton skins

vegetable oil, for deep-frying

sliced lime, to garnish

1 To make the filling, mix together the crabmeat, water chestnuts, chili, scallion, cornstarch, sherry, soy sauce, and lime juice.

2 Spread out the wonton skins on a work counter and spoon one portion of the filling into the center of each wonton wrapper.

3 Dampen the edges of the wonton skins with a little water and fold them in half to form triangles. Fold the two pointed ends in towards the center, moisten with a little water to secure, and then pinch together to seal.

4 Heat the oil for deep-frying in a wok or deep-fryer to 350°F–375°F or until a cube of bread browns in 30 seconds. Fry the wontons, in batches, for 2–3 minutes, until golden brown and crisp. Remove the wontons from the oil and leave to drain on paper towels.

5 Serve the wontons hot, garnished with slices of lime.

COOK'S TIP

Handle wonton skins carefully as they can be easily damaged. Make sure that the wontons are sealed well and secured before deep-frying to prevent the filling coming out and the wontons unwrapping.

Thai Potato Crab Cakes

These small crab cakes are based on a traditional Thai recipe. They make a delicious snack when served with this sweet and sour cucumber sauce.

NUTRITIONAL INFORMATION

Calories 254   Sugars 9g
Protein . . . . .12g   Fat 6g
Carbohydrate . . .40g   Saturates 1g

10 MINS   30 MINS

SERVES 4

INGREDIENTS

1 lb mealy potatoes, diced

6 oz white crabmeat, drained if canned

4 scallions, chopped

1 tsp light soy sauce

½ tsp sesame oil

1 tsp chopped lemon grass

1 tsp lime juice

3 tbsp all-purpose flour

2 tbsp vegetable oil

salt and pepper

SAUCE

4 tbsp finely chopped cucumber

2 tbsp clear honey

1 tbsp garlic wine vinegar

½ tsp light soy sauce

1 chopped red chili

TO GARNISH

1 red chili, sliced

cucumber slices

1 Cook the diced potatoes in a saucepan of boiling water for 10 minutes until cooked through. Drain well and mash.

2 Mix the crab meat into the potato with the scallions, soy sauce, sesame oil, lemon grass, lime juice, and flour. Season with salt and pepper.

3 Divide the potato mixture into 8 portions of equal size and shape them into small circles, using floured hands.

4 Heat the oil in a wok or skillet and cook the cakes, 4 at a time, for 5-7 minutes, turning once. Keep warm and repeat with the remaining crab cakes.

5 Meanwhile, make the sauce. In a small serving bowl, mix the cucumber, honey, vinegar, soy sauce, and chopped red chili.

6 Garnish the cakes with the sliced red chili and cucumber slices and serve with the sauce.

Crêpes with Curried Crab

Home-made crêpes are delicious – here, white crab meat is lightly flavored with curry spices and tossed in a low-fat dressing.

NUTRITIONAL INFORMATION

Calories ....279 Sugars 9g
Protein ....25g Fat 7g
Carbohydrate ...31g Saturates 1g

 40 MINS   25 MINS

SERVES 4

INGREDIENTS

4 oz buckwheat flour

1 large egg, beaten

1¼ cups skimmed milk

4½ oz frozen spinach, thawed, well-drained, and chopped

2 tsp vegetable oil

FILLING

12 oz white crabmeat

1 tsp mild curry powder

1 tbsp mango chutney

1 tbsp reduced-calorie mayonnaise

2 tbsp low-fat unsweetened yogurt

2 tbsp fresh cilantro, chopped

TO SERVE

green salad

lemon wedges

1 Sift the flour into a bowl and remove any husks that remain in the strainer. Make a well in the center of the flour and add the egg. Whisk in the milk, then blend in the spinach. Transfer to a jug and leave for 30 minutes.

2 To make the filling, mix together all the ingredients, except the cilantro, in a bowl, cover, and chill until required. Whisk the batter. Brush a small crepe pan with a little oil, heat until hot, and pour in enough batter to cover the base thinly. Cook for 1–2 minutes, turn over, and cook for 1 minute until golden. Repeat to make 8 pancakes, layering them on a plate with baking parchment.

3 Stir the cilantro into the crab mixture. Fold each pancake into quarters. Open one fold and fill with the crab mixture. Serve warm, with a green salad and lemon wedges.

VARIATION

Try lean diced chicken in a light white sauce or peeled shrimp instead of the crab.

Fat Horses

A mixture of meats is flavored with coconut milk, fish sauce and cilantro in this curious-sounding dish.

NUTRITIONAL INFORMATION

Calories	195	Sugars	.........1g
Protein	........23g	Fat	...........11g
Carbohydrate	....1g	Saturates	.......6g

 10 MINS   30 MINS

SERVES 4

I N G R E D I E N T S

2 tbsp creamed coconut

4½ oz lean pork

4½ oz chicken breast, skin removed

½ cup canned crab meat, drained

2 eggs

2 garlic cloves, minced

4 scallions, trimmed and chopped

1 tbsp fish sauce

1 tbsp chopped fresh cilantro leaves and
stems

1 tbsp dark brown sugar

salt and pepper

TO GARNISH

finely sliced daikon or turnip

chives

red chili

sprigs of fresh cilantro

1 Mix the coconut with 3 tbsp of hot water. Stir to dissolve the coconut.

2 Put the pork, chicken, and crab meat into a food processor or blender and process for 10–15 seconds until ground, or chop them finely by hand and put in a mixing bowl.

3 Add the coconut mixture to the food processor or blender with the eggs, garlic, scallions, fish sauce, cilantro, and sugar. Season to taste and process for a few more seconds. Alternatively, mix these ingredients into the chopped pork, chicken, and crab meat.

4 Grease 6 ramekin dishes with a little butter. Spoon in the ground mixture, leveling the surface. Place them in a steamer, then set the steamer over a pan of gently boiling water. Cook until set – about 30 minutes.

5 Lift out the dishes and leave to cool for a few minutes. Run a knife around the edge of each dish, then invert onto warmed plates. Serve garnished with finely sliced daikon or turnip, chives, red chili, and sprigs of fresh cilantro.

Crab Ravioli

These small packets are made from wonton skins and filled with mixed vegetables and crabmeat for a melt-in-the-mouth starter.

NUTRITIONAL INFORMATION

Calories	292	Sugars	.........1g
Protein	........25g	Fat	..........17g
Carbohydrate	....11g	Saturates	.......5g

 20 MINS   25 MINS

SERVES 4

I N G R E D I E N T S

1 lb crabmeat (fresh or canned and drained)

½ red bell pepper, seeded and finely diced

4½ oz Chinese lcabbage, shredded

1 oz beansprouts, roughly chopped

1 tbsp light soy sauce

1 tsp lime juice

16 wonton skins

1 small egg, beaten

2 tbsp peanut oil

1 tsp sesame oil

salt and pepper

1 Mix together the crabmeat, bell pepper, Chinese cabbage, beansprouts, soy sauce, and lime juice. Season and leave to stand for 15 minutes.

2 Spread out the wonton skins on a work counter. Spoon a little of the crabmeat mixture into the center of each skin. Brush the edges with egg and fold in half, pushing out any air. Press the edges together to seal.

3 Heat the peanut oil in a preheated wok or skillet. Fry the ravioli, in batches, for 3–4 minutes, turning, until browned. Remove with a draining spoon and drain on paper towels.

4 Heat any remaining filling in the wok or skillet over a gentle heat until hot. Serve the ravioli with the hot filling and sprinkled with sesame oil.

COOK'S TIP

Make sure that the edges of the ravioli are sealed well and that all of the air is pressed out to prevent them from opening during cooking.

Mussels in White Wine

This soup of mussels, cooked in white wine with onions and cream, can be served as an appetizer or a main dish with plenty of crusty bread.

NUTRITIONAL INFORMATION

Calories 396   Sugars 2g
Protein . . . . .23g   Fat 24g
Carbohydrate . . . .8g   Saturates 15g

5–10 MINS   25 MINS

SERVES 4

INGREDIENTS

3 quarts cups fresh mussels

¼ cup butter

1 large onion, chopped very finely

2–3 garlic cloves, minced

1½ cups dry white wine

⅔ cup water

2 tbsp lemon juice

good pinch of finely grated lemon peel

1 bouquet garni sachet

1 tbsp all-purpose flour

4 tbsp light or thick cream

2–3 tbsp chopped fresh parsley

salt and pepper

warm crusty bread, to serve

1 Scrub the mussels in several changes of cold water to remove all mud, sand, barnacles, etc. Pull off all the beards. All of the mussels must be tightly closed; if they don't close when given a sharp tap, they must be discarded.

2 Melt half the butter in a large saucepan. Add the onion and garlic, and fry gently until soft but not colored.

3 Add the wine, water, lemon juice and peel, bouquet garni, and plenty of seasoning. Bring to a boil, cover, and simmer for 4–5 minutes.

4 Add the mussels to the pan, cover tightly, and simmer for 5 minutes, shaking the pan frequently, until all the mussels have opened. Discard any mussels which have not opened. Remove the bouquet garni.

5 Remove the empty half shell from each mussel. Blend the remaining butter with the flour and whisk into the soup, a little at a time. Simmer gently for 2–3 minutes until slightly thickened.

6 Add the cream and half the parsley to the soup and reheat gently. Adjust the seasoning. Ladle the mussels and soup into warmed large soup bowls, sprinkle with the remaining parsley, and serve with plenty of warm crusty bread.

Deep-Fried Seafood

Deep-fried seafood is popular all around the Mediterranean coast, where fish of all kinds are fresh and abundant.

NUTRITIONAL INFORMATION

Calories 393   Sugars 0.2g
Protein ....27g   Fat 26g
Carbohydrate ...12g   Saturates 3g

5 MINS   15 MINS

SERVES 4

INGREDIENTS

7 oz prepared squid

7 oz raw jumbo shrimp, peeled

5 ½ oz whitebait

oil, for deep-frying

1 ½ oz all-purpose flour

1 tsp dried basil

salt and pepper

TO SERVE

garlic mayonnaise (see page 85)

lemon wedges

1 Carefully rinse the squid, shrimp and whitebait under cold running water, completely removing any dirt or grit.

2 Using a sharp knife, slice the squid into rings, leaving the tentacles whole.

3 Heat the oil in a large saucepan to 350°–375°F or until a cube of bread browns in 30 seconds.

4 Place the flour in a bowl, add the basil and season with salt and pepper to taste. Mix together well.

5 Roll the squid, shrimp, and whitebait in the seasoned flour until coated all over. Carefully shake off any excess flour.

6 Cook the seafood in the heated oil, in batches, for 2–3 minutes or until crispy and golden all over. Remove all of the seafood with a draining spoon and leave to drain thoroughly on paper towels.

7 Transfer the deep-fried seafood to serving plates, garnish with garlic mayonnaise and a few lemon wedges, and serve.

Roasted Seafood

Vegetables become deliciously sweet and juicy when they are roasted, and they go particularly well with fish and seafood.

NUTRITIONAL INFORMATION

Calories 280	Sugars 5g	
Protein 15g	Fat 12g	
Carbohydrate ...28g	Saturates 2g	

15 MINS   50 MINS

SERVES 4

INGREDIENTS

1 lb 5 oz new potatoes

3 red onions, cut into wedges

2 zucchini, sliced into chunks

8 garlic cloves, peeled

2 lemons, cut into wedges

4 sprigs rosemary

4 tbsp olive oil

12 oz shell-on shrimp, preferably uncooked

2 small squid, chopped into rings

4 tomatoes, quartered

1 Scrub the potatoes to remove any excess dirt. Cut any large potatoes in half. Place the potatoes in a large roasting pan, together with the onions, zucchini, garlic, lemon, and rosemary sprigs.

VARIATION

Most vegetables are suitable for roasting in the oven. Try adding 1 lb pumpkin, squash, or eggplant, if you prefer.

2 Pour over the oil and toss to coat all of the vegetables in the oil. Cook in a preheated oven, at 400°F for 40 minutes, turning occasionally, until the potatoes are tender.

3 Once the potatoes are tender, add the shrimp, squid, and tomatoes, tossing to coat them in the oil, and roast for 10 minutes. All of the vegetables should be cooked through and slightly charred for full flavor.

4 Transfer the roasted seafood and vegetables to warm serving plates and serve hot.

Rice & Tuna Bell Peppers

Grilled mixed sweet bell peppers are filled with tender tuna, corn, nutty brown and wild rice, and grated, reduced-fat cheese.

NUTRITIONAL INFORMATION

Calories	332	Sugars	.......13g
Protein	........27g	Fat	...........8g
Carbohydrate	...42g	Saturates	......4g

10 MINS   35 MINS

SERVES 4

INGREDIENTS

⅓ cup wild rice

⅓ cup brown rice

4 assorted medium bell peppers

7 oz can tuna fish in brine, drained and flaked

11½ oz can corn kernels (with no added sugar or salt), drained

3½ oz reduced-fat sharp Cheddar cheese, grated

1 bunch fresh basil leaves, shredded

2 tbsp dry white bread crumbs

1 tbsp Parmesan cheese, freshly grated

salt and pepper

fresh basil leaves, to garnish

crisp salad leaves, to serve

1 Place the wild rice and brown rice in different saucepans, cover with water, and cook for about 15 minutes or according to the directions on the package. Drain the rice well.

2 Meanwhile, preheat the broiler to medium. Halve the bell peppers, remove the seeds and stalks, and arrange the peppers on the broiler rack, cut side down. Cook for 5 minutes, turn over and cook for a further 4–5 minutes.

3 Transfer the cooked rice to a mixing bowl and add the flaked tuna and drained corn. Gently fold in the grated cheese. Stir the basil leaves into the rice mixture and season with salt and pepper to taste.

4 Divide the tuna and rice mixture into 8 equal portions. Pile each portion into each cooked bell-pepper half. Mix together the bread crumbs and Parmesan cheese and sprinkle over each bell pepper.

5 Place the bell peppers back under the broiler for 4–5 minutes until hot and golden-brown.

6 Serve the bell peppers immediately, garnished with basil and accompanied with fresh, crisp salad leaves.

Baked Tuna & Ricotta Rigatoni

Ribbed tubes of pasta are filled with tuna and ricotta cheese and then baked in a creamy sauce.

NUTRITIONAL INFORMATION

Calories	949	Sugars	.........5g
Protein	........51g	Fat	..........48g
Carbohydrate	...85g	Saturates	......26g

10 MINS   45 MINS

SERVES 4

INGREDIENTS

butter, for greasing

1 lb dried rigatoni

1 tbsp olive oil

7 oz can flaked tuna, drained

8 oz ricotta cheese

½ cup heavy cream

2 ⅔ cups grated Parmesan cheese

4 oz sun-dried tomatoes, drained
    and sliced

salt and pepper

1 Lightly grease a large baking dish with butter.

2 Bring a large saucepan of lightly salted water to a boil. Add the rigatoni and olive oil and cook for 8–10 minutes until just tender, but still firm to the bite. Drain the pasta and set aside until cool enough to handle.

3 Meanwhile, in a bowl, mix together the tuna and ricotta cheese to form a soft paste. Spoon the mixture into a piping bag and use to fill the rigatoni. Arrange the filled pasta tubes side by side in the prepared baking dish.

4 To make the sauce, mix the cream and Parmesan cheese and season with salt and pepper to taste. Spoon the sauce over the rigatoni and top with the sun-dried tomatoes, arranged in a criss-cross pattern. Bake in a preheated oven at 400°F for 20 minutes. Serve hot straight from the dish.

VARIATION

For a vegetarian alternative of this recipe, simply substitute a mixture of pitted and chopped black olives and chopped walnuts for the tuna. Follow exactly the same cooking method.

Pancakes with Smoked Fish

These are delicious as an appetizer or light supper dish and you can vary the filling with whichever fish you prefer.

NUTRITIONAL INFORMATION

Calories 399	Sugars 6g
Protein 36g	Fat 18g
Carbohydrate ...25g	Saturates 10g

15 MINS | 1 HR 20 MINS

Makes 12 pancakes

INGREDIENTS

PANCAKES

3 ½ oz flour

½ tsp salt

1 egg, beaten

1 ¼ cups milk

1 tbsp oil, for frying

SAUCE

1 lb smoked haddock, skinned

1 ¼ cups milk

3 tbsp butter or margarine

1 ½ oz flour

1 ¼ cups fish stock

2 ¾ oz Parmesan cheese, grated

3 ½ oz frozen English peas, defrosted

3 ½ oz shrimp, cooked and peeled

1 ¾ oz Gruyère cheese, grated

salt and pepper

1 To make the pancake batter, sift the flour and salt into a large bowl and make a well in the center. Add the egg and, using a wooden spoon, begin to draw in the flour. Slowly add the milk and beat together to form a smooth batter. Set aside until required.

2 Place the fish in a large skillet, add the milk, and bring to a boil. Simmer for 10 minutes or until the fish begins to flake. Drain thoroughly, reserving the milk.

3 Melt the butter in a saucepan. Add the flour, mix to a paste, and cook for 2–3 minutes. Remove the pan from the heat and add the reserved milk a little at a time, stirring to make a smooth sauce. Repeat with the fish stock. Return to the heat and bring to a boil, stirring. Stir in the Parmesan and season with salt and pepper to taste.

4 Grease a skillet with oil. Add 2 tablespoons of the pancake batter, swirling it around the pan, and cook for 2–3 minutes. Loosen the sides with a spatula and flip over the pancake. Cook for 2–3 minutes until golden; repeat. Stack the pancakes with sheets of baking parchment between them and keep warm in the oven.

5 Stir the flaked fish, peas, and shrimp into half of the sauce and use to fill each pancake. Pour over the remaining sauce, top with the Gruyère and bake for 20 minutes until golden.

Penne with Fried Mussels

This is quick and simple, but one of the nicest of Italian fried fish dishes, served with penne.

NUTRITIONAL INFORMATION

Calories 537	Sugars 2g	
Protein 22g	Fat 24g	
Carbohydrate ...62g	Saturates 3g	

🥄 10 MINS   🕐 25 MINS

SERVES 6

INGREDIENTS

3 ½ cups dried penne

½ cup olive oil

1 lb mussels, cooked and shelled

1 tsp sea salt

⅔ cup flour

3 ½ oz sun-dried tomatoes, sliced

2 tbsp chopped fresh basil leaves

salt and pepper

1 lemon, thinly sliced, to garnish

1 Bring a large saucepan of lightly salted water to a boil. Add the penne and 1 tbsp of the olive oil, and cook for 8–10 minutes, or until the pasta is just tender but still firm to the bite.

2 Drain the pasta thoroughly and place in a large, warm serving dish. Set aside and keep warm while you cook the mussels.

3 Lightly sprinkle the mussels with the sea salt. Season the flour with salt and pepper to taste, sprinkle into a bowl, and toss the mussels in the flour until well coated.

4 Heat the remaining oil in a large skillet. Add the mussels and fry, stirring frequently, until golden brown.

5 Toss the mussels with the penne and sprinkle with the sun-dried tomatoes and basil leaves. Garnish with slices of lemon and serve immediately.

COOK'S TIP

Sun-dried tomatoes, used in Italy for a long time, have become popular elsewhere only quite recently. They are dried and then preserved in oil. They have a concentrated, roasted flavor and a dense texture. They should be drained and chopped or sliced before using.

Pasta & Anchovy Sauce

This is an ideal dish for cooks in a hurry, as it is prepared in minutes from store-cupboard ingredients.

NUTRITIONAL INFORMATION

Calories 712   Sugars 4g
Protein ....25g   Fat 34g
Carbohydrate ...81g   Saturates 8g

 10 MINS   25 MINS

SERVES 4

INGREDIENTS

3 fl oz olive oil

2 garlic cloves, minced

2 oz can anchovy fillets, drained

1 lb dried spaghetti

2 oz pesto sauce

2 tbsp finely chopped fresh oregano

1 cup grated Parmesan cheese, plus extra
   for serving (optional)

salt and pepper

2 fresh oregano sprigs, to garnish

1 Reserve 1 tbsp of the oil and heat the remainder in a small saucepan. Add the garlic and fry for 3 minutes.

2 Lower the heat, stir in the anchovies and cook, stirring occasionally, until the anchovies have disintegrated.

3 Bring a large saucepan of lightly salted water to a boil. Add the spaghetti and the remaining olive oil, and cook for 8–10 minutes, or until just tender but still firm to the bite.

4 Add the pesto sauce and chopped fresh oregano to the anchovy mixture and then season with pepper to taste.

5 Drain the spaghetti, using a draining spoon, and transfer to a warm serving dish. Pour the pesto sauce over the spaghetti and then sprinkle over the grated Parmesan cheese.

6 Garnish with oregano sprigs and serve with extra cheese, if using.

COOK'S TIP

If you find canned anchovies too salty, soak them in a saucer of cold milk for 5 minutes, drain and pat dry with kitchen towels before using. The milk absorbs the salt.

Spinach & Anchovy Pasta

This colorful light meal can be made with a variety of different pasta, including spaghetti and linguine.

NUTRITIONAL INFORMATION

Calories	.619	Sugars	.5g
Protein	.21g	Fat	.31g
Carbohydrate	...67g	Saturates	.3g

 10 MINS   25 MINS

SERVES 4

I N G R E D I E N T S

2 lb fresh, young spinach leaves

14 oz dried fettuccine

6 tbsp olive oil

3 tbsp pine kernels

3 garlic cloves, minced

8 canned anchovy fillets, drained and
   chopped

salt

1 Trim off any tough spinach stalks. Rinse the spinach leaves and place them in a large saucepan with only the water that is clinging to them after washing. Cover and cook over a high heat, shaking the pan from time, until the spinach has wilted but retains its color. Drain well, set aside, and keep warm.

COOK'S TIP

If you are in a hurry, you can use frozen spinach. Thaw and drain it thoroughly, pressing out as much moisture as possible. Cut the leaves into strips and add to the dish with the anchovies in step 4.

2 Bring a large saucepan of lightly salted water to a boil. Add the fettuccine and 1 tablespoon of the oil and cook for 8–10 minutes until it is just tender, but still firm to the bite.

3 Heat 4 tablespoons of the remaining oil in a saucepan. Add the pine nuts and fry until golden. Remove the pine nuts from the pan and set aside until required.

4 Add the garlic to the pan and fry until golden. Add the anchovies and stir in the spinach. Cook, stirring, for 2-3 minutes, until heated through. Return the pine nuts to the pan.

5 Drain the fettuccine, toss in the remaining olive oil, and transfer to a warm serving dish. Spoon the anchovy and spinach sauce over the fettucine, toss lightly, and serve immediately.

Potatoes, Olives, & Anchovies

This side dish makes a delicious accompaniment for broiled fish or for lamb chops. The fennel adds a subtle aniseed flavor.

NUTRITIONAL INFORMATION

Calories	202	Sugars	.........2g
Protein	.........7g	Fat	..........12g
Carbohydrate	...19g	Saturates	.......1g

 10 MINS   30 MINS

SERVES 4

INGREDIENTS

1 lb baby new potatoes, scrubbed

2 tbsp olive oil

2 fennel bulbs, trimmed and sliced

2 sprigs rosemary, stalks removed

2¾ oz mixed olives

8 canned anchovy fillets, drained and
chopped

1 Bring a large saucepan of water to a boil and cook the potatoes for 8–10 minutes or until tender. Remove the potatoes from the saucepan using a draining spoon and set aside to cool slightly.

2 Once the potatoes are just cool enough to handle, cut them into wedges, using a sharp knife.

COOK'S TIP

Fresh rosemary is a particular favorite with Italians, but you can experiment with your favorite herbs in this recipe, if you prefer.

3 Pit the mixed olives and cut them in half, using a sharp knife.

4 Using a sharp knife, chop the anchovy fillets into smaller strips.

5 Heat the oil in a large skillet. Add the potato wedges, sliced fennel, and rosemary. Cook for 7–8 minutes or until the potatoes are golden.

6 Stir in the olives and anchovies and cook for 1 minute or until completely warmed through.

7 Transfer to serving plates and serve immediately.

Tuna & Anchovy Pâté

An excellent tangy combination which can be used for a sandwich filling or as a dip. The pâté will keep well in the refrigerator for up to one week.

NUTRITIONAL INFORMATION

Calories 183	Sugars 3g	
Protein 25g	Fat 6g	
Carbohydrate 9g	Saturates 2g	

🍲 1¼ HOURS   🕐 25 MINS

SERVES 6

INGREDIENTS

PATE

1¾ oz can anchovy fillets, drained

14 oz can tuna fish in brine, drained

¾ cup low-fat cottage cheese

½ cup skimmed milk soft cheese

1 tbsp horseradish relish

½ tsp grated orange peel

white pepper

MELBA CROUTONS

4 slices, thick sliced wholewheat bread

TO GARNISH

orange slices

fresh dill sprigs

1 To make the pâté, separate the anchovy fillets and pat well with paper towels to remove all traces of oil.

2 Place the anchovy fillets and remaining pâté ingredients into a blender or food processor. Blend for a few seconds until smooth. Alternatively, finely chop the anchovy fillets and flake the tuna, then beat together with the remaining ingredients; this will make a more textured pâté.

3 Transfer to a mixing bowl, cover, and chill for 1 hour.

4 To make the melba croutons, place the bread slices under a preheated medium broiler for 2–3 minutes on each side until lightly browned.

5 Using a serrated knife, slice off the crusts and slide the knife between the toasted edges of the bread.

6 Stamp out circles using a 2-inch round cutter and place on a cookie sheet. Alternatively, cut each piece of toast in half diagonally. Bake in a preheated oven at 300°F for 15–20 minutes until curled and dry.

7 Spoon the pâté onto serving plates and garnish with orange slices and fresh dill sprigs. Serve with the freshly baked melba croutons.

Olive & Anchovy Pâté

The flavor of olives is accentuated by the anchovies. Serve the pâté as an appetizer on thin pieces of toast with a very dry white wine.

NUTRITIONAL INFORMATION

Calories	214	Sugars	.........1g
Protein	.........2g	Fat	..........22g
Carbohydrate	....1g	Saturates	.......8g

 5–10 MINS 35 MINS

SERVES 4

I N G R E D I E N T S

6 oz black olives, pitted and chopped

finely grated peel and juice of 1 lemon

1½ oz unsalted butter

4 canned anchovy fillets, drained and rinsed

2 tbsp extra virgin olive oil

½ oz ground almonds

fresh herbs, to garnish

1 If you are making the pâté by hand, chop the olives very finely and then mash them along with the lemon peel, juice, and butter, using a fork or potato masher. Alternatively, place the roughly chopped olives, lemon peel, juice, and butter in a food processor and blend until all of the ingredients are finely chopped.

2 Chop the drained anchovies and add them to the olive and lemon mixture. Mash the pâté by hand or blend in a food processor for 20 seconds.

3 Gradually whisk in the olive oil and stir in the ground almonds. Place the black olive pâté in a serving bowl. Leave the pâté to chill in the refrigerator for about 30 minutes. Serve the pâté accompanied by thin pieces of toast, if wished.

COOK'S TIP

This pâté will keep for up to 5 days in a serving bowl in the refrigerator if you pour a thin layer of extra-virgin olive oil over the top of the pâté to seal it. Then use the oil to brush on the toast before spreading the pâté.

Smoked Fish & Potato Pâté

This smoked fish pâté is given a tart fruity flavor by the gooseberries, which complement the fish perfectly.

NUTRITIONAL INFORMATION

Calories	.418	Sugars	.4g
Protein	.18g	Fat	.25g
Carbohydrate	.32g	Saturates	.6g

 20 MINS   10 MINS

SERVES 4

INGREDIENTS

1 lb 7 oz mealy potatoes, diced

10½ oz smoked mackerel, skinned and flaked

2¾ oz cooked gooseberries

2 tsp lemon juice

2 tbsp low-fat crème fraîche

1 tbsp capers

1 gherkin, chopped

1 tbsp chopped dill pickle

1 tbsp chopped fresh dill

salt and pepper

lemon wedges, to garnish

toast or warm crusty bread, to serve

1 Cook the diced potatoes in a saucepan of boiling water for 10 minutes until tender, then drain well.

2 Place the cooked potatoes in a food processor or blender.

3 Add the skinned and flaked smoked mackerel and process for 30 seconds until fairly smooth. Alternatively, place the ingredients in a bowl and mash with a fork.

4 Add the cooked gooseberries, lemon juice, and crème fraîche to the fish and potato mixture. Blend for a further 10 seconds or mash well.

5 Stir in the capers, chopped gherkin, and dill pickle, and chopped fresh dill. Season well with salt and pepper.

6 Turn the fish pâté into a serving dish, garnish with lemon wedges, and serve with slices of toast or warm crusty bread cut into chunks or slices.

COOK'S TIP

Use stewed, canned, or bottled cooked gooseberries for convenience and to save time, or when fresh gooseberries are out of season.

Red Mullet & Coconut Loaf

This fish and coconut loaf is ideal to take along on picnics, as it can be served cold as well as hot.

NUTRITIONAL INFORMATION

Calories 138	Sugars 12g
Protein 11g	Fat 1g
Carbohydrate . . .23g	Saturates 0g

  15 MINS   1¼ HOURS

SERVES 4-6

INGREDIENTS

8 oz red mullet fillets, skinned

2 small tomatoes, seeded and chopped finely

2 green bell peppers, chopped finely

1 onion, chopped finely

1 fresh red chili, chopped finely

2½ cups bread crumbs

2½ cups coconut liquid

salt and pepper

HOT PEPPER SAUCE

½ cup tomato ketchup

1 tsp West Indian hot pepper sauce

¼ tsp hot mustard

TO GARNISH

lemon twists

sprigs of fresh chervil

COOK'S TIP

Be careful when preparing chilies because the juices can irritate the skin, especially the face. Wash your hands after handling them or wear clean kitchen gloves to prepare them if preferred.

1 Finely chop the fish and mix with the tomatoes, bell peppers, onion, and chili.

2 Stir in the bread crumbs, coconut liquid, and seasoning. If using fresh coconut, use a hammer and screwdriver or the tip of a sturdy knife to poke out the three eyes in the top of the coconut and pour out the liquid.

3 Grease and base-line a 1 lb 2 oz loaf pan and add the fish.

4 Bake in a preheated oven at 400°F for 1–1¼ hours until set.

5 To make the hot pepper sauce, mix together the tomato ketchup, hot pepper sauce, and mustard until smooth and creamy.

6 To serve, cut the loaf into slices, garnish with lemon twists and chervil, and serve hot or cold with the hot pepper sauce.

Potato & Tuna Quiche

The base for this quiche is made from mashed potato instead of pastry, giving a softer-textured shell for the tasty tuna filling.

NUTRITIONAL INFORMATION

Calories	383	Sugars	.........5g
Protein	........25g	Fat	..........15g
Carbohydrate	...40g	Saturates	......6g

20 MINS   1 HOUR

SERVES 4

INGREDIENTS

1 lb mealy potatoes, diced

2 tbsp butter

6 tbsp all-purpose flour

FILLING

1 tbsp vegetable oil

1 shallot, chopped

1 garlic clove, minced

1 red bell pepper, diced

6 oz can tuna in brine, drained

1¾ oz canned corn, drained

⅔ cup skimmed milk

3 eggs, beaten

1 tbsp chopped fresh dill

1¾ oz sharp low-fat cheese, grated

salt and pepper

TO GARNISH

fresh dill sprigs

lemon wedges

1 Cook the potatoes in a pan of boiling water for 10 minutes or until tender. Drain and mash the potatoes. Add the butter and flour and mix to form a dough.

2 Knead the potato dough on a floured surface and press the mixture into a 8-in flan pan. Prick the base with a fork.

Line with baking parchment and baking beans and bake blind in a preheated oven 400°F for 20 minutes.

3 Heat the oil in a skillet, add the shallot, garlic, and bell pepper and fry gently for 5 minutes. Drain well and spoon the mixture into the flan shell. Flake the tuna and arrange it over the top with the corn.

4 In a bowl, mix the milk, eggs, and chopped dill and season.

5 Pour the egg and dill mixture into the flan shell and sprinkle the grated cheese on top.

6 Bake in the oven for 20 minutes or until the filling has set. Garnish the quiche with fresh dill and lemon wedges. Serve with mixed vegetables or salad.

Tuna-Stuffed Tomatoes

Deliciously sweet roasted tomatoes are filled with homemade lemon mayonnaise and tuna.

NUTRITIONAL INFORMATION

Calories 196	Sugars 2g	
Protein 9g	Fat 17g	
Carbohydrate 2g	Saturates 3g	

  5–10 MINS   🕐 25 MINS

SERVES 4

I N G R E D I E N T S

4 plum tomatoes

2 tbsp sun-dried tomato paste

2 egg yolks

2 tsp lemon juice

finely grated peel of 1 lemon

4 tbsp olive oil

4 oz can tuna, drained

2 tbsp capers, rinsed

salt and pepper

T O   G A R N I S H

2 sun-dried tomatoes, cut into strips

fresh basil leaves

1 Halve the tomatoes and scoop out the seeds. Divide the sun-dried tomato paste among the tomato halves and spread around the inside of the skin.

2 Place on a cookie sheet and roast in a preheated oven at 400°F for 12–15 minutes. Leave to cool slightly.

3 Meanwhile, make the mayonnaise. In a food processor, blend the egg yolks and lemon juice with the lemon peel until smooth. Once mixed and with the motor still running slowly, add the olive oil. Stop the processor as soon as the mayonnaise has thickened. Alternatively, use a hand whisk, beating the mixture continuously until it thickens.

4 Add the tuna and capers to the mayonnaise and season.

5 Spoon the tuna mayonnaise mixture into the tomato shells and garnish with sun-dried tomato strips and basil leaves. Return to the oven for a few minutes or serve chilled.

COOK'S TIP

For a picnic, do not roast the tomatoes, just scoop out the seeds, drain, cut-side down on paper towels for 1 hour, and fill with the mayonnaise mixture. They are firmer and easier to handle this way. If you prefer, shop-bought mayonnaise may be used instead – just stir in the lemon peel.

Crostini alla Fiorentina

Serve as a starter, or simply spread on small pieces of crusty fried bread (crostini) as an appetizer with drinks.

NUTRITIONAL INFORMATION

Calories	393	Sugars	.........2g
Protein	........17g	Fat	..........25g
Carbohydrate	...19g	Saturates	.......9g

  10 MINS ⏱ 40-45 MINS

SERVES 4

INGREDIENTS

3 tbsp olive oil

1 onion, chopped

1 celery stalk, chopped

1 carrot, chopped

1–2 garlic cloves, minced

4½ oz chicken livers

4½ oz calf's, lamb's, or pig's liver

⅔ cup red wine

1 tbsp tomato paste

2 tbsp chopped fresh parsley

3–4 canned anchovy fillets, chopped finely

2 tbsp stock or water

2–3 tbsp butter

1 tbsp capers

salt and pepper

small pieces of fried crusty bread, to serve

chopped parsley, to garnish

1 Heat the oil in a pan, add the onion, celery, carrot, and garlic, and cook gently for 4–5 minutes or until the onion is soft, but not colored.

2 Meanwhile, rinse and dry the chicken livers. Dry the calf's or other liver, and slice into strips. Add the liver to the pan and fry gently for a few minutes until the strips are well sealed on all sides.

3 Add half of the wine and cook until it has mostly evaporated. Then add the rest of the wine, tomato paste, half of the parsley, the anchovy fillets, stock or water, a little salt, and plenty of black pepper.

4 Cover the pan and leave to simmer, stirring occasionally, for 15–20 minutes or until tender and most of the liquid has been absorbed.

5 Leave the mixture to cool a little, then either coarsely mince or put into a food processor and process to a chunky purée.

6 Return to the pan and add the butter, capers, and remaining parsley. Heat through gently until the butter melts. Adjust the seasoning and turn out into a bowl. Serve warm or cold, spread on the slices of crusty bread, and sprinkled with chopped parsley.

Niçoise with Pasta Shells

This is an Italian variation of the traditional Niçoise salad from southern France.

NUTRITIONAL INFORMATION

Calories	484	Sugars	.........5g
Protein	........28g	Fat	..........26g
Carbohydrate	...35g	Saturates	.......4g

 45 MINS   30 MINS

SERVES 4

INGREDIENTS

12 oz dried small pasta shells

1 tbsp olive oil

4 oz French beans

1¾ oz can anchovies, drained

⅛ cup milk

2 small crisp lettuces

1 lb or 3 large beef tomatoes

4 hard-cooked eggs

8 oz can tuna, drained

1 cup pitted black olives

salt and pepper

VINAIGRETTE DRESSING

2 fl oz extra virgin olive oil

1 fl oz white wine vinegar

1 tsp wholegrain mustard

salt and pepper

1 Bring a large saucepan of lightly salted water to a boil. Add the pasta and the olive oil and cook for 8–10 minutes or until tender, but still firm to the bite. Drain and refresh in cold water.

2 Bring a small saucepan of lightly salted water to a boil. Add the beans and cook for 10–12 minutes, until tender but still firm to the bite. Drain, refresh in cold water, drain thoroughly once more, and then set aside.

3 Put the anchovies in a shallow bowl, pour over the milk, and set aside for 10 minutes. Meanwhile, tear the lettuces into large pieces. Blanch the tomatoes in boiling water for 1–2 minutes, then drain, skin, and roughly chop the flesh. Shell the eggs and cut into quarters. Cut the tuna into large chunks.

4 Drain the anchovies and the pasta. Put all of the salad ingredients, the beans, and the olives into a large bowl and gently mix together.

5 To make the vinaigrette dressing, beat together all of the dressing ingredients and keep in the refrigerator until required. Just before serving, pour the vinaigrette dressing over the salad.

COOK'S TIP

It is very convenient to make salad dressings in a screw top jar. Put all the ingredients in the jar, cover securely, and shake well to mix and emulsify the oil.

Pasta Niçoise Salad

Based on the classic French salad niçoise, this recipe has a light olive oil dressing with the tang of capers and the fragrance of fresh basil.

NUTRITIONAL INFORMATION

Calories	214	Sugars	.........2g
Protein	........26g	Fat	...........7g
Carbohydrate	...14g	Saturates	......1g

15 MINS   35 MINS

SERVES 4

I N G R E D I E N T S

8 oz pasta bows

6 oz green beans, topped and tailed

12 oz fresh tuna steaks

4 oz baby plum tomatoes, halved

8 anchovy fillets, drained on paper towels

2 tbsp capers in brine, drained

1 oz pitted black olives in brine, drained

fresh basil leaves, to garnish

salt and pepper

D R E S S I N G

1 tbsp olive oil

1 garlic clove, minced

1 tbsp lemon juice

½ tsp finely grated lemon peel

1 tbsp shredded fresh basil leaves

1 Cook the pasta in lightly salted boiling water according to the directions on the package until just cooked. Drain well, set aside, and keep warm.

2 Bring a small saucepan of lightly salted water to a boil and cook the green beans for 5–6 minutes until just tender. Drain well and toss into the pasta. Set aside and keep warm.

3 Preheat the broiler to medium. Rinse and pat the tuna steaks dry on paper towels. Season on both sides with black pepper. Place the tuna steaks on the broiler rack and cook for 4–5 minutes on each side until cooked through.

4 Drain the tuna on paper towels and flake into bite-sized pieces. Toss the tuna into the pasta along with the tomatoes, anchovies, capers, and olives. Set aside and keep warm.

5 Meanwhile, prepare the dressing. Mix all the ingredients together and season well. Pour the dressing over the pasta mixture and mix carefully. Transfer to a warmed serving bowl and serve sprinkled with fresh basil leaves.

VARIATION

Any pasta shape is suitable for this salad – to make it even more colorful, use different pasta.

Tuscan Bean & Tuna Salad

The combination of beans and tuna is a favorite in Tuscany. The hint of honey and lemon in the dressing makes this salad very refreshing.

NUTRITIONAL INFORMATION

Calories 224	Sugars 4g
Protein 19g	Fat 10g
Carbohydrate . . .16g	Saturates 2g

30 MINS   0 MINS

SERVES 4

INGREDIENTS

1 small white onion or 2 scallions, finely
  chopped

2 x 14 oz cans butter beans, drained

2 medium tomatoes

6½ oz can tuna, drained

2 tbsp flat leaf parsley, chopped

2 tbsp olive oil

1 tbsp lemon juice

2 tsp clear honey

1 garlic clove, minced

1 Place the chopped onions or scallions and butter beans in a bowl and mix well to combine.

2 Using a sharp knife, cut the tomatoes into wedges.

3 Add the tomatoes to the onion and bean mixture.

4 Flake the tuna with a fork and add it to the onion and bean mixture together with the parsley.

5 In a screw-top jar, mix together the olive oil, lemon juice, honey, and garlic. Shake the jar until the dressing emulsifies and thickens.

6 Pour the dressing over the bean salad. Toss the ingredients together using 2 spoons and serve.

VARIATION

Substitute fresh salmon for the tuna if you wish to create a luxurious version of this recipe for a special occasion.

Tuna, Bean, & Anchovy Salad

Serve this dish as part of a selection of *antipasti*, or for a summer lunch with hot garlic bread.

NUTRITIONAL INFORMATION

Calories 397	Sugars 8g
Protein 23g	Fat 30g
Carbohydrate ...10g	Saturates 4g

 35 MINS   0 MINS

SERVES 4

INGREDIENTS

1 lb 2 oz tomatoes

7 oz can tuna fish, drained

2 tbsp chopped fresh parsley

½ cucumber

1 small red onion, sliced

8 oz cooked green beans

1 small red bell pepper, cored and seeded

1 small crisp lettuce

6 tbsp Italian-style dressing

3 hard-cooked eggs

2 oz can anchovies, drained

12 black olives, pitted

1 Cut the tomatoes into wedges, flake the tuna, and put both into the bowl with the parsley.

2 Cut the cucumber in half lengthways, then cut into slices. Slice the onion. Add the cucumber and onion to the bowl.

3 Cut the beans in half, chop the bell pepper, and add both to the bowl with the lettuce leaves. Pour over the dressing and toss to mix, then spoon into a salad bowl. Cut the eggs into quarters, arrange over the top with the anchovies, and scatter with the olives.

Lentil & Tuna Salad

In this recipe, lentils, combined with spices, lemon juice, and tuna, make a wonderfully tasty and filling salad.

NUTRITIONAL INFORMATION

Calories	227	Sugars	.........2g
Protein	........19g	Fat	...........9g
Carbohydrate	...19g	Saturates	.......1g

  25 MINS   0 MINS

SERVES 4

INGREDIENTS

3 tbsp virgin olive oil

1 tbsp lemon juice

1 tsp wholegrain mustard

1 garlic clove, minced

½ tsp cumin powder

½ tsp ground coriander

1 small red onion

2 ripe tomatoes

14 oz can lentils, drained

6½ can tuna, drained

2 tbsp fresh cilantro, chopped

pepper

1 Using a sharp knife, peel the tomatoes and then chop them into fine dice.

2 Using a sharp knife, finely chop the red onion.

3 To make the dressing, whisk together the virgin olive oil, lemon juice, mustard, garlic, cumin powder, and ground coriander in a small bowl. Set aside until required.

4 Mix together the chopped onion, diced tomatoes, and drained lentils in a large bowl.

5 Flake the tuna and stir it into the onion, tomato, and lentil mixture.

6 Stir in the chopped fresh cilantro.

7 Pour the dressing over the lentil and tuna salad and season with pepper to taste. Serve at once.

COOK'S TIP

Lentils are a good source of protein and contain important vitamins and minerals. Buy them dried for soaking and cooking yourself, or buy canned varieties for speed and convenience.

Potato & Tuna Salad

This colorful dish is a variation of the classic Salade Niçoise. Packed with tuna and vegetables; it is both filling and delicious.

NUTRITIONAL INFORMATION

Calories	225	Sugars	.........5g
Protein	........21g	Fat	..........5g
Carbohydrate	...27g	Saturates	......2g

40 MINS   20 MINS

SERVES 4

INGREDIENTS

1 lb new potatoes, scrubbed and quartered

1 green bell pepper, sliced

1¾ oz canned corn, drained

1 red onion, sliced

10½ oz canned tuna in brine, drained and flaked

2 tbsp chopped pitted black olives

salt and pepper

lime wedges, to garnish

DRESSING

2 tbsp low-fat mayonnaise

2 tbsp soured cream

1 tbsp lime juice

2 garlic cloves, minced

finely grated peel of 1 lime

1 Cook the potatoes in a saucepan of boiling water for 15 minutes until tender. Drain and leave to cool in a mixing bowl.

2 Gently stir in the sliced green bell pepper, corn, and sliced red onion.

3 Spoon the potato mixture into a large serving bowl and arrange the flaked tuna and chopped black olives over the top.

4 Season the salad generously with salt and pepper.

5 To make the dressing, mix together the mayonnaise, soured cream, lime juice, garlic, and lime peel in a bowl.

6 Spoon the dressing over the tuna and olives, garnish with lime wedges and serve.

COOK'S TIP

Green beans and hard-cooked egg slices can be added to the salad for a more traditional Salade Niçoise.

Sweet & Sour Tuna Salad

Small navy beans, zucchini, and tomatoes are briefly cooked in a sweet and sour sauce before being mixed with tuna.

NUTRITIONAL INFORMATION

Calories	245	Sugars	.........5g
Protein	........22g	Fat	...........8g
Carbohydrate	...24g	Saturates	......1g

 15 MINS   10 MINS

SERVES 4

INGREDIENTS

2 tbsp olive oil

1 onion, chopped

2 garlic cloves, minced

2 zucchini, sliced

4 tomatoes, skinned

14 oz can small navy beans, drained and rinsed

10 black olives, halved and pitted

1 tbsp capers

1 tsp superfine sugar

1 tbsp wholegrain mustard

1 tbsp white wine vinegar

7 oz can tuna fish, drained

2 tbsp chopped fresh parsley

chopped fresh parsley, to garnish

crusty bread, to serve

1 Heat the oil in a skillet and fry the onion and garlic for 5 minutes until soft.

2 Add the zucchini and cook for 3 minutes, stirring occasionally.

3 Cut the tomatoes in half then into thin wedges.

4 Add the tomatoes to the pan with the beans, olives, capers, sugar, mustard, and vinegar.

5 Simmer for 2 minutes, stirring gently, then allow to cool slightly.

6 Flake the tuna fish and stir into the bean mixture with the parsley.

7 Garnish with parsley and serve lukewarm with crusty bread.

COOK'S TIP

Capers are the flower buds of the caper bush, which is native to the Mediterranean region. Capers are preserved in vinegar and salt and give a distinctive flavor to this salad. They are much used in Italian and Provençale cooking.

Smoked Trout & Apple Salad

Smoked trout and horseradish are natural partners, but with apple and watercress this makes a wonderful first course.

NUTRITIONAL INFORMATION

Calories	133	Sugars	........11g
Protein	........12g	Fat	..........5g
Carbohydrate	....11g	Saturates	......1g

10 MINS   0 MINS

SERVES 4

INGREDIENTS

2 orange-red eating apples, such as Cox's Orange

2 tbsp French dressing

½ bunch watercress

1 smoked trout, about 6 oz

HORSERADISH DRESSING

½ cup low-fat unsweetened yogurt

½–1 tsp lemon juice

1 tbsp horseradish sauce

milk (optional)

salt and pepper

TO GARNISH

1 tbsp chopped chives

chive flowers (optional)

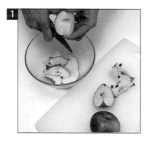

1 Leaving the skin on, cut the apples into quarters and remove the core. Slice the apples into a bowl and toss in the French dressing to prevent them from browning.

2 Break the watercress into sprigs and arrange on 4 serving plates.

3 Skin the trout and take out the bone. Carefully remove any fine bones that remain. Flake the trout into large pieces and arrange between the watercress with the apple.

4 To make the horseradish dressing, whisk all the ingredients together, adding a little milk if too thick, then drizzle over the trout. Sprinkle the chopped chives and flowers (if using) over the trout, then serve.

COOK'S TIP

To make Melba toast, toast thinly sliced bread, cut off the crusts, and carefully slice in half horizontally using a sharp knife. Cut in half diagonally and place toasted side down in a warm oven for 15–20 minutes until the edges start to curl and the toast is crisp.

Seafood Salad

Seafood is plentiful in Italy and each region has its own seafood salad. The dressing needs to be chilled for several hours so prepare in advance.

NUTRITIONAL INFORMATION

Calories	.471	Sugars	.2g
Protein	.34g	Fat	.33g
Carbohydrate	.4g	Saturates	.5g

🥘 45–55 MINS   🕐 40 MINS

SERVES 4

INGREDIENTS

6 oz squid rings, defrosted if frozen

2½ cups water

⅔ cup dry white wine

8 oz hake or monkfish, cut into cubes

16–20 mussels, scrubbed and debearded

20 clams in shells, scrubbed, if available
  (otherwise use extra mussels)

4½–6 oz peeled shrimp

3–4 scallions, trimmed and
  sliced (optional)

radicchio and curly endive leaves, to serve

lemon wedges, to garnish

DRESSING

6 tbsp olive oil

1 tbsp wine vinegar

2 tbsp chopped fresh parsley

1–2 garlic cloves, minced

salt and pepper

GARLIC MAYONNAISE

5 tbsp thick mayonnaise

2–3 tbsp fromage blanc or unsweetened
  yogurt

2 garlic cloves, minced

1 tbsp capers

2 tbsp chopped fresh parsley or mixed herbs

1 Poach the squid in the water and wine for 20 minutes or until nearly tender. Add the fish and continue to cook gently for 7–8 minutes or until tender. Strain, reserving the fish. Pour the stock into a clean pan.

2 Bring the fish stock to a boil and add the mussels and clams. Cover the pan and simmer gently for about 5 minutes or until the shells open. Discard any that remain closed.

3 Drain the shellfish and remove from their shells. Put into a bowl with the cooked fish and add the shrimp and scallions, if using.

4 For the dressing, whisk together the oil, vinegar, parsley, garlic, salt, and pepper to taste. Pour over the fish, mixing well. Cover and chill for several hours.

5 Arrange small leaves of radicchio and curly endive on 4 plates and spoon the fish salad into the center. Garnish with lemon wedges. Combine all the ingredients for the garlic mayonnaise and serve with the salad.

Sweet & Sour Fish Salad

This refreshing blend of pink and white fish mixed with fresh pineapple and bell peppers makes an interesting starter or a light meal.

NUTRITIONAL INFORMATION

Calories	168	Sugars	.........5g
Protein	........24g	Fat	..........6g
Carbohydrate	....5g	Saturates	......1g

🥗 35 MINS 🕐 10 MINS

SERVES 4

I N G R E D I E N T S

8 oz trout fillets

8 oz white fish fillets (such as haddock or cod)

1¼ cups water

1 stalk lemon grass

2 lime leaves

1 large red chili

1 bunch scallions, trimmed and shredded

4 oz fresh pineapple flesh, diced

1 small red bell pepper, seeded and diced

1 bunch watercress, washed and trimmed

fresh snipped chives, to garnish

D R E S S I N G

1 tbsp sunflower oil

1 tbsp rice wine vinegar

pinch of chili powder

1 tsp clear honey

salt and pepper

1 Rinse the fish, place in a skillet, and pour over the water. Bend the lemon grass in half to bruise it and add to the pan with the lime leaves. Prick the chili with a fork and add to the pan. Bring to a boil and simmer for 7–8 minutes. Let cool.

2 Drain the fish fillet thoroughly, flake the flesh away from the skin and place in a bowl. Gently stir in the scallions, pineapple, and bell pepper.

3 Arrange the washed watercress on 4 serving plates and spoon the cooked fish mixture on top.

4 To make the dressing, mix all the ingredients together and season well. Spoon over the fish and serve garnished with chives.

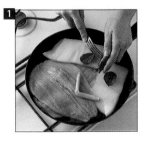

Hot & Sweet Salad

This salad is made by mixing fruit and vegetables with the sharp, sweet, and fishy flavors of the dressing.

NUTRITIONAL INFORMATION

Calories 169   Sugars 8g
Protein ....14g   Fat 8g
Carbohydrate ....11g   Saturates 1g

15 MINS   0 MINS

SERVES 4

INGREDIENTS

9 oz white cabbage, finely shredded

2 tomatoes, skinned, seeded and chopped

9 oz cooked green beans, halved if large

4½ oz peeled shrimp

1 papaya, peeled, seeded, and chopped

1-2 fresh red chilies, seeded and very finely sliced

scant ⅓ cup roasted salted peanuts, ground

handful of lettuce or baby spinach leaves, shredded or torn into small pieces

DRESSING

4 tbsp lime juice

2 tbsp fish sauce

sugar, to taste

pepper

1 Mix the white cabbage with the tomatoes, green beans, shrimp, three-quarters of the papaya, and half of the chilies in a large mixing bowl.

2 Stir in two-thirds of the ground peanuts and mix well.

3 Line the rim of a serving plate with the lettuce or spinach leaves and pile the salad mixture into the center.

4 To make the dressing, beat the lime juice with the fish sauce and add sugar and pepper to taste. Drizzle over the salad.

5 Scatter the top with the remaining papaya, chilies, and ground peanuts. Serve at once.

COOK'S TIP

To skin tomatoes, make a cross at the base with a very sharp knife and then immerse in a bowl of boiling water for a few minutes. Remove with a draining spoon and peel off the skin.

Neapolitan Seafood Salad

This delicious mix of seafood, salad greens, and ripe tomatoes conjures up all the warmth and sunshine of Naples.

NUTRITIONAL INFORMATION

Calories	1152	Sugars	.........3g
Protein	........67g	Fat	..........81g
Carbohydrate	...35g	Saturates	......12g

 6½ HOURS   🕐 25 MINS

SERVES 4

I N G R E D I E N T S

1 lb prepared squid, cut into strips

1 lb 10 oz cooked mussels

1 lb cooked cockles in brine

⅔ cup white wine

1¼ cups olive oil

2 cups dried campanelle or other small
   pasta shapes

juice of 1 lemon

1 bunch chives, snipped

1 bunch fresh parsley, finely chopped

4 large tomatoes

mixed salad greens

salt and pepper

sprig of fresh basil, to garnish

VARIATION

You can substitute cooked scallops for the mussels and clams in brine for the cockles, if you prefer. The seafood needs to be marinated for 6 hours, so prepare well in advance.

1 Put all of the seafood into a large bowl, pour over the wine, and half of the olive oil, and set aside for 6 hours.

2 Put the seafood mixture into a saucepan and simmer over a low heat for 10 minutes. Set aside to cool.

3 Bring a large saucepan of lightly salted water to a boil. Add the pasta and 1 tbsp of the remaining olive oil and cook for 8–10 minutes or until tender, but still firm to the bite. Drain thoroughly and refresh in cold water.

4 Strain off about half of the cooking liquid from the seafood and discard the rest. Mix in the lemon juice, chives, parsley, and the remaining olive oil. Season to taste with salt and pepper. Drain the pasta and add to the seafood.

5 Cut the tomatoes into quarters. Shred the salad greens and arrange them at the base of a salad bowl. Spoon in the seafood salad and garnish with the tomatoes and a sprig of basil. Serve.

Mussel Salad

A colorful combination of cooked mussels tossed together with broiled red bell peppers and salad leaves in a lemon dressing.

NUTRITIONAL INFORMATION

Calories 124	Sugars 5g	
Protein 16g	Fat 5g	
Carbohydrate 5g	Saturates 1g	

40 MINS   10 MINS

SERVES 4

INGREDIENTS

2 large red bell peppers

12 oz cooked shelled mussels, thawed if frozen

1 head of radicchio

1 oz arugula leaves

8 cooked New Zealand mussels in their shells

TO SERVE

lemon wedges

crusty bread

DRESSING

1 tbsp olive oil

1 tbsp lemon juice

1 tsp finely grated lemon peel

2 tsp clear honey

1 tsp French mustard

1 tbsp snipped fresh chives

salt and pepper

1 Preheat the broiler to hot. Halve and seed the bell peppers and place them skin-side up on the rack.

2 Cook for 8–10 minutes until the skin is charred and blistered and the flesh is soft. Leave to cool for 10 minutes, then peel off the skin.

3 Slice the bell pepper flesh into thin strips and place in a bowl. Gently mix in the shelled mussels and set aside until required.

4 To make the dressing, mix all of the ingredients until well blended.

5 Mix into the bell pepper and mussel mixture until coated.

6 Remove the central core of the radicchio and shred the leaves. Place in a serving bowl with the arugula leaves and toss together.

7 Pile the mussel mixture into the center of the leaves and arrange the large mussels in their shells around the edge of the dish. Serve with lemon wedges and crusty bread.

Pasta & Noodles

Nutritionists recommend a diet high in complex carbohydrates; pasta and noodles supply high energy levels and constant blood-sugar levels. They are also the natural

partners for fish and seafood. Both are cooked quickly to preserve their flavor and texture, they are packed with nutritional goodness, and the varieties are almost infinite. The superb recipes in this chapter, which draw on European recipes, in particular Italian, as well as Chinese flavors, demonstrate the full range of these qualities. There are quick and satisfying suppers, unusual and sophisticated dishes, and ideas to suit all tastes.

Lemon Sole & Haddock Ravioli

This delicate-tasting dish is surprisingly satisfying for even the hungriest appetites. Prepare the Italian Red Wine Sauce well in advance.

NUTRITIONAL INFORMATION

Calories	977	Sugars	....7g
Protein	....67g	Fat	....40g
Carbohydrate	...93g	Saturates	....17g

  9³⁄₄ HOURS   25 MINS

SERVES 4

INGREDIENTS

1 lb lemon sole fillets, skinned

1 lb haddock fillets, skinned

3 eggs beaten

1 lb cooked potato gnocchi (shop bought)

3 cups fresh bread crumbs

¼ cup heavy cream

1 lb basic pasta dough (shop bought)

1¼ cups red wine sauce

⅔ cup freshly grated Parmesan cheese

salt and pepper

1 Flake the lemon sole and haddock fillets with a fork and transfer the flesh to a large mixing bowl.

2 Mix the eggs, cooked potato gnocchi, bread crumbs, and cream in a bowl until thoroughly combined. Add the fish to the bowl containing the gnocchi and season the mixture with salt and pepper to taste.

3 Roll out the pasta dough on to a lightly floured surface and cut out 3 inch rounds using a cutter.

4 Place a spoonful of the fish stuffing on each round. Dampen the edges slightly and fold the pasta circles over, pressing together to seal.

5 Bring a large saucepan of lightly salted water to a boil. Add the ravioli and cook for 15 minutes.

6 Drain the ravioli, using a draining spoon, and transfer to a large serving dish. Pour over the red wine sauce, sprinkle over the Parmesan cheese, and serve immediately.

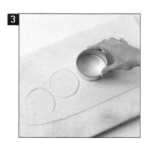

COOK'S TIP

For square ravioli, divide the dough in two. Wrap half in plastic wrap; thinly roll out the other half. Cover; roll out the remaining dough. Pipe the filling at regular intervals and brush the spaces in between with water or beaten egg. Lift the second sheet of dough into position with a rolling pin and press between the filling to seal. Cut with a ravioli cutter or a knife.

Trout with Smoked Bacon

Most trout available nowadays is farmed rainbow trout, however, if you can, buy wild brown trout for this recipe.

NUTRITIONAL INFORMATION

Calories 802	Sugars 8g
Protein 68g	Fat 36g
Carbohydrate ...54g	Saturates 10g

 35 MINS 25 MINS

SERVES 4

I N G R E D I E N T S

butter, for greasing

4 x 9½ oz trout, gutted and cleaned

12 anchovies in oil, drained and chopped

2 apples, peeled, cored, and sliced

4 fresh mint sprigs

juice of 1 lemon

12 slices rindless smoked fatty bacon

1 lb dried tagliatelle

1 tbsp olive oil

salt and pepper

T O   G A R N I S H

2 apples, cored and sliced

4 fresh mint sprigs

1 Grease a deep cookie sheet with butter.

2 Open up the cavities of each trout and rinse with warm salt water.

3 Season each cavity with salt and pepper. Divide the anchovies, sliced apples, and mint sprigs between each of the cavities. Sprinkle the lemon juice into each cavity.

4 Carefully cover the whole of each trout, except the head and tail, with three slices of smoked bacon in a spiral.

5 Arrange the trout on the cookie sheet with the loose ends of bacon tucked underneath. Season with pepper and bake in a preheated oven at 400°F for 20 minutes, turning the trout over after 10 minutes.

6 Meanwhile, bring a large pan of lightly salted water to a boil. Add the tagliatelle and olive oil and cook for about 12 minutes, until tender but still firm to the bite. Drain the pasta and transfer to a large, warm serving dish.

7 Remove the trout from the oven and arrange on the tagliatelle. Garnish with sliced apples and fresh mint sprigs and serve immediately.

Fillets of Red Mullet & Pasta

This simple recipe perfectly complements the sweet flavor and delicate texture of the fish.

NUTRITIONAL INFORMATION

Calories 457   Sugars 3g
Protein ....39g   Fat 12g
Carbohydrate ...44g   Saturates 5g

 15 MINS   1 HOUR

SERVES 4

I N G R E D I E N T S

2 lb 4 oz red mullet fillets

1¼ cups dry white wine

4 shallots, finely chopped

1 garlic clove, crushed

3 tbsp finely chopped mixed fresh herbs

finely grated peel and juice of 1 lemon

pinch of freshly grated nutmeg

3 anchovy fillets, roughly chopped

2 tbsp dheavy cream

1 tsp ccornstarch

1 lb dried vermicelli

1 tbsp olive oil

salt and pepper

TO GARNISH

1 fresh mint sprig

lemon slices

lemon peel

1 Put the red mullet fillets in a large casserole. Pour over the wine and add the shallots, garlic, herbs, lemon peel and juice, nutmeg, and anchovies. Season. Cover and bake in a preheated oven at 350°F for 35 minutes.

2 Transfer the mullet to a warm dish. Set aside and keep warm.

3 Pour the cooking liquid into a pan and bring to a boil. Simmer for 25 minutes, until reduced by half. Mix the cream and cornstarch and stir into the sauce to thicken.

4 Meanwhile, bring a pan of lightly salted water to a boil. Add the vermicelli and oil and cook for 8–10 minutes, until tender but still firm to the bite. Drain the pasta and transfer to a warm serving dish.

5 Arrange the red mullet fillets on top of the vermicelli and pour over the sauce. Garnish with a fresh mint sprig, slices of lemon, and strips of lemon peel and serve immediately.

Red Mullet & Amaretto Sauce

This succulent fish and pasta dish is ideal for serving on a warm, summer's evening – preferably *al fresco*.

NUTRITIONAL INFORMATION

Calories	806	Sugars	.........6g
Protein	........64g	Fat	..........34g
Carbohydrate	...64g	Saturates	......16g

 15 MINS 25 MINS

SERVES 4

INGREDIENTS

3¾ cup all-purpose flour

8 red mullet fillets

2 tbsp butter

⅔ cup fish stock

1 tbsp crushed almonds

1 tsp pink peppercorns

1 orange, peeled and cut into segments

1 tbsp orange liqueur

grated peel of 1 orange

1 lb dried orecchiette

1 tbsp olive oil

⅔ cup heavy cream

4 tbsp amaretto

salt and pepper

TO GARNISH

2 tbsp snipped fresh chives

1 tbsp toasted almonds

1 Season the flour with salt and pepper and sprinkle into a shallow bowl. Press the fish fillets into the flour to coat. Melt the butter in a skillet. Add the fish and fry over a low heat for 3 minutes, until browned.

2 Add the fish stock to the pan and cook for 4 minutes. Carefully remove the fish, cover with foil, and keep warm.

3 Add the almonds, pink peppercorns, half the orange, the orange liqueur, and orange peel to the pan. Simmer until the liquid has reduced by half.

4 Meanwhile, bring a large pan of lightly salted water to a boil. Add the orecchiette and oil and cook for 15 minutes, until tender but still firm to the bite.

5 Meanwhile, season the sauce with salt and pepper and stir in the cream and amaretto. Cook for 2 minutes. Return the fish to the pan to coat with the sauce.

6 Drain the pasta and transfer to a serving dish. Top with the fish fillets and their sauce. Garnish with the remaining orange segments, the chives, and toasted almonds. Serve immediately.

Smoked Fish Lasagne

Use smoked cod or haddock in this delicious lasagne. It is a great way to make a little go a long way.

NUTRITIONAL INFORMATION

Calories 483	Sugars 8g
Protein 36g	Fat 24g
Carbohydrate ...32g	Saturates 12g

 20 MINS 1¼ HOURS

SERVES 4

INGREDIENTS

2 tsp olive or vegetable oil

1 garlic clove, crushed

1 small onion, chopped finely

4½ oz mushrooms, sliced

14 oz can chopped tomatoes

1 small zucchini, sliced

⅔ cup vegetable stock or water

2 tbsp butter or margarine

1¼ cups skimmed milk

¼ cup pall-purpose flour

1 cup grated sharp Cheddar cheese

1 tbsp chopped fresh parsley

4½ oz (6 sheets) pre-cooked lasagne

12 oz skinned and boned smoked cod or
     haddock, cut into chunks

salt and pepper

fresh parsley sprigs to garnish

1 Heat the oil in a saucepan and fry the garlic and onion for about 5 minutes. Add the mushrooms and cook for 3 minutes, stirring.

2 Add the tomatoes, zucchini, and stock or water and simmer, uncovered, for 15–20 minutes until the vegetables are soft. Season.

3 Put the butter or margarine, milk, and flour into a small saucepan and heat, whisking constantly, until the sauce boils and thickens. Remove from the heat and add half of the cheese and all of the parsley. Stir gently to melt the cheese and season to taste.

4 Spoon the tomato sauce mixture into a large, shallow baking dish and top with half of the lasagne sheets. Scatter the chunks of fish evenly over the top, then pour over half of the cheese sauce. Top with the remaining lasagne sheets and then spread the rest of the cheese sauce on top. Sprinkle with the remaining cheese.

5 Bake in a preheated oven at 375°F for 40 minutes, until the top is golden brown and bubbling. Garnish with parsley sprigs and serve hot.

Pasta & Fish Pudding

A tasty mixture of creamy fish and pasta cooked in a bowl, unmolded and drizzled with tomato sauce presents macaroni in a new guise.

NUTRITIONAL INFORMATION

Calories	454	Sugars	.........1g
Protein	........30g	Fat	..........30g
Carbohydrate	...17g	Saturates	......16g

10 MINS   2 HOURS

SERVES 4

INGREDIENTS

1 cup dried short-cut macaroni or other
   short pasta

1 tbsp olive oil

1 tbsp butter, plus extra for greasing

1 lb white fish fillets, such as cod or
   haddock

2–3 fresh parsley sprigs

6 black peppercorns

½ cup heavy cream

2 eggs, separated

2 tbsp chopped fresh dill or parsley

pinch of freshly grated nutmeg

⅔ cup freshly grated Parmesan cheese

salt and pepper

fresh dill or parsley sprigs, to garnish

Tomato sauce, to serve

1 Bring a pan of salted water to a boil. Add the pasta and oil and cook for 8–10 minutes until tender, but still firm to the bite. Drain the pasta and return to the pan. Add the butter, cover, and keep warm.

2 Place the fish in a skillet. Add the parsley sprigs, peppercorns, and enough water to cover. Bring to a boil, cover and simmer for 10 minutes. Lift out the fish and set aside to cool. Reserve the cooking liquid.

3 Skin the fish and cut into bite-size pieces. Put the pasta in a bowl. Mix the cream, egg yolks, chopped dill, or parsley, nutmeg, and cheese, pour into the pasta and mix. Spoon in the fish without breaking it. Add enough of the reserved cooking liquid to make a moist, but firm mixture. Whisk the egg whites until stiff, then fold them into the mixture.

4 Grease a heatproof bowl and spoon in the fish mixture to within 1½ inches of the rim. Cover with waxed baking paper and foil and tie securely with string.

5 Stand the bowl on a trivet in a saucepan. Add boiling water to reach halfway up the sides. Cover and steam for 1½ hours.

6 Invert the pudding on to a serving plate. Pour over a little tomato sauce. Garnish and serve with the remaining tomato sauce.

Spaghetti al Tonno

The classic Italian combination of pasta and tuna is enhanced in this recipe with a delicious parsley sauce.

NUTRITIONAL INFORMATION

Calories	1065	Sugars	.........3g
Protein	........27g	Fat	..........85g
Carbohydrate	...52g	Saturates	......18g

10 MINS   15 MINS

SERVES 4

I N G R E D I E N T S

7 oz can tuna, drained

2 oz can anchovies, drained

1⅛ cups olive oil

1 cup roughly chopped flat leaf parsley

⅔ cup crème fraîche

1 lb dried spaghetti

2 tbsp butter

salt and pepper

black olives, to garnish

crusty bread, to serve

1 Remove any bones from the tuna. Put the tuna into a food processor or blender, together with the anchovies, 1 cup of the olive oil, and the flat leaf parsley. Process until the sauce is very smooth.

VARIATION

If liked, add 1–2 garlic cloves to the sauce, substitute ½ cup chopped fresh basil for half the parsley and garnish with capers instead of black olives.

2 Spoon the crème fraîche into the food processor or blender and process again for a few seconds to blend thoroughly. Season with salt and pepper to taste.

3 Bring a large pan of lightly salted water to a boil. Add the spaghetti and the remaining olive oil and cook for 8–10 minutes until tender but still firm to the bite.

4 Drain the spaghetti, return to the pan, and place over a medium heat. Add the butter and toss well to coat. Spoon in the sauce and quickly toss into the spaghetti, using 2 forks.

5 Remove the pan from the heat and divide the spaghetti between 4 warm individual serving plates. Garnish with the olives and serve immediately with warm, crusty bread.

Poached Salmon with Penne

Fresh salmon and pasta in a mouthwatering lemon and watercress sauce – a wonderful summer evening treat.

NUTRITIONAL INFORMATION

Calories	968	Sugars	.........3g
Protein	........59g	Fat	..........58g
Carbohydrate	...49g	Saturates	......19g

 10 MINS   30 MINS

SERVES 4

INGREDIENTS

4 x 9½ oz fresh salmon steaks

4 tbsp butter

¾ cup dry white wine

sea salt

8 peppercorns

fresh dill sprig

fresh tarragon sprig

1 lemon, sliced

1 lb dried penne

2 tbsp olive oil

lemon slices and fresh watercress,
   to garnish

LEMON & WATERCRESS SAUCE

2 tbsp butter

¼ cup all-purpose flour

⅝ cup warm milk

juice and finely grated peel of 2 lemons

2 oz watercress, chopped

salt and pepper

1 Put the salmon in a large, non-stick pan. Add the butter, wine, a pinch of sea salt, the peppercorns, dill, tarragon, and lemon. Cover, bring to a boil, and simmer for 10 minutes.

2 Using a fish slice, carefully remove the salmon. Strain and reserve the cooking liquid. Remove and discard the salmon skin and center bones. Place on a warm dish, cover, and keep warm.

3 Meanwhile, bring a saucepan of salted water to a boil. Add the penne and 1 tbsp of the oil and cook for 8–10 minutes until tender but still firm to the bite. Drain and sprinkle over the remaining olive oil. Place on a warm serving dish, top with the salmon steaks, and keep warm.

4 To make the sauce, melt the butter and stir in the flour for 2 minutes. Stir in the milk and about 7 tbsp of the reserved cooking liquid. Add the lemon juice and peel and cook, stirring, for a further 10 minutes.

5 Add the watercress to the sauce, stir gently, and season to taste with salt and pepper.

6 Pour the sauce over the salmon and penne, garnish with slices of lemon and fresh watercress, and serve.

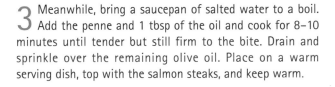

Salmon Lasagne Rolls

Sheets of green lasagne are filled with a mixture of fresh salmon and oyster mushrooms. This recipe has been adapted for the microwave.

NUTRITIONAL INFORMATION

Calories 352   Sugars 5g
Protein ....19g   Fat 19g
Carbohydrate ...25g   Saturates 9g

20 MINS   35 MINS

SERVES 4

I N G R E D I E N T S

8 sheets green lasagne

1 onion, sliced

1 tbsp butter

½ red bell pepper, chopped

1 zucchini, diced

1 tsp chopped gingerroot

4½ oz oyster mushrooms, preferably
    yellow, chopped coarsely

8 oz fresh salmon fillet, skinned, and
    cut into chunks

2 tbsp dry sherry

2 tsp cornstarch

3 tbsp all-purpose flour

1½ tbsp butter

1¼ cups milk

¼ cup Cheddar cheese, grated

¼ cup fresh white bread crumbs

salt and pepper

salad leaves, to serve

1 Place the lasagne sheets in a large shallow dish. Cover with plenty of boiling water. Cook on HIGH power for 5 minutes. Leave to stand, covered, for a few minutes before draining. Rinse in cold water and lay the sheets out on a clean work surface.

2 Put the onion and butter into a bowl. Cover and cook on HIGH power for 2 minutes. Add the bell pepper, zucchini, and gingerroot. Cover and cook on HIGH power for 3 minutes.

3 Add the mushrooms and salmon to the bowl. Mix the sherry into the cornstarch and stir into the bowl. Cover and cook on HIGH power for 4 minutes until the fish flakes when tested with a fork. Season to taste.

4 Whisk the flour, butter, and milk in a bowl. Cook on HIGH power for 3–4 minutes, whisking every minute, to give a sauce of coating consistency. Stir in half the cheese and season with salt and pepper to taste.

5 Spoon the salmon filling in equal quantities along the shorter side of each lasagne sheet. Roll up to enclose the filling. Arrange in a lightly oiled large rectangular dish. Pour over the sauce and sprinkle over the remaining cheese and the bread crumbs.

6 Cook on HIGH power for 3 minutes until heated through. If possible, lightly brown under a preheated broiler before serving. Serve with salad.

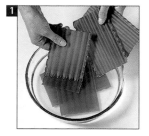  

Spaghetti & Smoked Salmon

Made in moments, this is a luxurious dish to astonish and delight unexpected guests.

NUTRITIONAL INFORMATION

Calories	803	Sugars	.........3g
Protein	........21g	Fat	..........49g
Carbohydrate	...52g	Saturates	......27g

 10 MINS   20 MINS

SERVES 4

INGREDIENTS

1 lb dried buckwheat spaghetti

2 tbsp olive oil

½ cup crumbled Feta cheese

salt

fresh cilantro or parsley leaves, to garnish

SAUCE

1¼ cups heavy cream

⅝ cup whiskey or brandy

4½ oz smoked salmon

pinch of cayenne pepper

pepper

2 tbsp chopped fresh cilantro or parsley

1 Bring a large pan of lightly salted water to a boil. Add the spaghetti and 1 tbsp of the olive oil and cook for 8–10 minutes until tender, but still firm to the bite. Drain the spaghetti, return to the pan and sprinkle over the remaining olive oil. Cover, shake the pan, set aside, and keep warm.

2 Pour the cream into a small saucepan and bring to simmering point, but do not let it boil. Pour the whiskey or brandy into another small saucepan and bring to simmering point, but do not allow it to boil. Remove both saucepans from the heat and mix together the cream and whiskey or brandy.

3 Cut the smoked salmon into thin strips and add to the cream mixture. Season to taste with cayenne and pepper. Just before serving, stir in the fresh cilantro or parsley.

4 Transfer the spaghetti to a warm serving dish, pour over the sauce, and toss thoroughly with 2 large forks. Scatter over the crumbled Feta cheese, garnish with the cilantro or parsley leaves, and serve immediately.

Shrimp Pasta Bake

This dish is ideal for a substantial supper. You can use whatever pasta you like, but the tricolor varieties will give the most colorful results.

NUTRITIONAL INFORMATION

Calories	723	Sugars	.........9g
Protein	........56g	Fat	..........8g
Carbohydrate	...114g	Saturates	......2g

10 MINS   50 MINS

SERVES 4

I N G R E D I E N T S

8 oz tricolor pasta shapes

1 tbsp vegetable oil

6 oz button mushrooms, sliced

1 bunch scallions, trimmed and chopped

14 oz can tuna in brine, drained and flaked

6 oz peeled shrimp, thawed if frozen

2 tbsp cornstarch

1¾ cups skimmed milk

4 medium tomatoes, sliced thinly

1 oz fresh bread crumbs

1 oz reduced-fat Cheddar cheese, grated

salt and pepper

TO SERVE

wholemeal bread

fresh salad

1 Preheat the oven to 375°F. Bring a large saucepan of water to a boil and cook the pasta according to the directions on the package. Drain well.

2 Heat the vegetable oil in a skillet and fry the mushrooms and most of the scallions for 4–5 minutes until softened.

3 Place the cooked pasta in a bowl and mix in the scallions, mushrooms, tuna, and shrimp.

4 Blend the cornstarch with a little milk to make a paste. Pour the remaining milk into a saucepan and stir in the paste. Heat, stirring, until the sauce begins to thicken. Season well. Add the sauce to the pasta mixture and mix well. Transfer to an ovenproof gratin dish and place on a cookie sheet.

5 Arrange the tomato slices over the pasta and sprinkle with the bread crumbs and cheese. Bake for 25–30 minutes until golden. Serve sprinkled with the reserved scallions and accompanied with bread and salad.

Pasta & Shrimp Packets

This is the ideal dish when you have unexpected guests because the packets can be prepared in advance and put in the oven when you are ready to eat.

NUTRITIONAL INFORMATION

Calories ....640 Sugars 1g
Protein ....50g Fat 29g
Carbohydrate ...42g Saturates 4g

15 MINS   30 MINS

SERVES 4

INGREDIENTS

1 lb dried fettuccine

⅝ cup pesto sauce (shop bought)

4 tsp extra virgin olive oil

1 lb 10 oz large raw shrimp, peeled and
  deveined

2 garlic cloves, crushed

½ cup dry white wine

salt and pepper

1 Cut out 4 x 12 inch squares of greaseproof paper.

2 Bring a large saucepan of lightly salted water to a boil. Add the fettuccine and cook for 2–3 minutes until just softened. Drain and set aside.

3 Mix together the fettuccine and half of the pesto sauce. Spread out the paper squares and put 1 tsp olive oil in the center of each. Divide the fettuccine between the the squares, divide the shrimp, and place it on top of the fettuccine.

4 Mix together the remaining pesto sauce and the garlic and spoon it over the shrimp. Season each packet with salt and black pepper and sprinkle with the white wine.

5 Dampen the edges of the waxed paper and wrap the packets loosely, twisting the edges to seal.

6 Place the parcels on a cookie sheetand bake in a preheated oven at 400°F for 10–15 minutes. Transfer the parcels to 4 individual serving plates and serve.

COOK'S TIP

Traditionally, these parcels are designed to look like money bags. The resemblance is more effective with waxed paper than with foil.

Macaroni & Seafood Bake

This adaptation of an eighteenth-century Italian dish is baked until it is golden brown and sizzling, then cut into wedges like a cake.

NUTRITIONAL INFORMATION

Calories 478	Sugars 6g
Protein 27g	Fat 17g
Carbohydrate ...57g	Saturates 7g

🥄 30 MINS 🕐 50 MINS

SERVES 4

I N G R E D I E N T S

3 cups dried short-cut macaroni

1 tbsp olive oil, plus extra for brushing

6 tbsp butter, plus extra for greasing

2 small fennel bulbs, thinly sliced and
   fronds reserved

6 oz mushrooms, thinly sliced

6 oz peeled, cooked shrimp

pinch of cayenne pepper

1¼ cups Béchamel sauce

⅔ cup freshly grated Parmesan cheese

2 large tomatoes, sliced

1 tsp dried oregano

salt and pepper

1 Bring a saucepan of salted water to a boil. Add the pasta and oil and cook for 8–10 minutes until tender but still firm to the bite. Drain the pasta and return to the pan.

2 Add 2 tbsp of the butter to the pasta, cover, shake the pan, and keep warm.

3 Melt the remaining butter in a saucepan. Fry the fennel for 3–4 minutes. Stir in the mushrooms and fry for a further 2 minutes.

4 Stir in the shrimp, then remove the pan from the heat.

5 Stir the cayenne pepper and shrimp mixture into the Béchamel sauce, stirring.

6 Pour into a greased baking dish and spread evenly. Sprinkle over the Parmesan cheese and arrange the tomato slices in a ring around the edge. Brush the tomatoes with olive oil and then sprinkle over the oregano.

7 Bake in a preheated oven at 350°F for 25 minutes or until golden brown. Serve immediately.

Saffron Mussel Tagliatelle

Saffron is the most expensive spice in the world, but you only ever need a small quantity. Saffron threads or powdered saffron may be used.

NUTRITIONAL INFORMATION

Calories	854	Sugars	........3g
Protein	........43g	Fat	..........49g
Carbohydrate	...57g	Saturates	......28g

 15 MINS   35 MINS

SERVES 4

I N G R E D I E N T S

2 lb 4 oz mussels

⅔ cup white wine

1 medium onion, finely chopped

2 tbsp butter

2 garlic cloves, crushed

2 tsp cornstarch

1¼ cups heavy cream

pinch of saffron threads or saffron powder

juice of ½ lemon

1 egg yolk

1 lb dried tagliatelle

1 tbsp olive oil

salt and pepper

3 tbsp chopped fresh parsley, to garnish

1 Scrub and debeard the mussels under cold running water. Discard any that do not close when sharply tapped. Put the mussels in a pan with the wine and onion. Cover and cook over a high heat, shaking the pan, for 5–8 minutes, until the shells open.

2 Drain and reserve the cooking liquid. Discard any mussels that are still closed. Reserve a few mussels for the garnish and remove the remainder from their shells.

3 Strain the cooking liquid into a pan. Bring to a boil and reduce by about half. Remove the pan from the heat.

4 Melt the butter in a saucepan. Add the garlic and cook, stirring frequently, for 2 minutes, until golden brown. Stir in the cornstarch and cook, stirring, for 1 minute. Gradually stir in the cooking liquid and the cream. Crush the saffron threads and add to the pan. Season with salt and pepper to taste and simmer over a low heat for 2–3 minutes, until thickened.

5 Stir in the egg yolk, lemon juice, and shelled mussels. Do not allow the mixture to boil.

6 Meanwhile, bring a pan of salted water to a boil. Add the pasta and oil and cook for 8–10 minutes until tender, but still firm to the bite. Drain and transfer to a serving dish. Add the mussel sauce and toss. Garnish with the parsley and reserved mussels and serve.

Pasta Shells with Mussels

Serve this aromatic seafood dish to family and friends who admit to a love of garlic.

NUTRITIONAL INFORMATION

Calories	686	Sugars	.........2g
Protein	........30g	Fat	..........45g
Carbohydrate	...36g	Saturates	......27g

 15 MINS   25 MINS

SERVES 6

I N G R E D I E N T S

2 lb 12 oz mussels

1 cup dry white wine

2 large onions, chopped

½ cup unsalted butter

6 large garlic cloves, finely chopped

5 tbsp chopped fresh parsley

1¼ cups heavy cream

14 oz dried pasta shells

1 tbsp olive oil

salt and pepper

crusty bread, to serve

1 Scrub and debeard the mussels under cold running water. Discard any mussels that do not close immediately when sharply tapped. Put the mussels into a large saucepan, together with the wine and half of the onions. Cover and cook over a medium heat, shaking the pan frequently, for 2–3 minutes, or until the shells open.

2 Remove the pan from the heat. Drain the mussels and reserve the cooking liquid. Discard any mussels that have not opened. Strain the cooking liquid through a clean cloth into a glass pitcher or bowl and reserve.

3 Melt the butter in a pan over a medium heat. Add the remaining onion and fry until translucent. Stir in the garlic and cook for 1 minute. Gradually stir in the reserved cooking liquid. Stir in the parsley and cream and season to taste with salt and pepper. Bring to simmering point over a low heat.

4 Meanwhile, bring a large pan of lightly salted water to a boil. Add the pasta and oil and cook for 8–10 minutes

until just tender but still firm to the bite. Drain the pasta, return to the pan, cover, and keep warm.

5 Reserve a few mussels for the garnish and remove the remainder from their shells. Stir the shelled mussels into the cream sauce and warm briefly.

6 Transfer the pasta to a serving dish. Pour over the sauce and toss to coat. Garnish with the reserved mussels.

Mussel & Scallop Spaghetti

Juicy mussels and scallops poached gently in white wine are the perfect accompaniment to pasta to make a sophisticated meal.

NUTRITIONAL INFORMATION

Calories 301   Sugars 1g
Protein . . . . .42g   Fat 5g
Carbohydrate . . .17g   Saturates 1g

 55 MINS   🕐 30 MINS

SERVES 4

I N G R E D I E N T S

8 oz dried wholewheat spaghetti

2 slices rindless lean slab bacon, chopped

2 shallots, chopped finely

2 celery stalk, chopped finely

⅔ cup dry white wine

⅔ cup fresh fish stock (see page 14)

1 lb 2 oz fresh mussels, prepared

8 oz shelled queen or bay scallops

1 tbsp chopped fresh parsley

salt and pepper

1 Cook the spaghetti in a saucepan of boiling water according to the packet instructions, or until the pasta is cooked but still firm to the bite – this will take about 10 minutes.

2 Meanwhile, gently dry-fry the bacon in a large nonstick skillet for 2–3 minutes. Stir in the shallots, celery, and wine. Simmer gently, uncovered, for 5 minutes until softened.

3 Add the stock, mussels, and scallops, cover and cook for 6–7 minutes more. Discard any mussels that remain unopened after cooking.

4 Drain the spaghetti and add to the skillet. Add the parsley, season to taste, and toss together. Continue to cook for 1–2 minutes to heat through. Pile on to warmed serving plates, spooning over the cooking juices.

Vermicelli with Clams

A quickly-cooked recipe that transforms store-cupboard ingredients into a dish with style.

NUTRITIONAL INFORMATION

Calories ....520 Sugars 2g
Protein ....26g Fat 13g
Carbohydrate ....71g Saturates 4g

 10 MINS   25 MINS

SERVES 4

I N G R E D I E N T S

14 oz dried vermicelli, spaghetti or
   other long pasta

2 tbsp olive oil

2 tbsp butter

2 onions, chopped

2 garlic cloves, chopped

2 x 7 oz jars clams in brine

½ cup white wine

4 tbsp chopped fresh parsley

½ tsp dried oregano

pinch of freshly grated nutmeg

salt and pepper

TO GARNISH

2 tbsp Parmesan cheese shavings

fresh basil sprigs

1 Bring a large pan of lightly salted water to a boil. Add the pasta and half of the olive oil and cook for 8–10 minutes until tender but still firm to the bite. Drain, return to the pan, and add the butter. Cover the pan, shake well, and keep warm.

2 Heat the remaining oil in a pan over a medium heat. Add the onions and fry until they are translucent. Stir in the garlic and cook for 1 minute.

3 Strain the liquid from 1 jar of clams and add the liquid to the pan, with the wine. Stir, bring to simmering point, and simmer for 3 minutes. Drain the second jar of clams and discard the liquid.

4 Add the clams, parsley, and oregano to the pan and season with pepper and nutmeg. Lower the heat and cook until the sauce is heated through.

5 Transfer the pasta to a warm serving dish and pour over the sauce. Sprinkle with the Parmesan cheese, garnish with the basil and serve immediately.

COOK'S TIP

There are many different types of clams found along almost every coast in the world. Those traditionally used in this dish are the tiny ones – only 1-2 inches across – known in Italy as vongole.

Farfallini Buttered Lobster

This is one of those dishes that looks almost too lovely to eat – but you should!

NUTRITIONAL INFORMATION

Calories	686	Sugars	.........1g
Protein	........45g	Fat	..........36g
Carbohydrate	...44g	Saturates	......19g

30 MINS   25 MINS

SERVES 4

INGREDIENTS

2 x 1 lb 9 oz lobsters, split into halves

juice and grated peel of 1 lemon

½ cup butter

4 tbsp fresh white bread crumbs

2 tbsp brandy

5 tbsp heavy cream or crème fraîche

1 lb dried farfallini

1 tbsp olive oil

⅔ cup freshly grated Parmesan cheese

salt and pepper

TO GARNISH

1 kiwi fruit, sliced

4 unpeeled, cooked jumbo shrimp

fresh dill sprigs

 1 Carefully discard the stomach sac, vein and gills from each lobster. Remove all the meat from the tail and chop. Crack the claws and legs, remove the meat, and chop. Transfer the meat to a bowl and add the lemon juice and grated lemon peel.

2 Clean the shells thoroughly and place in a warm oven at 1325°F to dry out.

3 Melt 2 tbsp of the butter in a skillet. Add the bread crumbs and fry for about 3 minutes until crisp and golden brown.

4 Melt the remaining butter in a saucepan. Add the lobster meat and heat through gently. Add the brandy and cook for a further 3 minutes, add the cream or crème fraîche, and season to taste with salt and pepper.

5 Meanwhile, bring a large pan of lightly salted water to a boil. Add the farfallini and olive oil and cook for 8–10 minutes until tender but still firm to the bite. Drain and spoon the pasta into the clean lobster shells.

6 Top with the buttered lobster and sprinkle with a little grated Parmesan cheese and the bread crumbs. Broil for 2–3 minutes, until golden brown.

7 Transfer the lobster shells to a warm serving dish, garnish with the lemon slices, kiwi fruit, jumbo shrimp, and dill sprigs and serve immediately.

Baked Scallops & Pasta

This is another tempting seafood dish where the eye is delighted as much as the taste-buds.

NUTRITIONAL INFORMATION

Calories 725   Sugars 2g
Protein . . . . .38g   Fat 48g
Carbohydrate . . .38g   Saturates 25g

 20 MINS   30 MINS

SERVES 4

INGREDIENTS

12 scallops

3 tbsp olive oil

3 cups small, dried whole wheat pasta shells

⅔ cup fish stock

1 onion, chopped

juice and finely grated peel of 2 lemons

⅔ cup heavy cream

2 cups grated Cheddar cheese

salt and pepper

crusty brown bread, to serve

1 Remove the scallops from their shells. Scrape off the skirt and the black intestinal thread. Reserve the white part (the flesh) and the orange part (the coral or roe). Carefully ease the flesh and coral from the shell with a short, strong knife.

2 Wash the shells thoroughly and dry them well. Put the shells on a cookie sheet, sprinkle lightly with two thirds of the olive oil, and set aside.

3 Meanwhile, bring a large saucepan of lightly salted water to a boil. Add the pasta shells and remaining olive oil and cook for 8–10 minutes or until tender, but still firm to the bite. Drain well and spoon about 1 oz of pasta into each scallop shell.

4 Put the scallops, fish stock, lemon peel, and onion in a baking dish and season with pepper. Cover with foil and bake in an oven at 350°F for 8 minutes.

5 Remove the dish from the oven. Remove the foil and, using a draining spoon, transfer the scallops to the shells. Add 1 tablespoon of the cooking liquid to each shell, together with a drizzle of lemon juice and a little cream, and top with the grated cheese.

6 Increase the oven temperature to 450°F and return the scallops to the oven for a further 4 minutes.

7 Serve the scallops in their shells with crusty brown bread and butter.

Seafood Lasagne

You can use any fish and any sauce you like in this recipe: try smoked finnan haddie and whiskey sauce or cod with cheese sauce.

NUTRITIONAL INFORMATION

Calories	790	Sugars	........23g
Protein	........55g	Fat	.........32g
Carbohydrate	...74g	Saturates	......19g

 30 MINS   45 MINS

SERVES 4

I N G R E D I E N T S

1 lb finnan haddie, filleted, skin removed, and flesh flaked

4 oz shrimp

4 oz sole fillet, skin removed and flesh sliced

juice of 1 lemon

4 tbsp butter

3 leeks, very thinly sliced

½ cup all purpose flour

about 2⅓ cups milk

2 tbsp honey

1¾ cups grated Mozzarella cheese

1 lb pre-cooked lasagne

⅔ cup freshly grated Parmesan cheese

pepper

  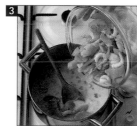

1 Put the haddie fillet, shrimp, and sole fillet into a large bowl and season with pepper and lemon juice according to taste. Set aside while you make the sauce.

2 Melt the butter in a large saucepan. Add the leeks and cook, stirring, for 8 minutes. Add the flour and cook, stirring, for 1 minute. Gradually stir in enough milk to make a thick, creamy sauce.

3 Blend in the honey and Mozzarella cheese and cook for 3 minutes more. Remove the pan from the heat and mix in the fish and shrimp.

4 Make alternate layers of fish sauce and lasagne in an ovenproof dish, finishing with a layer of fish sauce on top. Generously sprinkle over the grated Parmesan cheese and bake in a preheated oven at 350°F for 30 minutes. Serve immediately.

VARIATION
For a cider sauce, substitute 1 finely chopped shallot for the leeks, 1½ cups cider and 1½ cups heavy cream for the milk, and 1 tsp mustard for the honey. For a Tuscan sauce, substitute 1 chopped fennel bulb for the leeks; omit the honey.

Seafood Medley

You can use almost any kind of sea fish in this recipe. Red sea bream is an especially good choice.

NUTRITIONAL INFORMATION

Calories 699	Sugars 4g
Protein 56g	Fat 35g
Carbohydrate ...35g	Saturates 20g

🦐 🦐 🦐

 20 MINS   🕐 30 MINS

SERVES 4

INGREDIENTS

12 raw jumbo shrimp

12 raw small shrimp

1 lb fillet of sea bream

4 tbsp butter

12 scallops, shelled

4½ oz freshwater shrimp

juice and finely grated peel of 1 lemon

pinch of saffron powder or threads

4 cups vegetable stock

⅔ cup rose petal vinegar

1 lb dried farfalle

1 tbsp olive oil

⅔ cup white wine

1 tbsp pink peppercorns

4 oz baby carrots

⅔ cup heavy cream or fromage blanc

salt and pepper

carefully add a pinch of saffron powder or a few strands of saffron to the cooking juices (not to the seafood).

3 Remove the seafood from the pan, set aside, and keep warm.

4 Return the pan to the heat and add the stock. Bring to a boil and reduce by one third. Add the rose petal vinegar and cook for 4 minutes, until reduced.

5 Bring a pan of salted water to a boil. Add the farfalle and oil and cook for 8–10 minutes until tender but still firm to the bite. Drain the pasta, transfer to a serving plate, and top with the seafood.

6 Add the wine, peppercorns, and carrots to the pan and reduce the sauce for 6 minutes. Add the cream or fromage blanc and simmer for 2 minutes.

7 Pour the sauce over the seafood and pasta and serve immediately.

1 Peel and devein the shrimp and small shrimp. Thinly slice the sea bream. Melt the butter in a skillet, add the sea bream, scallops, shrimp, and small shrimp and cook for 1–2 minutes.

2 Season with pepper to taste. Add the lemon juice and grated peel. Very

Spaghetti & Seafood Sauce

Peeled shrimp from the freezer can become the star ingredient in this colorful and tasty dish.

NUTRITIONAL INFORMATION

Calories ....498 Sugars 5g
Protein ....32g Fat 23g
Carbohydrate ...43g Saturates 11g

30 MINS   35 MINS

SERVES 4

INGREDIENTS

8 oz dried spaghetti, broken into 6 inch
   pieces

2 tbsp olive oil

1 ¼ cups chicken stock

1 tsp lemon juice

1 small cauliflower, cut into flowerets

2 carrots, thinly sliced

4 oz snow peas

4 tbsp butter

1 onion, sliced

8 oz zucchini, sliced

1 garlic clove, chopped

12 oz frozen, cooked, peeled shrimp,
   defrosted

2 tbsp chopped fresh parsley

⅓ cup freshly grated Parmesan cheese

½ tsp paprika

salt and pepper

4 unpeeled, cooked shrimp, to garnish

1 Bring a pan of lightly salted water to a boil. Add the spaghetti and 1 tbsp of the olive oil and cook for 8–10 minutes until tender but still firm to the bite. Drain the spaghetti and return to the pan. Toss with the remaining olive oil, cover, and keep warm.

2 Bring the chicken stock and lemon juice to a boil. Add the cauliflower and carrots and cook for 3–4 minutes. Remove from the pan and set aside. Add the snow peas to the pan and cook for 1–2 minutes. Set aside with the other vegetables.

3 Melt half of the butter in a skillet over a medium heat. Add the onion and zucchini and fry for about 3 minutes. Add the garlic and shrimp and cook for a further 2–3 minutes until thoroughly heated through.

4 Stir in the reserved vegetables and heat through. Season to taste and stir in the remaining butter.

5 Transfer the spaghetti to a warm serving dish. Pour over the sauce and add the chopped parsley. Toss well with 2 forks until coated. Sprinkle over the Parmesan cheese and paprika, garnish with the unpeeled shrimp, and serve immediately.

Seafood Chow Mein

Use whatever seafood is available for this delicious noodle dish – mussels or crab would also be suitable.

NUTRITIONAL INFORMATION

Calories 281	Sugars 1g	
Protein 15g	Fat 18g	
Carbohydrate . . .16g	Saturates 2g	

15 MINS   15 MINS

SERVES 4

INGREDIENTS

3 oz squid, cleaned

3-4 fresh scallops

3 oz raw shrimp, shelled

½ egg white, lightly beaten

1 tbsp cornstarch paste

9½ oz egg noodles

5-6 tbsp vegetable oil

2 tbsp light soy sauce

2 oz snow peas

½ tsp salt

½ tsp sugar

1 tsp Chinese rice wine

2 scallions, finely shredded

a few drops of sesame oil

COOK'S TIP

Chinese rice wine, made from glutinous rice, is also known as yellow wine because of its golden amber color. If it is unavailable, a good dry or medium sherry is an acceptable substitute.

1 Open up the squid and score the inside in a criss-cross pattern, then cut into pieces about the size of a postage stamp. Soak the squid in a bowl of boiling water until all the pieces curl up. Rinse in cold water and drain.

2 Cut each scallop into 3-4 slices. Cut the shrimp in half lengthways if large. Mix the scallops and shrimp with the egg white and cornstarch paste.

3 Cook the noodles in boiling water according to the packet instructions, drain, and rinse under cold water. Drain well, then toss with about 1 tablespoon of oil.

4 Heat 3 tablespoons of oil in a preheated wok. Add the noodles and 1 tablespoon of the soy sauce and stir-fry for 2-3 minutes. Remove to a large serving dish.

5 Heat the remaining oil in the wok and add the snow peas and seafood. Stir-fry for about 2 minutes, then add the salt, sugar, wine, remaining soy sauce, and about half the scallions. Blend well and add a little stock or water if necessary. Pour the seafood mixture on top of the noodles and sprinkle with sesame oil. Garnish with the remaining scallions and serve.

Cellophane Noodles & Shrimp

Jumbo shrimp are cooked with orange juice, bell peppers, soy sauce, and vinegar, and served on a bed of cellophane noodles.

NUTRITIONAL INFORMATION

Calories	118	Sugar	.........4g
Protein	.........7g	Fat	...........4g
Carbohydrate	...15g	Saturates	.......1g

10 MINS   25 MINS

SERVES 4

INGREDIENTS

6 oz cellophane noodles

1 tbsp vegetable oil

1 garlic clove, crushed

2 tsp grated fresh gingerroot

24 raw jumbo shrimp, peeled and deveined

1 red bell pepper, seeded and thinly sliced

1 green bell pepper, seeded, and thinly sliced

1 onion, chopped

2 tbsp light soy sauce

juice of 1 orange

2 tsp wine vinegar

pinch of brown sugar

⅔ cup fish stock

1 tbsp cornstarch

2 tsp water

orange slices, to garnish

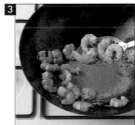  

1 Cook the noodles in a pan of boiling water for 1 minute. Drain well, rinse under cold water, and then drain again.

2 Heat the oil in a wok and stir-fry the garlic and ginger for 30 seconds.

3 Add the shrimp and stir-fry for 2 minutes. Remove with a draining spoon and keep warm.

4 Add the bell peppers and onion to the wok and stir-fry for 2 minutes. Stir in the soy sauce, orange juice, vinegar, sugar, and stock. Return the shrimp to the wok and cook for 8-10 minutes, until cooked through.

5 Blend the cornstarch with the water and stir into the wok. Bring to a boil, add the noodles, and cook for 1-2 minutes. Garnish and serve.

VARIATION
Lime or lemon juice and slices may be used instead of the orange. Use 3-5½ tsp of these juices.

Sweet & Sour Noodles

This delicious dish combines sweet and sour flavors with the addition of egg, rice noodles, colossal shrimp, and vegetables for a real treat.

NUTRITIONAL INFORMATION

Calories	352	Sugars 14g
Protein	........23g	Fat 17g
Carbohydrate	...29g	Saturates 3g

 10 MINS   10 MINS

SERVES 4

INGREDIENTS

3 tbsp fish sauce

2 tbsp distilled white vinegar

2 tbsp superfine or palm sugar

2 tbsp tomato paste

2 tbsp sunflower oil

3 cloves garlic, crushed

12 oz rice noodles, soaked in boiling water
    for 5 minutes

8 scallions, sliced

6 oz carrot, grated

1¼ cups beansprouts

2 eggs, beaten

8 oz peeled colossal shrimp

½ cup ground peanuts

1 tsp chili flakes, to garnish

1 Mix together the fish sauce, vinegar, sugar, and tomato paste.

2 Heat the sunflower oil in a large preheated wok.

3 Add the garlic to the wok and stir-fry for 30 seconds.

4 Drain the noodles thoroughly and add them to the wok together with the fish sauce and tomato paste mixture. Mix well to combine.

5 Add the scallions, carrot, and beansprouts to the wok and stir-fry for 2–3 minutes.

6 Move the contents of the wok to one side, add the beaten eggs to the empty part of the wok, and cook until the egg sets. Add the noodles, shrimp, and peanuts to the wok and mix well. Transfer to warm serving dishes and garnish with chili flakes. Serve hot.

COOK'S TIP

Chili flakes may be found in the spice section of large supermarkets.

Noodles with Shrimp

This is a simple dish using egg noodles and large shrimp, which give the dish a wonderful flavor, texture, and color.

NUTRITIONAL INFORMATION

Calories ....142 Sugars 0.4g
Protein ....11g Fat 7g
Carbohydrate ....11g Saturates 1g

🥔 5 MINS   🕐 10 MINS

SERVES 4

I N G R E D I E N T S

8 oz thin egg noodles

2 tbsp peanut oil

1 garlic clove, crushed

½ tsp ground star anise

1 bunch scallions, cut into 2-inch pieces

24 raw jumbo shrimp, peeled with tails intact

2 tbsp light soy sauce

2 tsp lime juice

lime wedges, to garnish

1 Blanch the noodles in a saucepan of boiling water for about 2 minutes.

2 Drain the noodles well, rinse under cold water, and drain thoroughly again. Keep warm and set aside until required.

3 Heat the peanut oil in a preheated wok or large skillet until almost smoking.

4 Add the crushed garlic and ground star anise to the wok and stir-fry for 30 seconds.

5 Add the scallions and jumbo shrimp to the wok and stir-fry for 2-3 minutes.

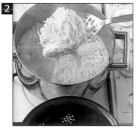

6 Stir in the light soy sauce, lime juice, and noodles and mix well.

7 Cook the mixture in the wok for about 1 minute until thoroughly heated through and all the ingredients are thoroughly incorporated.

8 Spoon the noodle and shrimp mixture into a warm serving dish. Transfer to serving bowls, garnish with lime wedges and serve immediately.

COOK'S TIP

If fresh egg noodles are available, these require very little cooking: simply place in boiling water for about 3 minutes, then drain and toss in oil. Noodles can be boiled and eaten plain, or stir-fried with meat and vegetables for a light meal or snack.

Noodles with Chili & Shrimp

This is a simple dish to prepare and is packed with flavor, making it an ideal choice for special occasions.

NUTRITIONAL INFORMATION

Calories	259	Sugars 9g
Protein	. . . . .28g	Fat 8g
Carbohydrate	. . .20g	Saturates 1g

10 MINS   5 MINS

SERVES 4

I N G R E D I E N T S

9 oz thin glass noodles

2 tbsp sunflower oil

1 onion, sliced

2 red chilies, seeded and very finely chopped

4 lime leaves, thinly shredded

1 tbsp fresh cilantro

2 tbsp palm or superfine sugar

2 tbsp fish sauce

1 lb raw jumbo shrimp, peeled

1 Place the noodles in a large bowl. Pour over enough boiling water to cover the noodles and leave to stand for 5 minutes. Drain thoroughly and set aside until required.

COOK'S TIP

If you cannot buy raw jumbo shrimp, use cooked shrimp instead and cook them with the noodles for 1 minute only, just to heat through.

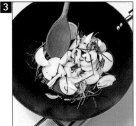  

2 Heat the sunflower oil in a large preheated wok or skillet until it is hot.

3 Add the onion, red chilies, and lime leaves to the wok and stir-fry for 1 minute.

4 Add the cilantro, palm or superfine sugar, fish sauce, and shrimp to the wok or skillet and stir-fry for a further 2 minutes or until the shrimp turn pink.

5 Add the drained noodles to the wok, toss to mix well, and stir-fry for 1–2 minutes or until heated through.

6 Transfer the noodles and shrimp to warm serving bowls and serve immediately.

Chili Small Shrimp Noodles

Cellophane or glass noodles are made from mung beans. They are sold dried, so they need soaking before use.

NUTRITIONAL INFORMATION

Calories 152	Sugars 2g	
Protein 11g	Fat 8g	
Carbohydrate ...10g	Saturates 1g	

 25 MINS   🕐 10 MINS

SERVES 4

I N G R E D I E N T S

2 tbsp light soy sauce

1 tbsp lime or lemon juice

1 tbsp fish sauce

4½ oz firm bean curd, cut into chunks

4½ oz cellophane noodles

2 tbsp sesame oil

4 shallots, sliced finely

2 garlic cloves, crushed

1 small red chili, seeded and chopped finely

2 celery stalks, sliced finely

2 carrots, sliced finely

⅔ cup cooked, peeled small shrimps

1 cup beansprouts

TO GARNISH

celery leaves

fresh chilies

1 Mix together the light soy sauce, lime or lemon juice, and fish sauce in a small bowl. Add the bean curd cubes and toss them until coated in the mixture. Cover and set aside for 15 minutes.

2 Put the noodles into a large bowl and cover with warm water. Leave them to soak for about 5 minutes and then drain them well.

3 Heat the sesame oil in a wok or large skillet. Add the shallots, garlic, and red chili, and stir-fry for 1 minute.

4 Add the sliced celery and carrots to the wok or pan and stir-fry for a further 2–3 minutes.

5 Tip the drained noodles into the wok or skillet and cook, stirring, for 2 minutes, then add the small shrimps, beansprouts, and bean curd, with the soy sauce mixture. Cook over a medium high heat for 2–3 minutes until heated through.

6 Transfer the mixture in the wok to a serving dish and garnish with celery leaves and chilies.

Noodles with Cod & Mango

Fish and fruit are tossed with a trio of bell peppers in this spicy dish served with noodles for a quick, healthy meal.

NUTRITIONAL INFORMATION

Calories 274   Sugars 11g
Protein ....25g   Fat 8g
Carbohydrate ...26g   Saturates 1g

10 MINS   25 MINS

SERVES 4

INGREDIENTS

9 oz packet egg noodles

1 lb skinless cod fillet

1 tbsp paprika

2 tbsp sunflower oil

1 red onion, sliced

1 orange bell pepper, seeded and sliced

1 green bell pepper, seeded and sliced

3½ oz baby corn-on-the-cobs, halved

1 mango, sliced

1 cup beansprouts

2 tbsp tomato catsup

2 tbsp soy sauce

2 tbsp medium sherry

1 tsp cornstarch

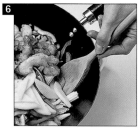

1 Place the egg noodles in a large bowl and cover with boiling water. Leave to stand for about 10 minutes.

2 Rinse the cod fillet and pat dry with paper towels. Cut the cod flesh into thin strips.

3 Place the cod strips in a large bowl. Add the paprika and toss well to coat the fish.

4 Heat the sunflower oil in a large preheated wok.

5 Add the onion, bell peppers, and baby corn-on-the-cobs to the wok and stir-fry for about 5 minutes.

6 Add the cod to the wok together with the sliced mango and stir-fry for a further 2–3 minutes or until the fish is tender.

7 Add the beansprouts to the wok and toss well to combine.

8 Mix together the tomato catsup, soy sauce, sherry, and cornstarch. Add the mixture to the wok and cook, stirring occasionally, until the juices thicken.

9 Drain the noodles thoroughly and transfer to warm serving bowls. Transfer the cod and mango stir-fry to separate serving bowls and serve immediately.

Oyster Sauce Noodles

Chicken and noodles are cooked and then tossed in an oyster sauce and egg mixture in this delicious recipe.

NUTRITIONAL INFORMATION

Calories 278	Sugars 2g
Protein 30g	Fat 12g
Carbohydrate ...13g	Saturates 3g

🍲 5 MINS 🕐 25 MINS

SERVES 4

INGREDIENTS

9 oz egg noodles

1 lb chicken thighs

2 tbsp peanut oil

3½ oz carrots, sliced

3 tbsp oyster sauce

2 eggs

3 tbsp cold water

1 Place the egg noodles in a large bowl or dish. Pour enough boiling water over the noodles to cover and leave to stand for 10 minutes.

2 Meanwhile, remove the skin from the chicken thighs. Cut the chicken flesh into small pieces, using a sharp knife.

VARIATION

Flavor the eggs with soy sauce or hoisin sauce as an alternative to the oyster sauce, if you prefer.

3 Heat the peanut oil in a large preheated wok or skillet, swirling the oil around the base of the wok until it is really hot.

4 Add the pieces of chicken and the carrot slices to the wok and stir-fry for about 5 minutes.

5 Drain the noodles thoroughly. Add the noodles to the wok and stir-fry for a further 2–3 minutes or until the noodles are heated through.

6 Beat together the oyster sauce, eggs, and 3 tablespoons of cold water. Drizzle the mixture over the noodles and stir-fry for a further 2–3 minutes or until the eggs set.

7 Transfer the mixture in the wok to warm serving bowls and serve hot.

Special Noodles

This dish combines meat, vegetables, shrimp, and noodles in a curried coconut sauce. Serve as a main meal or as an accompaniment.

NUTRITIONAL INFORMATION

Calories 409	Sugars 12g	
Protein 24g	Fat 23g	
Carbohydrate ...28g	Saturates 8g	

  5 MINS   25 MINS

SERVES 4

I N G R E D I E N T S

9 oz thin rice noodles

4 tbsp peanut oil

2 cloves garlic, crushed

2 red chilies, seeded and very finely chopped

1 tsp grated fresh gingerroot

2 tbsp Madras curry paste

2 tbsp rice wine vinegar

1 tbsp superfine sugar

8 oz cooked ham, finely shredded

1¼ cups canned water chestnuts, sliced

3½ oz mushrooms, sliced

¾ cup peas

1 red bell pepper, seeded and thinly sliced

3½ oz peeled shrimp

2 large eggs

4 tbsp coconut milk

¼ cup shredded coconut

2 tbsp chopped fresh cilantro

1 Place the rice noodles in a large bowl, cover with boiling water, and leave to soak for about 10 minutes. Drain the noodles thoroughly, then toss with 2 tablespoons of peanut oil.

2 Heat the remaining peanut oil in a large preheated wok until the oil is hot.

3 Add the garlic, chilies, ginger, curry paste, rice wine vinegar, and superfine sugar to the wok and stir-fry for 1 minute.

4 Add the ham, water chestnuts, mushrooms, peas, and red bell pepper to the wok and stir-fry for 5 minutes.

5 Add the noodles and shrimp to the wok and stir-fry for 2 minutes.

6 In a small bowl, beat together the eggs and coconut milk. Drizzle over the mixture in the wok and stir-fry until the egg sets.

7 Add the shredded coconut and chopped fresh cilantro to the wok and toss to combine. Transfer the noodles to warm serving dishes and serve immediately.

Curried Rice-Flour Noodles

Rice-flour noodles are also known as rice sticks. The ideal meat to use in this dish is barbecue pork.

NUTRITIONAL INFORMATION

Calories	223	Sugars	........2g
Protein	........15g	Fat	..........13g
Carbohydrate	....11g	Saturates	.......2g

15 MINS   15 MINS

SERVES 4

INGREDIENTS

7 oz rice-flour noodles

4½ oz cooked chicken or pork

62 oz peeled shrimp, defrosted if frozen

4 tbsp vegetable oil

1 medium onion, thinly shredded

4¼ oz fresh beansprouts

1 tsp salt

1 tbsp mild curry powder

2 tbsp light soy sauce

2 scallions, thinly shredded

1-2 small fresh green or red chili peppers, seeded and thinly shredded

1 Soak the rice-flour noodles in boiling water for about 8-10 minutes, rinse in cold water, and drain well. Set aside until required.

2 Using a sharp knife or meat cleaver, thinly slice the cooked meat.

3 Dry the shrimp on paper towels.

4 Heat the vegetable oil in a preheated wok or large skillet.

5 Add the shredded onion to the wok or pan and stir-fry until opaque. Add the beansprouts and stir-fry for 1 minute.

6 Add the drained noodles with the meat and shrimp, and continue stirring for another minute.

7 Mix together the salt, curry powder, and soy sauce in a little bowl.

8 Blend the sauce mixture into the wok, followed by the scallions and chili peppers. Stir-fry for one more minute, then serve immediately.

COOK'S TIP

Rice noodles are very delicate noodles made from rice flour. They become soft and pliable after being soaked for about 15 minutes. If you wish to store them after they have been soaked, toss them in a few drops of sesame oil and place them in a sealed container in the refrigerator.

Rice, Legumes, & Grains

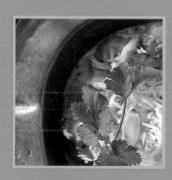

Rice, grains, and legumes are universally important staple foods; dieticians recommend a diet high in complex carbohydrates to prevent dips in blood-sugar levels which can lead to binge eating and low energy levels. They are highly nutritious as they provide an excellent source of protein, iron, calcium, and B vitamins. In addition, they are virtually fat-free and form a substantial base to which other ingredients can be added to produce innovative and healthy dishes. From risotto to gumbo, there is a treat here for everyone.

Fried Rice with Shrimp

Use either large peeled shrimp or tiger jumbo shrimp for this rice dish.

NUTRITIONAL INFORMATION

Calories . . . . . . .599 Sugars 0g
Protein . . . . .26g Fat 16g
Carbohydrate . . .94g Saturates 3g

  5 MINS   35 MINS

SERVES 4

I N G R E D I E N T S

1½ cups long-grain rice

2 eggs

4 tsp cold water

salt and pepper

3 tbsp sunflower oil

4 scallions, thinly sliced diagonally

1 garlic clove, crushed

4½ oz closed-cup or button mushrooms,
  thinly sliced

2 tbsp oyster or anchovy sauce

1 x 7 oz can water chestnuts, drained and
  sliced

9 oz peeled shrimp, defrosted if frozen

½ bunch watercress, roughly chopped

watercress sprigs, to garnish (optional)

1 Rinse the rice in cold water, drain and add to boiling water. Stir, cover and simmer gently for 12–13 minutes. Keep warm.

2 Beat each egg separately with 2 teaspoons of cold water and salt and pepper.

3 Heat 2 teaspoons of sunflower oil in a wok or large skillet, swirling it around until really hot. Pour in the first egg, swirl it around and leave to cook undisturbed until set. Remove to a plate or board and repeat with the second egg. Cut the omelets into 1 inch squares.

4 Heat the remaining oil in the wok and when really hot add the scallions and garlic and stir-fry for 1 minute. Add the mushrooms and continue to cook for a further 2 minutes.

5 Stir in the oyster or anchovy sauce and seasoning and add the water chestnuts and shrimp; stir-fry for 2 minutes.

6 Stir in the cooked rice and stir-fry for 1 minute, then add the watercress and omelet squares and stir-fry for a further 1-2 minutes until very hot. Serve at once garnished with sprigs of watercress, if liked.

Shrimp Biryani

The flavors of biryani are subtle, and despite the list of ingredients, it is easy to cook, making the curry suitable for every day.

NUTRITIONAL INFORMATION

Calories	177	Sugars	.........6g
Protein	........15g	Fat	...........6g
Carbohydrate	...18g	Saturates	.....0.5g

  2¹/₂ HOURS   45 MINS

SERVES 8

INGREDIENTS

1 tsp saffron strands

4 tbsp tepid water

2 shallots, chopped coarsely

3 garlic cloves, minced

1 tsp chopped gingerroot

2 tsp coriander seeds

½ tsp black peppercorns

2 cloves

2 green cardamom pods

1 inch piece cinnamon stick

1 tsp ground turmeric

1 fresh green chili, chopped

½ tsp salt

2 tbsp ghee

1 tsp whole black mustard seeds

1 lb uncooked tiger shrimp in their shells, or 14 oz uncooked and peeled

1¼ cups coconut milk

1¼ cups low-fat unsweetened yogurt

generous 1 cup basmati rice, soaked for 2 hours and drained

1 tbsp golden raisins

flaked slivered almonds, toasted and 1 scallion, sliced, to garnish

1 Soak the saffron in the tepid water for 10 minutes. Put the shallots, garlic, spices and salt into a spice grinder or mortar and pestle and grind to a paste.

2 Heat the ghee in a saucepan and add the mustard seeds. When they start to pop, add the shrimp and stir over a high heat for 1 minute. Stir in the spice mix, then the coconut milk and yogurt. Simmer for 20 minutes.

3 Bring a large saucepan of salted water to a boil. Add the rice to the pan. Boil for 12 minutes. Drain. Pile the rice on the shrimp. Spoon over the golden raisins and trickle the saffron water over the rice in lines. Cover the pan with a clean cloth and put the lid on tightly. Remove the pan from heat and leave to stand for 5 minutes. Serve, garnished with the almonds and sliced scallion.

Fish & Rice with Dark Rum

Based on a traditional Cuban recipe, this dish is similar to Spanish paella, but it has the added kick of dark rum.

NUTRITIONAL INFORMATION

Calories 547	Sugars 9g
Protein 27g	Fat 4g
Carbohydrate ...85g	Saturates 1g

2¼ HOURS   35 MINS

SERVES 4

INGREDIENTS

1 lb firm white fish fillets (such as cod or angler fish), skinned and cut into 1 inch cubes

2 tsp ground cumin

2 tsp dried oregano

2 tbsp lime juice

⅔ cup dark rum

1 tbsp dark muscovado sugar

3 garlic cloves, chopped finely

1 large onion, chopped

1 medium red bell pepper, seeded and sliced into rings

1 medium green bell pepper, seeded and sliced into rings

1 medium yellow bell pepper, seeded and sliced into rings

5 cups fish stock

2 cups long-grain rice

salt and pepper

crusty bread, to serve

TO GARNISH

fresh oregano leaves

lime wedges

1 Place the cubes of fish in a bowl and add the cumin, oregano, salt, and pepper, lime juice, rum, and sugar. Mix everything together well, cover and leave to chill for 2 hours.

2 Meanwhile, place the garlic, onion, and bell peppers in a large saucepan. Pour over the stock and stir in the rice. Bring to a boil, cover and leave to cook for 15 minutes.

3 Gently add the fish and the marinade juices to the pan. Bring back to a boil and simmer, uncovered, stirring occasionally but taking care not to break up the fish for 10 minutes until the fish is cooked and the rice is tender.

4 Season to taste and transfer to a warm serving plate. Garnish with fresh oregano and lime wedges and serve with crusty bread.

Crab Fried Rice

Canned crabmeat is used in this recipe for convenience, but fresh white crabmeat could be used – quite deliciously – in its place.

NUTRITIONAL INFORMATION

Calories	225	Sugars	.........1g
Protein	........12g	Fat	...........11g
Carbohydrate	...20g	Saturates	.......2g

🍞 5 MINS   🕐 25 MINS

SERVES 4

INGREDIENTS

⅔ cup long-grain rice

2 tbsp peanut oil

4½ oz canned white crabmeat, drained

1 leek, sliced

⅔ cup mung bean sprouts

2 eggs, beaten

1 tbsp light soy sauce

2 tsp lime juice

1 tsp sesame oil

salt

sliced lime, to garnish

1 Cook the rice in a saucepan of boiling salted water for 15 minutes. Drain well, rinse under cold running water, and drain again thoroughly.

2 Heat the peanut oil in a preheated wok until it is really hot.

3 Add the crabmeat, leek, and bean sprouts to the wok and stir-fry for 2–3 minutes. Remove the mixture from the wok with a draining spoon and set aside until required.

4 Add the eggs to the wok and cook, stirring occasionally, for 2–3 minutes, until they begin to set.

5 Stir the rice and the crabmeat, leek, and bean sprout mixture into the eggs in the wok.

6 Add the soy sauce and lime juice to the mixture in the wok. Cook for 1 minute, stirring to combine, and sprinkle with the sesame oil.

7 Transfer the crab fried rice to a serving dish, garnish with the sliced lime and serve immediately.

VARIATION

Cooked lobster may be used instead of the crab for a really special dish.

Rice with Crab & Mussels

Shellfish makes an ideal partner for rice. Mussels and crab add flavor and texture to this spicy dish.

NUTRITIONAL INFORMATION

Calories	336	Sugars	.........4g
Protein	........32g	Fat	..........10g
Carbohydrate	...33g	Saturates	.......1g

 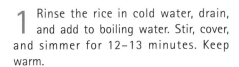

🖐 🖐 🖐

🍲 20 MINS   🕐 10 MINS

SERVES 4

I N G R E D I E N T S

1½ cups long-grain rice

6 oz white crabmeat, fresh, canned, or frozen (defrosted if frozen), or 8 crab sticks, defrosted if frozen

1 inch piece gingerroot, grated

4 scallions, thinly sliced diagonally

4½ oz snow peas, cut into 2-3 pieces

½ tsp turmeric

1 tsp ground cumin

2 x 7 oz jars mussels, well drained, or 12 oz frozen mussels, defrosted

1 x 15 oz can mung bean sprouts, well drained

salt and pepper

1 Rinse the rice in cold water, drain, and add to boiling water. Stir, cover, and simmer for 12–13 minutes. Keep warm.

2 Extract the crabmeat, if using fresh crab (see right). Flake the crabmeat or cut the crab sticks into 3 or 4 pieces.

3 Heat the oil in a preheated wok and stir-fry the ginger and scallions for a minute or so. Add the snow peas and continue to cook for a further minute. Sprinkle the turmeric, cumin, and seasoning over the vegetables and mix well.

4 Add the crabmeat and mussels and stir-fry for 1 minute. Stir in the cooked rice and bean sprouts and stir-fry for 2 minutes or until hot and well mixed.

COOK'S TIP

To prepare fresh crab, twist off the claws and legs, crack with a heavy knife, and pick out the meat with a skewer. Discard the gills and pull out the under shell; discard the stomach sac. Pull the soft meat from the shell. Cut open the body section and prise out the meat with a skewer.

Crab Congee

This is a typical Chinese breakfast dish although it is probably best served as a lunch or supper dish at a Western table!

NUTRITIONAL INFORMATION

Calories	...327	Sugars	...0.1g
Protein	...18g	Fat	...7g
Carbohydrate	...50g	Saturates	...2g

🍽 5 MINS   🕐 1¼ HOURS

SERVES 4

INGREDIENTS

1 cup short-grain rice

6¼ cups fish stock

½ tsp salt

3½ oz Chinese sausage, thinly sliced

8 oz white crabmeat

6 scallions, sliced

2 tbsp chopped fresh cilantro

freshly ground black pepper,
    to serve

1 Place the short-grain rice in a large preheated wok or skillet.

2 Add the fish stock to the wok or skillet and bring to a boil.

3 Reduce the heat, then simmer gently for 1 hour, stirring the mixture from time to time.

4 Add the salt, sliced Chinese sausage, white crabmeat, sliced scallions, and chopped fresh cilantro to the wok and heat through for about 5 minutes.

5 Add a little more water to the wok if the congee is too thick, stirring well.

6 Transfer the crab congee to warm serving bowls, sprinkle with freshly ground black pepper, and serve immediately.

COOK'S TIP

Always buy the freshest possible crabmeat; fresh is best, although frozen or canned will work for this recipe. In the West, crabs are almost always sold ready-cooked. The crab should feel heavy for its size, and when it is shaken, there should be no sound of water inside.

Genoese Seafood Risotto

This is cooked in a different way from any of the other risottos. First, you cook the rice, then you prepare a sauce, then you mix the two together.

NUTRITIONAL INFORMATION

Calories	424	Sugars	.........0g
Protein	........23g	Fat	..........17g
Carbohydrate	...46g	Saturates	......10g

 10 MINS   25 MINS

SERVES 4

I N G R E D I E N T S

5 cups hot fish or chicken stock

12 oz arborio rice, washed

3 tbsp butter

2 garlic cloves, chopped

9 oz mixed seafood, preferably raw, such as
   shrimp, squid, mussels, clams, and
   (small) shrimp

2 tbsp chopped oregano, plus extra
   for garnishing

1¾ oz Pecorino or Parmesan cheese, grated

1 In a large saucepan, bring the stock to a boil. Add the rice and cook for about 12 minutes, stirring, or until the rice is tender. Drain thoroughly, reserving any excess liquid.

2 Heat the butter in a large skillet and add the garlic, stirring.

3 Add the raw mixed seafood to the skillet and cook for 5 minutes. If you are using cooked seafood, fry for 2–3 minutes.

4 Stir the oregano into the seafood mixture in the skillet.

5 Add the cooked rice to the skillet and cook for 2–3 minutes, stirring, or until hot. Add the reserved stock if the mixture gets too sticky.

6 Add the Pecorino or Parmesan cheese and mix well.

7 Transfer the risotto to warm serving dishes and serve immediately.

COOK'S TIP

The Genoese are excellent cooks, and they make particularly delicious fish dishes flavored with the local olive oil.

Smoked Cod Polenta

Using polenta as a crust for a gratin dish gives a lovely crispy outer texture and a smooth inside. It works well with smoked fish and chicken.

NUTRITIONAL INFORMATION

Calories	616	Sugars	. . . . .3g
Protein	. . . . .41g	Fat	. . . . .24g
Carbohydrate	. . .58g	Saturates	. . . . . .12g

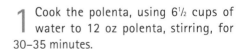 30 MINS   1¹/₄ HOURS

SERVES 4

INGREDIENTS

12 oz instant polenta

6½ cups water

7 oz chopped frozen spinach, defrosted

3 tbsp butter

1¾ oz Pecorino cheese, grated

¾ cup milk

1 lb smoked cod fillet, skinned and boned

4 eggs, beaten

salt and pepper

1 Cook the polenta, using 6½ cups of water to 12 oz polenta, stirring, for 30–35 minutes.

2 Stir the spinach, butter, and half of the Pecorino cheese into the polenta. Season to taste with salt and pepper.

3 Divide the polenta among 4 individual ovenproof dishes, spreading the polenta evenly across the bottom and up the sides of the dishes.

4 In a skillet, bring the milk to a boil. Add the fish and cook for 8–10 minutes, turning once, or until tender. Remove the fish with a draining spoon.

5 Remove the skillet from the heat. Pour the eggs into the milk in the skillet and mix together.

6 Using a fork, flake the fish into smaller pieces and place it in the center of the dishes.

7 Pour the milk and egg mixture over the fish.

8 Sprinkle with the remaining cheese and bake in a preheated oven, at 375°F, for 25–30 minutes or until set and golden. Serve hot.

VARIATION

Try using 12 oz cooked chicken breast with 2 tablespoons of chopped tarragon, instead of the smoked cod, if you prefer.

Aromatic Seafood Rice

This is one of those easy, delicious meals where the rice and fish are cooked together in one pan. Remove the whole spices before serving.

NUTRITIONAL INFORMATION

Calories 380   Sugar 2g
Protein ....40g   Fats 13g
Carbohydrates ...26g Saturates 5g

 20 MINS   25 MINS

SERVES 4

I N G R E D I E N T S

1¼ cups basmati rice

2 tbsp ghee or vegetable oil

1 onion, peeled and chopped

1 garlic clove, peeled and minced

1 tsp cumin seeds

½-1 tsp chili powder

4 cloves

1 cinnamon stick

2 tsp curry paste

8 oz peeled shrimp

1 lb white fish fillets (such as angler fish, cod, or haddock), skinned and boned and cut into bite-sized pieces

salt and freshly ground black pepper

2½ cups boiling water

⅓ cup frozen english peas

⅓ cup frozen corn kernels

1-2 tbsp lime juice

2 tbsp toasted shredded coconut

cilantro sprigs and lime slices, to garnish

1 Place the rice in a strainer and wash well under cold running water until the water runs clear, then drain well.

2 Heat the ghee or oil in a saucepan, add the onion, garlic, spices, and curry paste and fry very gently for 1 minute.

3 Stir in the rice and mix well until coated in the spiced oil. Add the shrimp and white fish and season well with salt and pepper. Stir lightly, then pour in the boiling water.

4 Cover and cook gently for 10 minutes, without uncovering the pan. Add the peas and corn, cover and continue cooking for a further 8 minutes. Remove from the heat and allow to stand for 10 minutes.

5 Uncover the pan, fluff up the rice with a fork, and transfer to a warm serving platter.

6 Sprinkle the dish with the lime juice and toasted coconut, and serve garnished with cilantro sprigs and lime slices.

Balti Cod & Red Lentils

The aniseed in this recipe gives a very delicate aroma to the fish and really enhances the flavor. Serve with wholewheat bread.

NUTRITIONAL INFORMATION

Calories	236	Sugars	.........3g
Protein	........29g	Fat	...........7g
Carbohydrate	...15g	Saturates	......1g

5 MINS   1 HOUR

SERVES 4

I N G R E D I E N T S

2 tbsp oil

¼ tsp ground asafetida (optional)

1 tbsp minced aniseed

1 tsp ground ginger

1 tsp chili powder

¼ tsp ground turmeric

1 cup split red lentils, washed

1 tsp salt

1 lb cod, skinned, filleted and cut into 1 inch cubes

1 fresh red chili, choppcd

3 tbsp low-fat unsweetened yogurt

2 tbsp chopped fresh cilantro

wholewheat bread, to serve

COOK'S TIP

Ground asafetida is easier to use than the type that comes on a block. It should only be used in small quantities. Do not be put off by the smell, which is very pungent.

1 Heat the oil in a Balti pan or wok, add the asafetida (if using), and fry for about 10 seconds to burn off the smell of the asafoetida.

2 Add the aniseed, ginger, chili powder, and turmeric and fry for 30 seconds.

3 Wash the lentils thoroughly then add to the pan with the salt and enough water to cover.

4 Bring to a boil, then simmer gently for 45 minutes, until the lentils are soft but not mushy.

5 Add the cod and red chili, bring to a boil and simmer for a further 10 minutes.

6 Stir in the yogurt and fresh cilantro into the fish mixture and serve with warm bread.

Low Fat Dishes

Naturally low in fat yet rich in minerals and proteins, white fish and shellfish are ideal to include in a low fat diet. There are so many different textures and flavors

available that they lend themselves to a wide range of cooking methods, as you will see from the recipes that follow. White fish such as cod, haddock, halibut, angler fish, and mullet are readily available and easy to cook. Shellfish such as shrimp, oysters, crab, and lobster may take a little longer to prepare but are well worth the effort. Oily fish — like salmon, trout, tuna, and mackerel — are high in fat and should be eaten in moderation.

Sole & Smoked Salmon Rolls

In this elegant dish, the delicate flavor of sole and salmon blend together perfectly with a light, citrus filling.

NUTRITIONAL INFORMATION

Calories 191   Sugars 3g
Protein . . . . .31g   Fat 4g
Carbohydrate . . . .9g   Saturates 1g

  1 HOUR   20 MINS

SERVES 4

I N G R E D I E N T S

1 cup fresh whole-wheat bread crumbs

½ tsp grated lime rind

1 tbsp lime juice

¼ cup low-fat soft cheese

4½ oz sole fillets

2 oz smoked salmon

⅔ cup fesh fish stock (see page 14)

⅔ cup low-fat unsweetened yogurt

1 tbsp chopped fresh chervil

salt and pepper

fresh chervil, to garnish

T O   S E R V E

selection of freshly steamed vegetables

lime wedges

COOK'S TIP

When buying fresh fish, choose fish with a bright eye and red gills. The fish should be firm to the touch, with just a slight 'fishy' smell.

1 In a mixing bowl, combine the bread crumbs, lime rind, and juice, soft cheese, and seasoning, to form a soft stuffing mixture.

2 Skin the sole fillets by inserting a sharp knife in between the skin and flesh at the tail end. Holding the skin in your fingers and keeping it taut, strip the flesh away from the skin.

3 Halve the sole fillets lengthways. Place strips of smoked salmon over the skinned side of each fillet, trimming the salmon as necessary.

4 Spoon one-eighth of the stuffing on to each fish fillet and press down along the fish with the back of a spoon. Carefully roll up from the head to the tail end. Place, seam-side down, in an ovenproof dish and pour in the stock. Bake in a preheated oven at 375°F for 15 minutes.

5 Using a slice, transfer the fish to a warm serving plate, cover and keep warm. Pour the cooking juices into a saucepan and add the yogurt and chopped chervil. Season to taste and heat gently without boiling. Garnish the fish rolls with chervil and serve with the yogurt sauce, and the steamed vegetables and lime wedges.

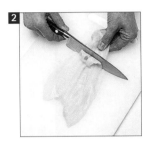

Ocean Pie

A tasty fish pie combining a mixture of fish and shellfish. You can use a wide variety of fish – whatever is available.

NUTRITIONAL INFORMATION

Calories 599	Sugars 8g
Protein 45g	Fat 21g
Carbohydrate ...58g	Saturates 4g

 15 MINS   1 HOUR

SERVES 4

INGREDIENTS

1 lb cod or haddock fillet, skinned

8 oz salmon steak

scant 2 cups skimmed milk

1 bay leaf

2 lb potatoes

⅓ cup peeled shrimp, thawed if frozen

¼ cup margarine

4 tbsp all-purpose flour

2–4 tbsp white wine

1 tsp chopped fresh dill or ½ tsp dried dill

2 tbsp drained capers

salt and pepper

few whole shrimp in their shells,
   to garnish

1 Put the fish into a saucepan with 1¼ cups of the milk, the bay leaf and seasoning. Bring to a boil, cover and simmer gently for 10–15 minutes until tender.

2 Coarsely chop the potatoes and cook in boiling salted water until tender.

3 Drain the fish, reserving 1¼ cups of the cooking liquid (make up with more milk if necessary). Flake the fish, discarding any bones and place in a shallow ovenproof dish. Add the shrimp.

4 Melt half the margarine in a saucepan, add the flour, and cook, stirring, for a minute or so. Gradually stir in the reserved stock and the wine and bring to a boil. Add the dill, capers, and seasoning to taste and simmer until thickened. Pour over the fish and mix well.

5 Drain the potatoes and mash, adding the remaining margarine, seasoning, and sufficient milk to give a piping consistency.

6 Put the mashed potato into a pastry bag. Use a large star tip and pipe over the fish. Cook in a preheated oven at 400°F for about 25 minutes until very hot and browned. Serve garnished with shrimp.

Smoky Fish Pie

This flavorsome and colorful fish pie is perfect for a light supper. The addition of smoked salmon gives it a touch of luxury.

NUTRITIONAL INFORMATION

Calories 523   Sugars 15g
Protein ....58g   Fat 6g
Carbohydrate ...63g   Saturates 2g

  15 MINS 🕐 1 HOUR

SERVES 4

I N G R E D I E N T S

2 lb smoked haddock or
   cod fillets

2½ cups skimmed milk

2 bay leaves

4 oz button mushrooms, quartered

4 oz frozen English peas

4 oz frozen corn kernels

1½ lb potatoes, diced

5 tbsp low-fat unsweetened
   yogurt

4 tbsp chopped fresh parsley

2 oz smoked salmon, sliced into
   thin strips

3 tbsp cornstarch

1 oz smoked cheese, grated

salt and pepper

1 Preheat the oven to 400°F. Place the fish in a pan and add the milk and bay leaves. Bring to a boil, cover and then simmer for 5 minutes.

2 Add the mushrooms, peas, and corn, bring back to a simmer, cover and cook for 5–7 minutes. Leave to cool.

3 Place the potatoes in a saucepan, cover with water, boil, and cook for 8 minutes. Drain well and mash with a fork or a potato masher. Stir in the yogurt, parsley, and seasoning. Set aside.

4 Using a draining spoon, remove the fish from the pan. Flake the cooked fish away from the skin and place in an ovenproof gratin dish. Reserve the cooking liquid.

5 Drain the vegetables, reserving the cooking liquid, and gently stir into the fish with the salmon strips.

6 Blend a little cooking liquid into the cornstarch to make a paste. Transfer the rest of the liquid to a saucepan and add the paste. Heat through, stirring, until thickened. Discard the bay leaves and season to taste. Pour the sauce over the fish and vegetables and mix. Spoon over the mashed potato so that the fish is covered, sprinkle with cheese and bake for 25–30 minutes.

COOK'S TIP

If possible, use smoked haddock or cod that has not been dyed bright yellow or artificially flavored to give the illusion of having been smoked.

Green Fish Curry

This dish has a wonderful fresh, hot, exotic taste resulting from the generous amount of fresh herbs, sharp fresh chilies, and coconut milk.

NUTRITIONAL INFORMATION

Calories 223	Sugars 2g	
Protein 44g	Fat 5g	
Carbohydrate 2g	Saturates 1g	

5 MINS   20 MINS

SERVES 4

INGREDIENTS

1 tbsp oil

2 scallions, sliced

1 tsp cumin seeds, ground

2 fresh green chilies, chopped

1 tsp coriander seeds, ground

4 tbsp chopped fresh cilantro

4 tbsp chopped fresh mint

1 tbsp chopped chives

⅔ cup coconut milk

4 white fish fillets, about 8 oz each

salt and pepper

basmati rice, to serve

1 mint sprig, to garnish

1 Heat the oil in a large skillet or shallow saucepan and add the scallions.

2 Stir-fry the scallions over a medium heat until they are softened but not colored.

3 Stir in the cumin, chilies, and ground coriander, and cook until fragrant.

4 Add the fresh cilantro, mint, chives, and coconut milk and season liberally.

5 Carefully place the fish in the skillet and poach for 10–15 minutes until the flesh flakes when tested with a fork.

6 Serve the fish fillets in the sauce with the rice. Garnish with a mint sprig.

COOK'S TIP

Never overcook fish – it is surprising how little time it takes compared to meat. It will continue to cook slightly while keeping warm in the oven and while being dished up and brought to the table.

Szechuan White Fish

Szechuan pepper is quite hot and should be used sparingly to avoid making the dish unbearably spicy.

NUTRITIONAL INFORMATION

Calories 225	Sugars 3g
Protein 20g	Fat 8g
Carbohydrate ...17g	Saturates 1g

5 MINS   20 MINS

SERVES 4

INGREDIENTS

12 oz white fish fillets

1 small egg, beaten

3 tbsp all-purpose flour

4 tbsp dry white wine

3 tbsp light soy sauce

vegetable oil, for frying

1 garlic clove, cut into slivers

½-inch piece fresh gingerroot, finely chopped

1 onion, finely chopped

1 celery stalk, chopped

1 fresh red chili, chopped

3 scallions, chopped

1 tsp rice wine vinegar

½ tsp ground Szechuan pepper

¾ cup fish stock

1 tsp superfine sugar

1 tsp cornstarch

2 tsp water

1 Cut the fish into 1½-inch cubes. Beat together the egg, flour, wine, and 1 tablespoon of soy sauce to make a batter. Dip the cubes of fish into the batter to coat well.

2 Heat the oil in a wok, reduce the heat slightly, and cook the fish, in batches, for 2–3 minutes, until golden brown. Remove with a draining spoon, drain on paper towels, set aside and keep warm.

3 Pour all but 1 tablespoon of oil from the wok and return to the heat. Add the garlic, ginger, onion, celery, chili, and scallions and stir-fry for 1–2 minutes. Stir in the remaining soy sauce and the vinegar.

4 Add the Szechuan pepper, fish stock, and superfine sugar to the wok. Mix the cornstarch with the water to form a smooth paste and stir it into the stock. Bring to a boil and cook, stirring, for 1 minute, until the sauce thickens and clears.

5 Return the fish cubes to the wok and cook for 1–2 minutes. Serve immediately.

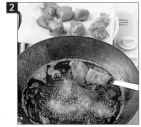

Yucatan Fish

Herbs, onion, green bell pepper, and pumpkin seeds are used to flavor this baked fish dish, which is first marinated in lime juice.

NUTRITIONAL INFORMATION

Calories 248   Sugars 2g
Protein ....33g   Fat 11g
Carbohydrate ....3g   Saturates 1g

 40 MINS   35 MINS

SERVES 4

I N G R E D I E N T S

4 cod cutlets or steaks or hake cutlets
  (about 6 oz each)

2 tbsp lime juice

salt and pepper

1 green bell pepper

1 tbsp olive oil

1 onion, chopped finely

1–2 garlic cloves, minced

1½ oz green pumpkin seeds

grated rind of ½ lime

1 tbsp chopped fresh cilantro
  or parsley

1 tbsp chopped fresh mixed herbs

2 oz button mushrooms,
  sliced thinly

2–3 tbsp fresh orange juice or
  white wine

TO GARNISH

lime wedges

fresh mixed herbs

1 Wipe the fish, place in a shallow ovenproof dish and pour the lime juice over. Turn the fish in the juice, season with salt and pepper, cover, and leave in a cool place for 15–30 minutes.

2 Halve the bell pepper, remove the seeds, and place under a preheated moderate broiler, skin-side upwards, until the skin burns and splits. Leave to cool slightly, then peel off the skin and chop the flesh.

3 Heat the oil in a pan and fry the onion, garlic, bell pepper, and pumpkin seeds gently for a few minutes until the onion is soft.

4 Stir in the lime rind, cilantro or parsley, mixed herbs, mushrooms, and seasoning, and spoon over the fish.

5 Spoon or pour the orange juice or wine over the fish, cover with foil or a lid and place in a preheated oven at 350°F for about 30 minutes, or until the fish is just tender.

6 Garnish the fish with lime wedges and fresh herbs and serve.

Fish & Yogurt Quenelles

These quenelles, made from a thick purée of fish and yogurt, can be prepared well in advance and stored in the refrigerator before poaching.

NUTRITIONAL INFORMATION

Calories 228	Sugars 7g
Protein 39g	Fat 2g
Carbohydrate ...14g	Saturates 1g

🍲 45 MINS   🕐 15 MINS

SERVES 4

I N G R E D I E N T S

1 lb 10 oz white fish fillets, such as cod or whiting, skinned

2 small egg whites

½ tsp ground coriander

1 tsp ground mace

⅔ cup low-fat unsweetened yogurt

1 small onion, sliced

salt and pepper

mixture of boiled Basmati rice and wild rice, to serve

S A U C E

1 bunch watercress, trimmed

1¼ cups chicken stock

2 tbsp cornstarch

⅔ cup low-fat unsweetened yogurt

2 tbsp low-fat crème fraîche

1 Cut the fish into pieces and process it in a food processor for about 30 seconds. Add the egg whites to the fish and process for a further 30 seconds until the mixture forms a stiff paste. Add the coriander, mace, seasoning, and the yogurt and process until smooth. Cover and chill for at least 30 minutes.

2 Spoon the mixture into a piping bag, and pipe into sausage shapes about 4 inches long. Alternatively, take rounded dessert spoons of the mixture and shape into ovals, using 2 spoons.

3 Bring about 2 inches of water to a boil in a skillet and add the onion for flavoring. Lower the quenelles into the water, using a fish slice or spoon. Cover the pan, keep the water at a gentle boil and poach the quenelles for 8 minutes, turning them once. Remove with a draining spoon and drain.

4 Roughly chop the watercress, reserving a few sprigs for garnish. Process the remainder with the chicken stock until well blended, then pour into a small pan. Stir the cornstarch into the yogurt and pour the mixture into the pan. Bring to a boil, stirring.

5 Stir in the crème fraîche, season, and remove from the heat. Garnish with the watercress sprigs. Serve with the rice.

Fish with Black Bean Sauce

Any firm and delicate fish steaks such as salmon or salmon trout can be cooked by the same method.

NUTRITIONAL INFORMATION

Calories ....194 Sugars 0.2g
Protein ....27g Fat 9g
Carbohydrate ....1g Saturates 1g

5 MINS   20 MINS

SERVES 6

I N G R E D I E N T S

1 sea bass, trout or turbot, weighing about 1 lb 9 oz, cleaned

1 tsp salt

1 tbsp sesame oil

2-3 scallions, cut in half lengthways

1 tbsp light soy sauce

1 tbsp Chinese rice wine or dry sherry

1 tbsp finely shredded gingerroot

1 tbsp oil

2 tbsp minced black bean sauce

2 finely shredded scallions

fresh cilantro leaves, to garnish (optional)

lemon slices, to garnish

1 Score both sides of the fish with diagonal cuts at 1 inch intervals. Rub both the inside and outside of the fish with salt and sesame oil.

2 Place the fish on top of the scallions on a heat-proof platter. Blend the soy sauce and wine with the ginger shreds and pour evenly all over the fish.

3 Place the fish on the platter in a very hot steamer (or inside a wok on a rack), cover and steam vigorously for 12–15 minutes.

4 Heat the oil until hot, then blend in the black bean sauce. Remove the fish from the steamer and place on a serving dish.

5 Pour the hot black bean sauce over the whole length of the fish and place the shredded scallions on top. Place the fish on a platter and serve garnished with cilantro leaves (if using) and lemon slices.

COOK'S TIP

If using fish steaks, rub them with the salt and sesame oil, but do not score with a knife. The fish may require less cooking, depending on the thickness of the steaks – test with a skewer after about 8 minutes to check whether they are done.

Pineapple & Fish Curry

This is a fiery hot Thai curry dish all the better for serving with refreshing (and cooling) fresh pineapple pieces.

NUTRITIONAL INFORMATION

Calories	249	Sugars	.........4g
Protein	........29g	Fat	..........9g
Carbohydrate	...15g	Saturates	......1g

🍤 15 MINS   🕐 15 MINS

SERVES 4

INGREDIENTS

2 pineapples

3 inch piece galangal, sliced

2 blades of lemongrass, bruised then chopped

5 sprigs fresh basil

1 lb firm white fish fillets (angler fish, halibut, or cod, for example), cubed

4½ oz peeled shrimp

2 tbsp vegetable oil

2 tbsp red curry paste

½ cup thick coconut milk or cream

2 tbsp fish sauce

2 tsp jaggery or demerara sugar

2-3 red chilies, seeded and cut into thin julienne strips

about 6 kaffir lime leaves, torn into pieces

cilantro sprigs, to garnish

COOK'S TIP

Angler fish, like sole, goes well with a many different types of sauces – cream, tomato, or hollandaise – and is delicious served cold with fresh mayonnaise.

1 Cut the pineapples in half lengthways. Remove the flesh, reserving the shells if using (see right). Remove the core from the pineapple flesh then dice into bite-sized pieces.

2 Place the galangal in a large shallow pan with the lemon grass and basil. Add the fish cubes and just enough water to cover. Bring to a boil, reduce the heat, and simmer for about 2 minutes.

3 Add the shrimp and cook for a further 1 minute or until the fish is just cooked. Remove from the flavored stock with a draining spoon and keep warm.

4 Heat the oil in a heavy-bottomed skeillet or wok. Add the curry paste and cook for 1 minute. Stir in the coconut milk or cream, fish sauce, brown sugar, chilies, and lime leaves.

5 Add the pineapple and cook until just heated through. Add the cooked fish and mix gently to combine.

6 Spoon into the reserved pineapple shells, if liked, and serve immediately, garnished with sprigs of cilantro.

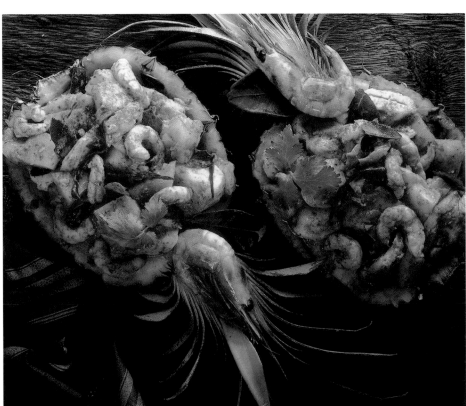

Bajan Fish

Bajan seasoning comes from Barbados and can be used with all kinds of meat, fish, poultry, and game. Add more chili if you like it really hot.

NUTRITIONAL INFORMATION

Calories	247	Sugars	.........4g
Protein	........27g	Fat	..........12g
Carbohydrate	....5g	Saturates	......1g

 45 MINS   15 MINS

SERVES 4

INGREDIENTS

1 lb 2 oz-1 lb 6 oz angler fish tails, boned and cubed

2 large carrots

6-8 oz baby corn-on-the-cobs

3 tbsp sunflower oil

1 yellow bell pepper, cored, seeded, and thinly sliced

1 tbsp wine vinegar

⅔ cup fish or vegetable stock

1 tbsp lemon juice

2 tbsp sherry

1 tsp cornstarch

salt and pepper

fresh herbs and lemon slices, to garnish

BAJAN SEASONING

1 small onion, quartered

2 shallots

3-4 garlic cloves, minced

4-6 large scallions, sliced

small handful of fresh parsley

2-3 sprigs of fresh thyme

small strip of green chili pepper, seeds removed, or ½-¼ tsp chili powder

½ tsp salt

¼ tsp freshly ground black pepper

2 tbsp brown rum or red wine vinegar

1 Process the ingredients for the Bajan seasoning very finely. Put the fish in a dish, spread with the seasoning to coat evenly. Cover and chill for 30 minutes.

2 Cut the carrots into narrow 1½ inch slices. Slice the baby-corn-on-the-cobs diagonally. Heat 2 tbsp of oil in the wok, swirling it around until really hot. Add the fish and stir-fry for 3-4 minutes. Remove to a bowl and keep warm.

3 Add the remaining oil and stir-fry the carrots and corn for 2 minutes. Add the bell pepper and stir-fry for another minute. Return the fish and juices to the wok and stir-fry for 1-2 minutes.

4 Blend the vinegar, stock, lemon juice, sherry, and seasoning with the cornstarch. Stir into the wok and boil until thickened. Serve garnished with herbs and lemon.

Angler Fish & Okra Balti

Okra can be bought both in large supermarkets and Asian food stores.

NUTRITIONAL INFORMATION

Calories	266	Sugars	.........4g
Protein	........46g	Fat	...........7g
Carbohydrate	....5g	Saturates	.......1g

1¼ HOURS   25 MINS

SERVES 4

I N G R E D I E N T S

1 lb 10 oz angler fish, cut into
   1¼ inch cubes

9 oz okra

2 tbsp oil

1 onion, sliced

1 garlic clove, minced

1 inch piece gingerroot, sliced

⅔ cup coconut milk or fish stock

2 tsp garam masala

M A R I N A D E

3 tbsp lemon juice

grated rind of 1 lemon

¼ tsp aniseed

½ tsp salt

½ tsp ground black pepper

T O   G A R N I S H

4 lime wedges

sprigs of fresh cilantro

1 To make the marinade, mix the ingredients together in a bowl. Stir the angler fish into the bowl and leave to marinate for 1 hour.

2 Bring a saucepan of water to a boil, add the okra and boil for 4–5 minutes. Drain and cut into ½ inch slices.

3 Heat the oil in a Balti pan or wok, add the onion and stir-fry until golden brown. Add the garlic and ginger and fry for 1 minute. Add the fish with the marinade and stir-fry for 2 minutes.

4 Stir in the okra, coconut milk or stock, and the garam masala and simmer for 10 minutes. Serve garnished with lime wedges and fresh cilantro.

VARIATION

Angler fish is a very meaty fish, resembling lobster, which could be used instead of angler fish for a special occasion.

Steamed Stuffed Snapper

Red mullet may be used instead of the snapper, although they are a little more difficult to stuff because of their size. Use one mullet per person.

NUTRITIONAL INFORMATION

Calories 406   Sugar 4g
Protein ....68g   Fat 9g
Carbohydrate ....9g   Saturates 0g

  20 MINS   10 MINS

SERVES 4

INGREDIENTS

3 lb whole snapper, cleaned and scaled

6 oz spinach

orange slices and shredded scallion, to garnish

STUFFING

2 cups cooked long-grain rice

1 tsp grated fresh gingerroot

2 scallions, finely chopped

2 tsp light soy sauce

1 tsp sesame oil

½ tsp ground star anise

1 orange, segmented and chopped

1 Rinse the fish inside and out under cold running water and pat dry with paper towels.

2 Blanch the spinach for 40 seconds, rinse in cold water and drain well, pressing out as much moisture as possible.

3 Arrange the spinach on a heat-proof plate and place the fish on top.

4 To make the stuffing, mix together the cooked rice, grated ginger, scallions, soy sauce, sesame oil, star anise, and orange in a bowl.

5 Spoon the stuffing into the body cavity of the fish, pressing it in well with a spoon.

6 Cover the plate and cook in a steamer for 10 minutes, or until the fish is cooked through.

7 Transfer the fish to a warmed serving dish, garnish with orange slices and shredded scallion and serve.

COOK'S TIP

The name snapper covers a family of tropical and subtropical fish that vary in color. They may be red, orange, pink, grey, or blue-green. Some are striped or spotted and they range in size from about 6 inches to 3 ft.

Crab-Stuffed Red Snapper

This popular fish is pinkish-red in color and has moist, tender flesh. For this recipe it is steamed, but it can also be baked or braised.

NUTRITIONAL INFORMATION

Calories	205	Sugars	.......0.1g
Protein	........36g	Fat	..........6g
Carbohydrate	...0.1g	Saturates	......1g

 10 MINS   25 MINS

SERVES 4

INGREDIENTS

4 red snappers, cleaned and scaled, about 6 oz each

2 tbsp dry sherry

salt and pepper

wedges of lime, to garnish

red chili strips, to garnish

stir-fried shredded vegetables, to serve

STUFFING

1 small red chili

1 garlic clove

1 scallion

½ tsp finely grated lime rind

1 tbsp lime juice

3½ oz white crabmeat, flaked

1 Rinse the fish and pat dry on paper towels. Season inside and out and place in a shallow dish. Spoon over the sherry and set aside.

2 Meanwhile, make the stuffing. Carefully halve, seed, and finely chop the chili. Place in a small bowl.

3 Peel and finely chop the garlic. Trim and finely chop the scallion. Add to the chili together with the grated lime rind, lime juice, and the flaked crabmeat.

4 Season with salt and pepper to taste and combine.

5 Spoon some of the stuffing into the cavity of each fish.

6 Bring a large saucepan of water to a boil. Arrange the fish in a steamer lined with baking parchment or in a large strainer and place over the boiling water on the cooker.

7 Cover and steam for 10 minutes. Turn the fish over and steam for a further 10 minutes or until the fish is cooked through.

8 Drain the fish and transfer to serving plates.

9 Garnish with wedges of lime and strips of chili, and serve the fish on a bed of stir-fried vegetables.

Indonesian-Style Spicy Cod

A delicious aromatic coating makes this dish rather special. Serve it with a crisp salad and crusty bread.

NUTRITIONAL INFORMATION

Calories 146   Sugars 2g
Protein ....19g   Fat 7g
Carbohydrate ....2g   Saturates 4g

  10 MINS   15 MINS

SERVES 4

INGREDIENTS

4 cod steaks

1 stalk lemon grass

1 small red onion, chopped

3 cloves garlic, chopped

2 fresh red chilies, seeded and chopped

1 tsp grated gingerroot

¼ tsp turmeric

2 tbsp butter, cut into small cubes

8 tbsp canned coconut milk

2 tbsp lemon juice

salt and pepper

red chilies, to garnish (optional)

1 Rinse the cod steaks and pat them dry on absorbent paper towels.

2 Remove and discard the outer leaves from the lemon grass and thinly slice the inner section.

3 Place the lemon grass, onion, garlic, chilies, ginger, and turmeric in a food processor and blend until the ingredients are finely chopped. Season with salt and pepper to taste.

4 With the processor running, add the butter, coconut milk, and lemon juice and process until well blended.

5 Place the fish in a shallow, non-metallic dish. Pour over the coconut mixture and turn the fish until it is well coated.

6 If you have one, place the fish steaks in a hinged basket, which will make them easier to turn. Grill over hot coals for 15 minutes or until the fish is cooked through, turning once. Serve garnished with red chilies (if using).

COOK'S TIP

If you prefer a milder flavor, omit the chilies altogether. For a hotter flavor, do not remove the seeds from the chilies.

Indian Cod with Tomatoes

Quick and easy–cod steaks are cooked in a rich tomato and coconut sauce to produce tender, succulent results.

NUTRITIONAL INFORMATION

Calories 194	Sugars 6g	
Protein 21g	Fat 9g	
Carbohydrate 7g	Saturates 1g	

 5 MINS   25 MINS

SERVES 4

I N G R E D I E N T S

3 tbsp vegetable oil

4 cod steaks, about 1 inch thick

salt and freshly ground black pepper

1 onion, peeled and finely chopped

2 garlic cloves, peeled and minced

1 red bell pepper, seeded and chopped

1 tsp ground coriander

1 tsp ground cumin

1 tsp ground turmeric

½ tsp garam masala

1 x 14 oz can chopped tomatoes

⅔ cup coconut milk

1-2 tbsp chopped fresh cilantro or parsley

VARIATION

The mixture may be flavored with a tablespoonful of curry powder or curry paste (mild, medium or hot, according to personal preference) instead of the mixture of spices at step 2, if wished.

1 Heat the oil in a skillet, add the fish steaks, season with salt and pepper, and fry until browned on both sides (but not cooked through). Remove from the pan and reserve.

2 Add the onion, garlic, red bell pepper, and spices and cook very gently for 2 minutes, stirring frequently. Add the tomatoes, bring to a boil and simmer for 5 minutes.

3 Add the fish steaks to the skillet and simmer gently for 8 minutes or until the fish is cooked through.

4 Remove from the skillet and keep warm on a serving dish. Add the coconut milk and cilantro or parsley to the skillet and reheat gently.

5 Spoon the sauce over the cod steaks and serve immediately.

Japanese Plaice

The marinade for this dish has a distinctly Japanese taste. Its subtle flavor goes well with any white fish.

NUTRITIONAL INFORMATION

Calories 207   Sugars 9g
Protein . . . . .22g   Fat 8g
Carbohydrate . . .10g   Saturates 1g

6 HOURS   10 MINS

SERVES 4

I N G R E D I E N T S

4 small plaice

6 tbsp soy sauce

2 tbsp sake or dry white wine

2 tbsp sesame oil

1 tbsp lemon juice

2 tbsp light muscovado sugar

1 tsp gingerroot, grated

1 clove garlic, minced

TO GARNISH

1 small carrot

4 scallion

1 Rinse the fish and pat them dry on paper towels.

2 Cut a few slashes into the sides of the fish so that they absorb the marinade.

3 Mix together the soy sauce, sake or wine, oil, lemon juice, sugar, ginger, and garlic in a large, shallow dish.

4 Place the fish in the marinade and turn them over so that they are well coated on both sides. Leave to stand in the refrigerator for 1–6 hours.

5 Meanwhile, prepare the garnish. Cut the carrot into evenly-sized thin sticks and clean and shred the scallions.

6 Grill the fish over hot coals for about 10 minutes, turning once.

7 Scatter the chopped scallions and carrot over the fish and transfer the fish to a serving dish. Serve immediately.

VARIATION

Use sole instead of the plaice and scatter over some toasted sesame seeds instead of the carrot and scallions, if you prefer.

Plaice Fillets with Grapes

Fish is ideal for a quick meal, especially when cut into strips as in this recipe – it takes only minutes to cook.

NUTRITIONAL INFORMATION

Calories . . . . . . .226 Sugars 6g
Protein . . . . .23g Fat 9g
Carbohydrate . . . .9g Saturates 4g

5 MINS   10 MINS

SERVES 4

I N G R E D I E N T S

1 lb plaice fillets, skinned

4 scallions, white and green parts, sliced diagonally

½ cup dry white wine

1 tbsp cornstarch

2 tbsp skimmed milk

2 tbsp chopped fresh dill

¼ cup heavy cream

4½ oz seedless green grapes

1 tsp lemon juice

salt and pepper

fresh dill sprigs, to garnish

T O   S E R V E

basmati rice

zucchini ribbons

1 Cut the fish into strips about 1¾ inches long and put into a skillet with the scallions, wine, and seasoning.

2 Bring to a boil, cover, and simmer for 4 minutes. Carefully transfer the fish to a warm serving dish. Cover and keep warm.

3 Mix the cornstarch and milk then add to the pan with the dill and cream. Bring to a boil, and boil, stirring, for 2 minutes until thickened.

4 Add the grapes and lemon juice and heat through gently for 1–2 minutes, then pour over the fish. Garnish with dill and serve with rice and zucchini ribbons.

COOK'S TIP

Dill has a fairly strong aniseed flavor that goes very well with fish. The feathery leaves are particularly attractive when used as a garnish.

Plaice with Mushrooms

The moist texture of broiled fish is complemented by the texture of the mushrooms.

NUTRITIONAL INFORMATION

Calories	243	Sugars	.........2g
Protein	........30g	Fat	..........13g
Carbohydrate	....2g	Saturates	......3g

🥔 🥔

10 MINS   ⏱ 20 MINS

SERVES 4

I N G R E D I E N T S

4 × 5½ oz white-skinned plaice fillets

2 tbsp lime juice

celery salt and pepper

⅓ cup low-fat spread

2½ cups mixed small mushrooms such as button, oyster, shiitake, chanterelle, or morel, sliced or quartered

4 tomatoes, skinned, seeded and chopped

basil leaves, to garnish

mixed salad, to serve

1   Line a broiler rack with baking parchment and place the fish on top.

2   Sprinkle over the lime juice and season with celery salt and pepper.

3   Place under a preheated moderate broiler and cook for 7–8 minutes without turning, until just cooked. Keep warm.

4   Meanwhile, gently melt the low fat spread in a non-stick skillet, add the mushrooms and fry for 4–5 minutes over a low heat until cooked through.

5   Gently heat the tomatoes in a small saucepan.

6   Spoon the mushrooms, with any pan juices, and the tomatoes over the plaice.

7   Garnish the broiled plaice with the basil leaves and serve with a mixed salad.

COOK'S TIP

Mushrooms are ideal in a low-fat diet, as they are packed full of flavor and contain no fat. More 'meaty' types of mushroom, such as crimini, will take slightly longer to cook.

Delicately Spiced Trout

The firm, sweet flesh of the trout is enhanced by the sweet-spicy flavor of the marinade and cooking juices.

NUTRITIONAL INFORMATION

Calories	374	Sugars	........13g
Protein	........38g	Fat	..........19g
Carbohydrate	...14g	Saturates	......3g

 45 MINS   20 MINS

SERVES 4

I N G R E D I E N T S

4 trout, each weighing 6–9 oz, cleaned

3 tbsp oil

1 tsp fennel seeds

1tsp onion seeds

1 garlic clove, minced

⅔ cup coconut milk or fish stock

3 tbsp tomato paste

⅓ cup golden raisins

½ tsp garam masala

TO GARNISH

¼ cup chopped cashew nuts

lemon wedges

sprigs of fresh cilantro

MARINADE

4 tbsp lemon juice

2 tbsp chopped fresh cilantro

1 tsp ground cumin

½ tsp salt

½ tsp ground black pepper

1 Slash the trout skin in several places on both sides with a sharp knife.

2 To make the marinade, mix all the ingredients together in a bowl.

3 Put the trout in a shallow dish and pour over the marinade. Leave to marinate for 30–40 minutes; turn the fish over during the marinating time.

4 Heat the oil in a Balti pan or wok and fry the fennel seeds and onion seeds until they start popping.

5 Add the minced garlic, coconut milk or fish stock, and tomato paste and bring the mixture in the wok to a boil.

6 Add the golden raisins, garam masala, and trout with the juices from the marinade. Cover and simmer for 5 minutes. Turn the trout over and simmer for a further 10 minutes.

7 Serve garnished with the nuts, lemon, and cilantro sprigs.

Soused Trout

In this recipe, fillets of trout are gently poached in a spiced vinegar, left to marinate for 24 hours, and served cold with a potato salad.

NUTRITIONAL INFORMATION

Calories 521   Sugars 3g
Protein . . . . .61g   Fat 20g
Carbohydrate . . .27g   Saturates 4g

24 HOURS   35 MINS

SERVES 4

INGREDIENTS

4 trout, about 8–12 oz each, filleted

1 onion, sliced very thinly

2 bay leaves, preferably fresh

sprigs of fresh parsley and dill, or other fresh herbs

10–12 black peppercorns

4–6 cloves

good pinch of salt

⅔ cup red wine vinegar

salad leaves, to garnish

POTATO SALAD

1 lb small new potatoes

2 tbsp French dressing

4 tbsp thick low-fat mayonnaise

3–4 scallions, sliced

1 Trim the trout fillets, cutting off any pieces of fin. If preferred, remove the skin – use a sharp knife and, beginning at the tail end, carefully cut the flesh from the skin, pressing the knife down firmly as you go.

2 Lightly grease a shallow ovenproof dish and lay the fillets in it, packing them fairly tightly together but keeping them in a single layer. Arrange the sliced onion, bay leaves and herbs over the fish.

3 Put the peppercorns, cloves, salt, and vinegar into a pan and bring almost to a boil. Remove from the heat and pour evenly over the fish. Leave to marinate in the refrigerator for 24 hours. Cover with foil and cook in a preheated oven at 325°F for 15 minutes. Leave until cold, and then chill thoroughly.

4 Cook the potatoes in boiling salted water for 10–15 minutes until just tender. Drain. While still warm, cut into large dice and place in a bowl. Combine the French dressing and mayonnaise, add to the potatoes while warm and toss evenly. Leave until cold, then sprinkle the potato salad with chopped scallions.

5 Pour a little of the juices over each portion of fish. Garnish with salad leaves and serve with the potato salad.

Baked Trout Mexican-Style

Make this dish as hot or as mild as you like by adjusting the amount of red chili. The green chilies are milder and add a pungency to the dish.

NUTRITIONAL INFORMATION

Calories 329	Sugars 5g	
Protein 53g	Fat 10g	
Carbohydrate 6g	Saturates 2g	

10 MINS   30 MINS

SERVES 4

I N G R E D I E N T S

4 trout, 8 oz each

1 small bunch fresh cilantro

4 shallots, shredded finely

1 small yellow bell pepper, seeded and very
  finely chopped

1 small red bell pepper, seeded and very
  finely chopped

2 green chilies, seeded and finely chopped

1–2 red chilies, seeded and finely chopped

1 tbsp lemon juice

1 tbsp white wine vinegar

2 tsp superfine sugar

salt and pepper

fresh cilantro, to garnish

salad leaves, to serve

COOK'S TIP

For the chili bean rice,
cook 1¼ cup long-
grain white rice. Drain and rinse a
14 oz can kidney beans and stir into the
rice with 1 tsp each of
ground cumin and coriander. Stir in
4 tbsp chopped fresh cilantro and
season.

1 Preheat the oven to 350°F. Wash the trout and pat dry with paper towels. Season and stuff with cilantro leaves.

2 Place the fish side by side in a shallow ovenproof dish. Sprinkle over the shallots, bell peppers, and chilies.

3 Mix together the lemon juice, vinegar and sugar in a bowl. Spoon over the trout and season with salt and pepper.

Cover the dish and bake for 30 minutes or until the fish is tender and the flesh is opaque.

4 Remove the the fish with a fish slice and drain. Transfer to warm serving plates and spoon the cooking juices over the fish. Garnish with fresh cilantro and serve with salad and chili bean rice (see Cook's Tip).

Herrings with Tarragon

The fish are filled with an orange-flavored stuffing and are wrapped in kitchen foil before being baked on the grill.

NUTRITIONAL INFORMATION

Calories	332	Sugars	.........4g
Protein	........21g	Fat	.........24g
Carbohydrate	....9g	Saturates	......6g

 15 MINS   35 MINS

SERVES 4

I N G R E D I E N T S

1 orange

4 scallions

1¾ oz fresh whole-wheat bread crumbs

1 tbsp fresh tarragon, chopped

4 herrings, cleaned and gutted

salt and pepper

green salad, to serve

TO GARNISH

2 oranges

1 tbsp light brown sugar

1 tbsp olive oil

sprigs of fresh tarragon

1 To make the stuffing, grate the rind from half of the orange, using a citrus zester.

2 Peel and chop all of the orange flesh on a plate in order to catch all of the juice.

3 Mix together the orange flesh, juice, rind, scallions, bread crumbs, and tarragon in a bowl. Season with salt and pepper to taste.

4 Divide the stuffing into 4 equal portions and use it to fill the body cavities of the fish.

5 Place each fish on to a square of lightly greased kitchen foil and wrap the foil around the fish so that it is completely enclosed. Grill over hot coals for 20–30 minutes until the fish are cooked through – the flesh should be white and firm to the touch.

6 Meanwhile make the garnish. Peel and thickly slice the 2 oranges and sprinkle over the sugar.

7 Just before the fish is cooked, drizzle a little oil over the orange slices and place them on the barbecue for about 5 minutes to heat through.

8 Transfer the fish to serving plates and garnish with the grilled orange slices and sprigs of fresh tarragon.

9 Serve the fish with a fresh green salad.

Baked Sea Bass

Seabass is often paired with subtle oriental flavors. For a special occasion, you may like to bone the fish.

NUTRITIONAL INFORMATION

Calories 140   Sugars 0.1g
Protein ....29g   Fat 1g
Carbohydrate ...0.1g   Saturates 0.2g

  10 MINS   15 MINS

SERVES 4–6

INGREDIENTS

2 sea bass, about 2 lb each, cleaned and scaled

2 scallions, green part only, cut into strips

2 inch piece ginger, peeled and cut into strips

2 garlic cloves, unpeeled, minced lightly

2 tbsp mirin or dry sherry

salt and pepper

TO SERVE

pickled sushi ginger (optional)

soy sauce

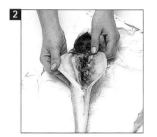

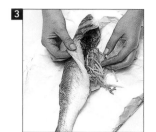

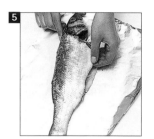

1 For each fish lay out a double thickness of foil and oil the top piece well, or lay a piece of silicon paper over the foil.

2 Place the fish in the middle and expose the cavity.

3 Divide the scallion and ginger between each cavity. Put a garlic clove in each cavity.

4 Pour over the mirin or dry sherry. Season the fish well.

5 Close the cavities and lay each fish on its side. Bring over the foil and fold the edges together to seal securely. Fold each end neatly.

6 Cook over a medium grill for 15 minutes, turning once.

7 To serve, remove the foil and cut each fish into 2 or 3 pieces.

8 Serve with the pickled ginger (if using) accompanied by soy sauce.

COOK'S TIP

Fresh sea bass is just as delicious when cooked very simply. Stuff the fish with garlic and chopped herbs, brush with olive oil, and bake in the oven.

Fragrant Tuna Steaks

Fresh tuna steaks are very meaty – they have a firm texture, yet the flesh is succulent. Steaks from the belly are best of all.

NUTRITIONAL INFORMATION

Calories	239	Sugars	.......0.1g
Protein	........42g	Fat	...........8g
Carbohydrate	...0.5g	Saturates	......2g

  15 MINS   15 MINS

SERVES 4

INGREDIENTS

4 tuna steaks, 6 oz each

½ tsp finely grated lime rind

1 garlic clove, minced

2 tsp olive oil

1 tsp ground cumin

1 tsp ground coriander

pepper

1 tbsp lime juice

fresh cilantro, to garnish

TO SERVE

avocado relish (see Cook's Tip, below)

lime wedges

tomato wedges

COOK'S TIP

For the avocado relish, peel and chop a small ripe avocado. Mix in 1 tbsp lime juice, 1 tbsp freshly chopped cilantro, 1 small finely chopped red onion and some chopped fresh mango or tomato. Season to taste.

1 Trim the skin from the tuna steaks, rinse and pat dry on absorbent paper towels.

2 In a small bowl, mix together the lime rind, garlic, olive oil, cumin, ground coriander, and pepper to make a paste.

3 Spread the paste thinly on both sides of the tuna. Heat a non-stick, ridged skillet until hot and press the tuna steaks into the pan to seal them. Lower the heat and cook for 5 minutes. Turn the fish over and cook for a further 4–5 minutes until the fish is cooked through. Drain on paper towels and transfer to a serving plate.

4 Sprinkle the lime juice and chopped cilantro over the fish. Serve with avocado relish (see Cook's Tip), and tomato and lime wedges.

Pan-Seared Halibut

Liven up firm steaks of white fish with a spicy, colorful relish. Use red onions for a slightly sweeter flavor.

NUTRITIONAL INFORMATION

Calories 197	Sugars 1g
Protein 31g	Fat 7g
Carbohydrate 2g	Saturates 1g

55 MINS   30 MINS

SERVES 4

INGREDIENTS

1 tsp olive oil

4 halibut steaks, skinned, 6 oz each

½ tsp cornstarch mixed with
  2 tsp cold water

salt and pepper

2 tbsp fresh chives, snipped, to garnish

RED ONION RELISH

2 tsp olive oil

2 medium red onions

6 shallots

1 tbsp lemon juice

2 tbsp red wine vinegar

2 tsp superfine sugar

⅔ cup fresh fish stock (see page 14)

1 To make the relish, peel and thinly shred the onions and shallots. Place in a small bowl and toss in the lemon juice.

2 Heat the oil in a pan and fry the onions and shallots for 3–4 minutes until just softened.

3 Add the vinegar and sugar and continue to cook for a further 2 minutes over a high heat. Pour in the stock and season well. Bring to a boil and simmer gently for a further 8–9 minutes until the sauce has thickened and is slightly reduced.

4 Brush a non-stick, ridged skillet with oil and heat until hot. Press the fish steaks into the pan to seal, lower the heat and cook for 4 minutes. Turn the fish over and cook for 4–5 minutes until cooked through. Drain on paper towels and keep warm.

5 Stir the cornstarch paste into the onion sauce and heat through, stirring, until thickened. Season to taste.

6 Pile the relish on to 4 warm serving plates and place a halibut steak on top of each. Garnish with chives.

COOK'S TIP

If raw onions make your eyes water, try peeling them under cold, running water. Alternatively, stand or sit well back from the onion so that your face is not directly over it.

Mackerel with Lime

The secret of this dish lies in the simple, fresh flavors which perfectly complement the fish.

NUTRITIONAL INFORMATION

Calories 302   Sugars 0g
Protein ....21g   Fat 24g
Carbohydrate ....0g   Saturates 4g

10 MINS   10 MINS

SERVES 4

I N G R E D I E N T S

4 small mackerel

¼ tsp ground coriander

¼ tsp ground cumin

4 sprigs fresh cilantro

3 tbsp chopped, fresh cilantro

1 red chili, seeded and chopped

grated rind and juice of 1 lime

2 tbsp sunflower oil

salt and pepper

1 lime, sliced, to garnish

chili flowers (optional), to garnish

salad leaves, to serve

1 To make the chili flowers (if using), cut the tip of a small chili lengthways into thin strips, leaving the chili intact at the stem end. Remove the seeds and place in iced water until curled.

COOK'S TIP

This recipe is suitable for other oily fish, such as trout, herring, or sardines.

2 Clean and gut the mackerel, removing the heads if preferred. Transfer the mackerel to a chopping board.

3 Sprinkle the fish with the ground spices and salt and pepper to taste. Sprinkle 1 teaspoon of chopped cilantro inside the cavity of each fish.

4 Mix together the chopped cilantro, chili, lime rind and juice and the oil in a small bowl. Brush the mixture liberally over the fish.

5 Place the fish in a hinged rack if you have one. Grill the fish over hot coals for 3–4 minutes on each side, turning once. Brush the fish frequently with the remaining basting mixture. Transfer to plates and garnish with chili flowers (if using) and lime slices, and serve with salad leaves.

Poached Salmon

Salmon steaks, poached in a well-flavored stock and served with a piquant sauce, make a delicious summer lunch or supper dish.

NUTRITIONAL INFORMATION

Calories	.712	Sugars	.5g
Protein	.66g	Fat	.47g
Carbohydrate	.6g	Saturates	.9g

10 MINS   30 MINS

SERVES 4

INGREDIENTS

1 small onion, sliced

1 small carrot, sliced

1 stalk celery, sliced

1 bay leaf

pared rind and juice of ½ orange

a few stalks of parsley

salt

5-6 black peppercorns

3 cups water

4 salmon steaks, about 12 oz each

salad leaves, to serve

lemon twists, to garnish

SAUCE

1 large avocado, peeled, halved, and stoned

½ cup low-fat unsweetened yogurt

grated zest and juice of ½ orange

black pepper

a few drops of hot red pepper sauce

1 Put the onion, carrot, celery, bay leaf, orange rind, orange juice, parsley stalks, salt, and peppercorns in a pan just large enough to take the salmon steaks in a single layer. Pour on the water, cover the pan and bring to a boil. Simmer the stock for 20 minutes.

2 Arrange the salmon steaks in the pan, return the stock to a boil and simmer for 3 minutes. Cover the pan, remove from the heat and leave the salmon to cool in the stock.

3 Roughly chop the avocado and place it in a blender or food processor with the yogurt, orange zest, and orange juice. Process until smooth, then season to taste with salt, pepper, and hot pepper sauce.

4 Remove the salmon steaks from the stock (reserve it to make fish soup or a sauce), skin them, and pat dry with paper towels.

5 Cover the serving dish with salad leaves, arrange the salmon steaks on top and spoon a little of the sauce into the center of each one. Garnish the fish with lemon twists, and serve the remaining sauce separately.

 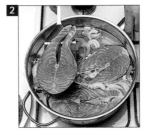 

Salmon Fillet with Herbs

This is a great party dish, as the salmon is cooked in one piece. The combination of the herbs and grill give a great flavor.

NUTRITIONAL INFORMATION

Calories 507   Sugars 0.4g
Protein . . . . .46g   Fat 35g
Carbohydrate . . .0.5g   Saturates 6g

 5 MINS   30 MINS

SERVES 4

I N G R E D I E N T S

½ large bunch dried thyme

5 fresh rosemary branches, 6–8 inches long

8 bay leaves

2 lb salmon fillet

1 bulb fennel, cut into 8 pieces

2 tbsp lemon juice

2 tbsp olive oil

TO SERVE

crusty bread

green salad

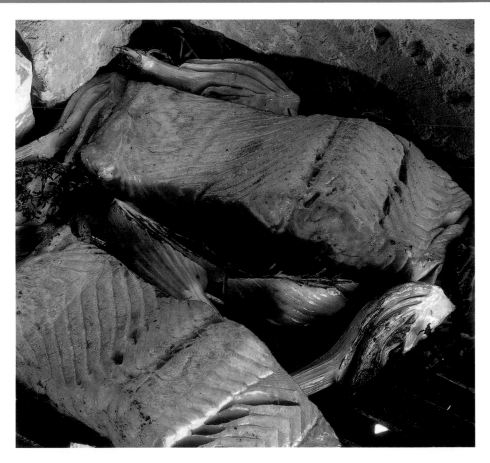

1 Make a base on a hot grill with the dried thyme, rosemary branches, and bay leaves, overlapping them so that they cover a slightly bigger area than the salmon.

2 Carefully place the salmon on top of the herbs.

3 Arrange the fennel around the edge of the fish.

4 Combine the lemon juice and oil and brush the salmon with it.

5 Cover the salmon loosely with a piece of foil, to keep it moist.

6 Cook for about 20–30 minutes, basting frequently with the lemon juice mixture.

7 Remove the salmon from the grill, cut it into slices and serve with the fennel.

8 Serve with slices of crusty bread and a green salad.

VARIATION

Use whatever combination of herbs you may have to hand – but avoid the stronger tasting herbs, such as sage and marjoram, which are unsuitable for fish.

Salmon with Caper Sauce

The richness of salmon is beautifully balanced by the tangy capers in this creamy herb sauce.

NUTRITIONAL INFORMATION

Calories 302	Sugars 0g
Protein 21g	Fat 24g
Carbohydrate 1g	Saturates 9g

 5 MINS   25 MINS

SERVES 4

I N G R E D I E N T S

4 salmon fillets, skinned

1 fresh bay leaf

few black peppercorns

1 tsp white wine vinegar

⅔ cup fish stock

3 tbsp heavy cream

1 tbsp capers

1 tbsp chopped fresh dill

1 tbsp chopped fresh chives

1 tsp cornstarch

2 tbsp skimmed milk

salt and pepper

new potatoes, to serve

TO GARNISH

fresh dill sprigs

chive flowers

1 Lay the salmon fillets in a shallow ovenproof dish. Add the bay leaf, peppercorns, vinegar, and stock.

2 Cover with foil and bake in a preheated oven at 350°F for 15–20 minutes until the flesh is opaque and flakes easily when tested with a fork.

3 Transfer the fish to warmed serving plates, cover and keep warm.

4 Strain the cooking liquid into a saucepan. Stir in the cream, capers, dill, and chives and seasoning to taste.

5 Blend the cornstarch with the milk. Add to the saucepan and heat, stirring, until thickened slightly. Boil for 1 minute.

6 Spoon the sauce over the salmon, garnish with dill sprigs and chive flowers.

7 Serve with new potatoes.

COOK'S TIP

Ask the fishmonger to skin the fillets for you. The cooking time for the salmon will depend on the thickness of the fish: the thin tail end of the salmon takes the least time to cook.

Salmon Yakitori

The Japanese sauce used here combines well with salmon, although it is usually served with chicken.

NUTRITIONAL INFORMATION

Calories 247	Sugars 10g
Protein 19g	Fat 11g
Carbohydrate . . .12g	Saturates 2g

20 MINS   15 MINS

SERVES 4

I N G R E D I E N T S

12 oz chunky salmon fillet

8 baby leeks

Y A K I T O R I   S A U C E

5 tbsp light soy sauce

5 tbsp fish stock

2 tbsp superfine sugar

5 tbsp dry white wine

3 tbsp sweet sherry

1 clove garlic, minced

1 Skin the salmon and cut the flesh into 2 inch chunks. Trim the leeks and cut them into 2 inch lengths.

2 Thread the salmon and leeks alternately on to 8 pre-soaked wooden skewers. Leave to chill in the refrigerator until required.

3 To make the sauce, place all of the ingredients in a small pan and heat gently, stirring, until the sugar has dissolved.

4 Bring to a boil, then reduce the heat and simmer for 2 minutes. Strain the sauce through a fine strainer and leave to cool until it is required.

5 Pour about one-third of the sauce into a small dish and set aside to serve with the kabobs.

6 Brush plenty of the remaining sauce over the skewers and cook directly on the rack.

7 If preferred, place a sheet of oiled kitchen foil on the rack and cook the salmon on that.

8 Grill the salmon and leek kabobs over hot coals for about 10 minutes or until cooked though, turning once.

9 Use a brush to baste frequently during cooking with the remaining sauce in order to prevent the fish and vegetables from drying out. Transfer the kabobs to a large serving platter and serve with a small bowl of the reserved sauce for dipping.

Sole Paupiettes

A delicate dish of sole fillets rolled up with spinach and shrimp, and served in a creamy ginger sauce.

NUTRITIONAL INFORMATION

Calories 253	Sugars 7g
Protein 24g	Fat 14g
Carbohydrate 9g	Saturates 5g

  10 MINS   45 MINS

SERVES 4

I N G R E D I E N T S

4½ oz fresh young spinach leaves

2 Dover soles or large lemon soles or plaice, filleted

4½ oz peeled shrimp, defrosted if frozen

2 tsp sunflower oil

2-4 scallions, finely sliced diagonally

2 thin slices gingerroot, finely chopped

⅔ cup fish stock or water

2 tsp cornstarch

4 tbsp single cream

6 tbsp low-fat unsweetened yogurt

salt and pepper

whole shrimp, to garnish (optional)

1 Strip the stalks off the spinach, wash and dry on paper towels. Divide the spinach between the seasoned fish fillets, laying the leaves on the skin side. Divide half the shrimp between them. Roll up the fillets from head to tail and secure with wooden cocktail sticks. Arrange the rolls on a plate in the base of a bamboo steamer.

2 Stand a low metal trivet in the wok and add enough water to come almost to the top of it. Bring to a boil.

Place the bamboo steamer on the trivet, cover with the steamer lid and then the wok lid, or cover tightly with a domed piece of foil. Steam gently for 30 minutes until the fish is tender and cooked right through.

3 Remove the fish rolls and keep warm. Empty the wok and wipe dry with paper towels. Heat the oil in the wok, swirling it around until really hot. Add the scallions and ginger and stir-fry for 1-2 minutes.

4 Add the stock to the wok and bring to a boil. Blend the cornstarch with the cream. Add the yogurt and remaining shrimp to the wok and heat gently until boiling. Add a little sauce to the blended cream and return it all to the wok. Heat gently until thickened and season to taste. Serve the paupiettes with the sauce spooned over and garnished with whole shrimp, if using.

Angler Fish with Coconut

This is a tasty kabob with a mild marinade. Allow the skewers to marinate for at least an hour before cooking.

NUTRITIONAL INFORMATION

Calories 193   Sugars 2g
Protein . . . . .39g   Fat 3g
Carbohydrate . . . .2g   Saturates 1g

4 HOURS   30 MINS

SERVES 4

I N G R E D I E N T S

1 lb angler fish tails

8 oz uncooked peeled shrimp

shredded coconut, toasted, to garnish (optional)

M A R I N A D E

1 tsp sunflower oil

½ small onion, finely grated

1 tsp gingerroot, grated

⅔ cup canned coconut milk

2 tbsp chopped, fresh cilantro

1 To make the marinade, heat the oil in a wok or saucepan and fry the onion and ginger for 5 minutes until just softened but not browned.

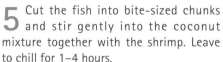

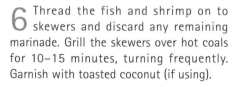

2 Add the coconut milk to the pan and bring to a boil. Boil rapidly for about 5 minutes or until reduced to the consistency of light cream.

3 Remove the pan from the heat and allow to cool completely.

4 When cooled, stir the cilantro into the coconut milk and pour into a shallow dish.

5 Cut the fish into bite-sized chunks and stir gently into the coconut mixture together with the shrimp. Leave to chill for 1–4 hours.

6 Thread the fish and shrimp on to skewers and discard any remaining marinade. Grill the skewers over hot coals for 10–15 minutes, turning frequently. Garnish with toasted coconut (if using).

COOK'S TIP

Look for uncooked shrimp in the freezer cabinet in large supermarkets. If you cannot obtain them, you can use cooked shrimp, but remember they only need heating through.

Lemony Angler Fish Skewers

A simple basting sauce is brushed over these tasty kabobs. When served with crusty bread, they make a perfect light meal.

NUTRITIONAL INFORMATION

Calories	191	Sugars	.........2g
Protein	........21g	Fat	...........11g
Carbohydrate	....1g	Saturates	......1g

10 MINS   15 MINS

SERVES 4

I N G R E D I E N T S

1 lb angler fish tail

2 zucchini

1 lemon

12 cherry tomatoes

8 bay leaves

S A U C E

3 tbsp olive oil

2 tbsp lemon juice

1 tsp chopped, fresh thyme

½ tsp lemon pepper

salt

T O   S E R V E

green salad leaves

fresh, crusty bread

1 Cut the angler fish into 2 inch chunks.

VARIATION

Use plaice fillets instead of the angler fish, if you prefer. Allow two fillets per person, and skin and cut each fillet lengthways into two. Roll up each piece and thread them on to the skewers.

2 Cut the zucchini into thick slices and the lemon into wedges.

3 Thread the angler fish, zucchini, lemon, tomatoes, and bay leaves on to 4 skewers.

4 To make the basting sauce, combine the oil, lemon juice, thyme, lemon pepper, and salt to taste in a small bowl.

5 Brush the basting sauce liberally all over the fish, lemon, tomatoes, and bay leaves on the skewers.

6 Cook the skewers on the grill for about 15 minutes over medium-hot coals, basting them frequently with the sauce, until the fish is cooked through. Transfer the skewers to plates and serve with green salad leaves and wedges of crusty bread.

Smoky Fish Skewers

The combination of fresh and smoked fish gives these kabobs a special flavor. Choose thick fish fillets to get good-sized pieces.

NUTRITIONAL INFORMATION

Calories	221	Sugars	. . . . .0g
Protein	. . . . .33g	Fat	. . . . .10g
Carbohydrate	. . . .0g	Saturates	. . . . . .1g

 4 HOURS   10 MINS

SERVES 4

INGREDIENTS

12 oz smoked cod fillet

12 oz cod fillet

8 large raw shrimp

8 bay leaves

fresh dill, to garnish (optional)

MARINADE

4 tbsp sunflower oil, plus a little for brushing

2 tbsp lemon or lime juice

rind of ½ lemon or lime, grated

¼ tsp dried dill

salt and pepper

1 Skin both types of cod and cut the flesh into bite-size pieces. Peel the shrimp, leaving just the tail.

2 To make the marinade, combine the oil, lemon or lime juice and rind, dill, and salt and pepper to taste in a shallow, non-metallic dish.

3 Place the prepared fish in the marinade and stir together until the fish is well coated on all sides. Leave the fish to marinate for 1–4 hours.

4 Thread the fish on to 4 skewers, alternating the 2 types of cod with the shrimp and bay leaves.

5 Cover the rack with lightly oiled kitchen foil and place the fish skewers on top of the foil.

6 Grill the fish skewers over hot coals for 5-10 minutes, basting with any remaining marinade, turning once.

7 Garnish the skewers with fresh dill (if using) and serve immediately.

COOK'S TIP

Cod fillet can be rather flaky, so choose the thicker end which is easier to cut into chunky pieces. Cook the fish on kitchen foil rather directly on the rack, so that if the fish breaks away from the skewer, it is not wasted.

Citrus Fish Kabobs

Use your favorite fish for this dish as long as it is firm enough to thread on to skewers. The tang of orange makes this a refreshing meal.

NUTRITIONAL INFORMATION

Calories 333	Sugars 10g
Protein 31g	Fat 14g
Carbohydrate . . .10g	Saturates 3g

2¹/₂ HOURS   10 MINS

SERVES 4

INGREDIENTS

1 lb firm white fish fillets (such as cod or
   angler fish)

1 lb thick salmon fillet

2 large oranges

1 pink grapefruit

1 bunch fresh bay leaves

1 tsp finely grated lemon rind

3 tbsp lemon juice

2 tsp clear honey

2 garlic cloves, minced

salt and pepper

TO SERVE

crusty bread

mixed salad

1 Skin the white fish and the salmon, rinse and pat dry on paper towels. Cut each fillet into 16 pieces.

2 Using a sharp knife, remove the skin and pith from the oranges and grapefruit. Cut out the segments of flesh, removing all remaining traces of the pith and dividing membrane.

3 Thread the pieces of fish with the orange and grapefruit segments and the bay leaves on to 8 skewers. Place the fish kabobs in a shallow dish.

4 In a small bowl, mix together the lemon rind and juice, the honey, and the garlic.

5 Pour over the fish kabobs and season well. Cover and chill for 2 hours, turning occasionally.

6 Preheat the broiler to medium. Remove the fish kabobs from the marinade and place on the rack.

7 Cook for 7–8 minutes, turning once, until cooked through.

8 Drain, transfer to serving plates and serve with crusty bread and a fresh mixed salad.

Oriental Shellfish Kabobs

These shellfish and vegetable kabobs are ideal for serving at parties. They are quick and easy to prepare and take next to no time to cook.

NUTRITIONAL INFORMATION

Calories 93   Sugars 1g
Protein ....15g   Fat 2g
Carbohydrate ....2g   Saturates 0.3g

2½ HOURS   5 MINS

MAKES 12

I N G R E D I E N T S

12 oz raw jumbo shrimp, peeled leaving tails intact

12 oz scallops, cleaned, trimmed and halved (quartered if large)

1 bunch scallions, sliced into 1 inch pieces

1 medium red bell pepper, seeded and cubed

3½ oz baby-corn-on-the-cobs, trimmed and sliced into ½ inch pieces

3 tbsp dark soy sauce

½ tsp hot chili powder

½ tsp ground ginger

1 tbsp sunflower oil

1 red chili, seeded and sliced, to garnish

D I P

4 tbsp dark soy sauce

4 tbsp dry sherry

2 tsp clear honey

1 inch piece gingerroot, peeled and grated

1 scallion, trimmed and sliced very finely

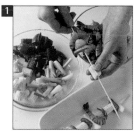

1 Divide the shrimp, scallops, scallions, bell pepper, and baby-corn-on-the-cobs into 12 portions and thread on to the skewers (soaked for 10 minutes in water to prevent them from burning). Cover the ends with foil so that they do not burn and place in a shallow dish.

2 Mix the soy sauce, chili powder and ground ginger and coat the kabobs. Cover and chill for about 2 hours.

3 Preheat the broiler to hot. Arrange the kabobs on the rack, brush with oil, and cook for 2–3 minutes on each side until the shrimp turn pink, the scallops become opaque, and the vegetables soften.

4 Mix together the dip ingredients.

5 Remove the foil and transfer the kabobs to a warm serving platter. Garnish with sliced chili and serve with the dip.

Shrimp Curry & Fruit Sauce

Serve this lightly-spiced dish as part of a buffet meal, or as a refreshingly different lunch dish, with a bowl of rice.

NUTRITIONAL INFORMATION

Calories	538	Sugars	.......28g
Protein	........40g	Fat	..........28g
Carbohydrate	...33g	Saturates	.....15g

 30 MINS   20 MINS

SERVES 4

INGREDIENTS

2 tbsp vegetable oil

2 tbsp butter

2 onions, finely chopped

2 garlic cloves, finely chopped

1 tsp cumin seeds, lightly minced

1 tsp ground turmeric

1 tsp paprika

½ tsp chili powder, or to taste

2 oz creamed coconut

1 x 14 oz can chopped tomatoes

1 tbsp tomato paste

1 lb frozen cooked shrimps, defrosted

½ cucumber, thinly diced

⅔ cup low-fat yogurt

2 hard-cooked eggs, quartered

salt

cilantro and onion rings, to garnish

FRUIT SAUCE

1¼ cups low-fat unsweetened yogurt

¼ tsp salt

1 garlic clove, minced

2 tbsp chopped mint

4 tbsp seedless raisins

1 small pomegranate

1 Heat the oil and butter in a skillet. Add the chopped onions and fry until translucent. Add the garlic and fry for a further minute, until softened but not browned.

2 Stir in the spices and cook for 2 minutes, stirring. Stir in the creamed coconut, chopped tomatoes, and tomato paste and bring to a boil. Simmer for 10 minutes, or until the sauce has thickened slightly. It should not be at all runny.

3 Remove the skillet from the heat and set aside to cool. Stir in the shrimps, cucumber, and yogurt. Taste the sauce and adjust the seasoning if necessary. Cover and chill until ready to serve.

4 To make the fruit sauce, place everything except the pomegrantes into a bowl. Cut the pomegranate in half, scoop out the seeds, discarding the white membrane, and stir into the fruit mixture, reserving a few for garnish.

5 Transfer the curry to a serving dish and arrange the hard-cooked egg, cilantro, and onion rings on top. Serve the sauce separately, sprinkled with the reserved pomegranate seeds.

Scallop Skewers

As the scallops are marinated, it is not essential that they are fresh; frozen shellfish are fine for a grill.

NUTRITIONAL INFORMATION

Calories	182	Sugars	.........0g
Protein	........29g	Fat	..........7g
Carbohydrate	....0g	Saturates	......1g

 30 MINS   10 MINS

SERVES 4

I N G R E D I E N T S

grated zest and juice of 2 limes

2 tbsp finely chopped lemon grass or 1 tbsp lemon juice

2 garlic cloves, minced

1 green chili, seeded and chopped

16 scallops, with corals

2 limes, each cut into 8 segments

2 tbsp sunflower oil

1 tbsp lemon juice

salt and pepper

TO SERVE

1 cup arugula salad

3 cups mixed salad greens

1 Soak 8 skewers in warm water for at least 10 minutes before you use them to prevent the food from sticking.

2 Combine the lime juice and zest, lemon grass, garlic and chili together in a mortarand pestle or spice grinder to make a paste.

3 Thread 2 scallops on to each of the soaked skewers. Cover the ends with foil to prevent them from burning.

4 Alternate the scallops with the lime segments.

5 Whisk together the oil, lemon juice, salt, and pepper to make the dressing.

6 Coat the scallops with the spice paste and place over a medium grill, basting occasionally.

7 Cook for 10 minutes, turning once.

8 Toss the arugula, mixed salad greens and dressing together well. Put into a serving bowl.

9 Serve the scallops very hot, 2 skewers on each plate, with the salad.

Scallops with Mushrooms

Scallops have a rich but delicate flavor. When sautéed with mushrooms and bathed in brandy and cream, they make a really special meal.

NUTRITIONAL INFORMATION

Calories	390	Sugars	.........1g
Protein	........31g	Fat	.........28g
Carbohydrate	....1g	Saturates	......4g

5 MINS   10 MINS

SERVES 2

INGREDIENTS

1 tbsp butter

8 oz shelled scallops

1 tbsp olive oil

1¾ oz oyster mushrooms, sliced

1¾ oz shiitake mushrooms, sliced

1 garlic clove, chopped

4 scallions, white and green parts sliced

3 tbsp heavy cream

1 tbsp brandy

salt and pepper

sprigs of fresh dill, to garnish

basmati rice to serve

1 Heat the butter in a heavy-bottomed skillet and fry the scallops for about 1 minute, turning occasionally.

2 Remove the scallops from the skillet with a draining spoon and keep warm.

3 Add the olive oil to the skillet and heat. Add the mushrooms, garlic, and scallions, and cook for 2 minutes, stirring constantly.

4 Return the scallops to the skillet. Add the heavy cream and brandy, stirring well to mix.

5 Season with salt and pepper to taste and heat to warm through.

6 Garnish with fresh dill sprigs and serve with rice.

COOK'S TIP

Scallops, which consist of a large, round white muscle with bright orange roe, are the most delicious seafood in the prettiest of shells. The rounded half of the shell can be used as a dish in which to serve the scallops.

Caribbean Shrimp

This is an ideal recipe for cooks who have difficulty in finding raw shrimp.

NUTRITIONAL INFORMATION

Calories 110	Sugars 15g	
Protein 5g	Fat 4g	
Carbohydrate . . .15g	Saturates 3g	

  🐚 🐚 🐚

40 MINS   🕑 15 MINS

SERVES 4

I N G R E D I E N T S

16 cooked colossal shrimp

1 small pineapple

flaked coconut, to garnish (optional)

M A R I N A D E

⅔ cup pineapple juice

2 tbsp white wine vinegar

2 tbsp dark muscovado sugar

2 tbsp shredded coconut

1 If they are unpeeled, peel the shrimp, leaving the tails attached if preferred.

2 Peel the pineapple and cut it in half lengthways. Cut one pineapple half into wedges then into chunks.

3 To make the marinade, mix together half of the pineapple juice and the vinegar, sugar, and coconut in a shallow, non-metallic dish. Add the peeled shrimp and pineapple chunks, and toss until well coated. Leave the shrimp and pineapple to marinate for at least 30 minutes.

4 Remove the pineapple and shrimp from the marinade and thread them on to skewers. Reserve the marinade.

5 Strain the marinade and place in a food processor. Roughly chop the remaining pineapple and add to the processor with the remaining pineapple juice. Process the pineapple for a few seconds to produce a thick sauce.

6 Pour the sauce into a small saucepan. Bring to a boil then simmer for about 5 minutes. If you prefer, you can heat up the sauce by the side of the grill.

7 Transfer the kabobs to the grill and brush with some of the sauce. Grill for about 5 minutes until the kabobs are very hot. Turn the kabobs, brushing occasionally with the sauce.

8 Serve the kabobs with extra sauce, sprinkled with shredded coconut (if using).

Butterfly Shrimp

These shrimp look stunning when presented on the skewers, and they will certainly be an impressive prelude to the main meal.

NUTRITIONAL INFORMATION

Calories 183	Sugars 0g	
Protein 28g	Fat 8g	
Carbohydrate 0g	Saturates 1g	

4½ HOURS 🕐 10 MINS

SERVES 2–4

INGREDIENTS

1 lb or 16 raw jumbo shrimp, shelled, leaving tails intact

juice of 2 limes

1 tsp cardamom seeds

2 tsp cumin seeds, ground

2 tsp coriander seeds, ground

½ tsp ground cinnamon

1 tsp ground turmeric

1 garlic clove, minced

1 tsp cayenne pepper

2 tbsp oil

cucumber slices, to garnish

1 Soak 8 wooden skewers in water for 20 minutes. Cut the shrimp lengthways in half down to the tail and flatten out to form a symmetrical shape.

2 Thread a shrimp on to 2 wooden skewers, with the tail between them, so that, when laid flat, the skewers hold the shrimp in shape. Thread another 3 shrimp on to these 2 skewers in the same way.

3 Repeat until you have 4 sets of 4 shrimp each.

4 Lay the skewered shrimp in a non-porous, non-metallic dish, and sprinkle over the lime juice.

5 Combine the spices and the oil, and coat the shrimp well in the mixture. Cover the shrimp and chill for 4 hours.

6 Cook over a hot grill or in a broiler pan lined with foil under a preheated broiler for 6 minutes, turning once.

7 Serve immediately, garnished with cucumber and accompanied by a sweet relish – walnut relish is ideal.

Shrimp Dansak

The spicy lentil purée sauce in this recipe is of Parsi origin and is popular throughout the Indian continent.

NUTRITIONAL INFORMATION

Calories	379	Sugars	.........5g
Protein	........45g	Fat	..........12g
Carbohydrate	...25g	Saturates	......2g

1¼ HOURS   1¼ HOURS

SERVES 4

I N G R E D I E N T S

1 lb 9 oz uncooked jumbo shrimp in their shells or 1 lb 7 oz peeled jumbo shrimp

1 tsp salt

1 dried bay leaf

3 garlic cloves, minced

⅓ cup split yellow peas, soaked for 1 hour in cold water and drained

¼ cup red lentils

1 carrot, chopped

1 potato, cut into large dice

3 tbsp drained canned corn

3 tbsp oil

2 onions, chopped

½ tsp yellow mustard seeds

1½ tsp coriander seeds, ground

½ tsp cumin seeds, ground

½ tsp fenugreek seeds, ground

1½ tsp ground turmeric

1 dried red chili

15 oz can tomatoes

½ tsp garam masala

3 tbsp chopped fresh cilantro

2 tbsp chopped fresh mint

1 Reserve 4 shrimp for garnish and peel the rest. Cook those for the garnish in boiling water for 3–5 minutes.

2 Fill a pan with water and add the salt, bay leaf, ⅓ of the garlic, and the split peas. Bring to a boil and cook for 15 minutes. Add the lentils, carrot, and potato and cook for a further 15 minutes. Drain, discarding the garlic and bay leaf, and blend with the corn until smooth.

3 Heat the oil in a large saucepan and cook the remaining garlic and onion for 3–4 minutes. Add the mustard seeds and when they start to pop, stir in the other spices. Add the peeled shrimp and stir for 1–2 minutes. Add the tomatoes and lentil purée, and simmer, uncovered, for 30–40 minutes. Stir in the garam masala and season. Serve sprinkled with cilantro and mint and garnished with the shrimp.

Spicy Shrimp

Basil and tomatoes are ideal flavorings for shrimp, spiced with cumin seeds and garlic.

NUTRITIONAL INFORMATION

Calories	208	Sugars	.........8g
Protein	........27g	Fat	...........8g
Carbohydrate	....8g	Saturates	......1g

5 MINS   20 MINS

SERVES 4

I N G R E D I E N T S

2 tbsp corn oil

1 onion

2 cloves garlic, minced

1 tsp cumin seeds

1 tbsp demerara sugar

14 oz can chopped tomatoes

1 tbsp sun-dried tomato paste

1 tbsp chopped fresh basil

1 lb peeled colossal shrimp

salt and pepper

1 Heat the corn oil in a large preheated wok.

2 Using a sharp knife, finely chop the onion. Add the onion and minced garlic to the wok and stir-fry for 2–3 minutes, or until softened.

3 Stir in the cumin seeds and stir-fry for 1 minute.

4 Add the sugar, chopped tomatoes, and tomato paste to the wok.

5 Bring the mixture to a boil, then reduce the heat and leave the sauce to simmer for 10 minutes.

6 Add the basil and shrimp to the mixture in the wok. Season to taste with salt and pepper.

7 Increase the heat and cook for a further 2–3 minutes or until the shrimp are completely cooked through. Transfer to a warm serving dish and serve immediately.

COOK'S TIP

Sun-dried tomato paste has a much more intense flavor than that of normal tomato paste. It adds a distinctive intensity to any tomato-based dish.

Balti Scallops

This is a wonderful recipe for a special occasion dish. Cooked with cilantro and tomatoes, the scallops have a spicy flavor.

NUTRITIONAL INFORMATION

Calories	258	Sugars	.........2g
Protein	........44g	Fat	...........8g
Carbohydrate	....3g	Saturates	......1g

1¼ HOURS   15 MINS

SERVES 4

INGREDIENTS

1 lb 10 oz shelled scallops

2 tbsp oil

2 onions, chopped

3 tomatoes, quartered

2 fresh green chilies, sliced

4 lime wedges, to garnish

MARINADE

3 tbsp chopped fresh cilantro

1 inch piece gingerroot, grated

1 tsp ground coriander

3 tbsp lemon juice

grated rind of 1 lemon

¼ tsp ground black pepper

½ tsp salt

½ tsp ground cumin

1 garlic clove, minced

1 To make the marinade, mix all the ingredients together in a bowl.

2 Put the scallops into a bowl. Add the marinade and turn the scallops until they are well coated.

3 Then cover and leave to marinate for 1 hour or overnight in the refrigerator.

4 Heat the oil in a Balti pan or wok, add the onions and stir-fry until softened.

5 Add the tomatoes and chilies and stir-fry for 1 minute.

6 Add the scallops and stir-fry for 6–8 minutes until the scallops are cooked through, but still succulent inside.

7 Serve garnished with lime wedges.

COOK'S TIP

It is best to buy the scallops fresh in the shell with the roe – you will need 3 lb – a fishstore will clean them and remove the shell for you.

Shrimp Bhuna

This is a fiery recipe with subtle undertones. As the flavor of the shrimp should be noticeable, the spices should not take over this dish.

NUTRITIONAL INFORMATION

Calories 141	Sugars 0.4g	
Protein 19g	Fat 7g	
Carbohydrate 1g	Saturates 1g	

15 MINS   20 MINS

SERVES 4–6

INGREDIENTS

2 dried red chilies, seeded if liked

3 fresh green chilies, finely chopped

1 tsp ground turmeric

3 garlic cloves, minced

½ tsp pepper

1 tsp paprika

2 tsp white wine vinegar

½ tsp salt

1 lb uncooked peeled colossal shrimp

3 tbsp oil

1 onion, chopped very finely

¾ cup water

2 tbsp lemon juice

2 tsp garam masala

sprigs of fresh cilantro, to garnish

COOK'S TIP

Garam masala should be used sparingly and is generally added to foods towards the end of their cooking time. It is also used sprinkled over cooked meats, vegetables and legumes as a garnish.

1 Combine the chilies, spices, vinegar, and salt in a non-metallic bowl. Stir in the shrimp and leave for 10 minutes.

2 Heat the oil in a large skillet or wok, add the onion and fry for 3–4 minutes until soft.

3 Add the shrimp and the contents of the bowl to the pan and stir-fry over a high heat for 2 minutes. Reduce the

heat, add the water and boil for 10 minutes, stirring occasionally, until the water is evaporated and the curry is fragrant.

4 Stir in the lemon juice and garam masala then transfer the mixture to a warm serving dish and garnish with fresh cilantro sprigs.

Curried Crab

If you can buy fresh crab, clean the shell and brush lightly with oil and use as a container for the crabmeat.

NUTRITIONAL INFORMATION

Calories	272	Sugars	........5g
Protein	........27g	Fat	..........16g
Carbohydrate	....5g	Saturates	......2g

5 MINS   15 MINS

SERVES 4

I N G R E D I E N T S

2 tbsp mustard oil

1 tbsp ghee

1 onion, chopped finely

2 inch piece gingerroot, grated

2 garlic cloves, peeled but left whole

1 tsp ground turmeric

1 tsp salt

1 tsp chili powder

2 fresh green chilies, chopped

1 tsp paprika

½ cup brown crabmeat

1½ cups white crabmeat

1 cup low-fat unsweetened yogurt

1 tsp garam masala

basmati rice, to serve

fresh cilantro, to garnish

1 Heat the mustard oil in a large, preferably non-stick, skillet, wok, or saucepan.

2 When it starts to smoke, add the ghee and onion. Stir for 3 minutes over a medium heat until the onion is soft.

3 Stir in the ginger and whole garlic cloves.

4 Add the turmeric, salt, chili powder, chilies, and paprika. Mix thoroughly.

5 Increase the heat and add the crabmeat and yogurt. Simmer, stirring occasionally, for 10 minutes until the sauce is thickened slightly.

6 Add garam masala to taste.

7 Serve hot, over plain basmati rice, with the fresh cilantro either chopped or in sprigs.

COOK'S TIP

For an unusual combination of flavors, mix the crabmeat with segments of grapefruit in a mayonnaise. Sprinkle with slivers of almonds.

Spiced Balti Seafood

Although shrimp are not a traditional ingredient of Balti cooking, they work well with Balti spices and cooking methods.

NUTRITIONAL INFORMATION

Calories ....194 Sugars 2g
Protein ....29g Fat 8g
Carbohydrate ....2g Saturates 1g

2¼ HOURS   15 MINS

SERVES 4

INGREDIENTS

1 garlic clove,

2 tsp freshly grated gingerroot

2 tsp ground coriander

2 tsp ground cumin

½ tsp ground cardamom

¼ tsp chili powder

2 tbsp tomato paste

5 tbsp water

3 tbsp chopped fresh cilantro

1 lb peeled cooked colossal shrimp

2 tbsp oil

2 small onions, sliced

1 fresh green chili, chopped

salt

1 Put the garlic, ginger, ground coriander, cumin, cardamom, chili powder, tomato paste, 4 tablespoons of the water, and 2 tablespoons of the fresh cilantro into a bowl. Mix all the ingredients together.

2 Add the shrimp to the bowl and leave to marinate for 2 hours.

3 Heat the oil in a karahi or wok, add the onions and stir-fry until golden brown.

4 Add the shrimp, marinade and the chili and stir-fry over a medium heat for 5 minutes. Add salt to taste, and the remaining tablespoon of water if the mixture is very dry. Stir-fry over a medium heat for 5 minutes.

5 Serve the shrimp immediately, garnished with the remaining fresh chopped cilantro.

COOK'S TIP

Shrimp lose less flavor if they are put without water in a tightly covered pan and set over a high heat to cook in their own juice.

Seafood in Red Curry Sauce

For something very quick and simple that sets your tastebuds alight, try this inspired dish of shrimp in a wonderfully spicy sauce.

NUTRITIONAL INFORMATION

Calories	175	Sugars	.........3g
Protein	........29g	Fat	...........5g
Carbohydrate	....3g	Saturates	......1g

10 MINS   10 MINS

SERVES 4

I N G R E D I E N T S

1 tbsp vegetable oil

6 scallions, trimmed and sliced

1 stalk lemongrass

½ inch piece of fresh gingerroot

1 cup coconut milk

2 tbsp Thai red curry paste

1 tbsp fish sauce

3 cups uncooked jumbo shrimp

1 tbsp chopped fresh cilantro

fresh chilies, to garnish

1 Heat the vegetable oil in a wok or large skillet and fry the scallions gently until softened, about 2 minutes.

2 Bruise the stalk of lemon grass using a meat mallet or rolling pin.

3 Peel and finely grate the piece of fresh gingerroot.

4 Add the bruised lemongrass and grated ginger root to the wok or skillet with the coconut milk, Thai red curry paste, and fish sauce. Heat the coconut milk until almost boiling.

5 Peel the shrimp, leaving the tails intact. Remove the black vein along the back of each shrimp.

6 Add the shrimp to the wok or skillet with the chopped cilantro and cook gently for 5 minutes.

7 Serve the shrimp with the sauce, garnished with fresh chilies.

VARIATION

Try this recipe using Thai green curry sauce instead of red. Both varieties are obtainable from many supermarkets – look for them in the oriental foods section.

Seafood Stir-Fry

This combination of assorted seafood and tender vegetables flavored with ginger makes an ideal light meal served with thread noodles.

NUTRITIONAL INFORMATION

Calories 226	Sugars 5g	
Protein 35g	Fat 7g	
Carbohydrate 6g	Saturates 1g	

5 MINS   15 MINS

SERVES 4

INGREDIENTS

3½ oz small, thin asparagus spears, trimmed

1 tbsp sunflower oil

1 inch piece gingerroot, cut into thin strips

1 medium leek, shredded

2 medium carrots, julienned

3½ oz baby-corn-on-the-cobs, quartered lengthwise

2 tbsp light soy sauce

1 tbsp oyster sauce

1 tsp clear honey

1 lb cooked, assorted shellfish, thawed if frozen

freshly cooked egg noodles, to serve

TO GARNISH

4 large cooked shrimp

small bunch fresh chives, freshly snipped

1 Bring a small saucepan of water to a boil and blanch the asparagus for 1–2 minutes.

2 Drain the asparagus, set aside, and keep warm.

3 Heat the oil in a wok or large skillet and stir-fry the ginger, leek, carrot, and corn for about 3 minutes. Do not allow the vegetables to brown.

4 Add the soy sauce, oyster sauce, and honey to the wok or skillet.

5 Stir in the cooked shellfish and continue to stir-fry for 2–3 minutes until the vegetables are just tender and the shellfish are thoroughly heated through. Add the blanched asparagus and stir-fry for about 2 minutes.

6 To serve, pile the cooked noodles on to 4 warm serving plates and spoon the seafood and vegetable stir-fry over them.

7 Garnish with the cooked shrimp and freshly snipped chives and serve immediately. Serve garnished with a large shrimp and freshly snipped chives.

Provençale-Style Mussels

These delicious large mussels are served hot with a tasty tomato and vegetable sauce. Mop up the delicious sauce with some crusty bread.

NUTRITIONAL INFORMATION

Calories	253	Sugars	.........8g
Protein	........31g	Fat	...........8g
Carbohydrate	....9g	Saturates	......1g

5 MINS   50 MINS

SERVES 4

INGREDIENTS

1 tbsp olive oil

1 large onion, finely chopped

1 garlic clove, finely chopped

1 small red bell pepper, seeded and finely chopped

sprig of rosemary

2 bay leaves

14 oz can chopped tomatoes

⅔ cup white wine

1 zucchini, diced finely

2 tbsp tomato paste

1 tsp superfine sugar

1¾ oz pitted black olives in brine, drained and chopped

1½ lb cooked green-lipped mussels in their shells

1 tsp orange rind

salt and pepper

crusty bread, to serve

2 tbsp chopped, fresh parsley, to garnish

1 Heat the olive oil in a large saucepan and gently fry the chopped onion, garlic, and bell pepper for 3–4 minutes until just softened.

2 Add the rosemary and bay leaves to the saucepan with the tomatoes and ⅓ cup wine. Season to taste, then bring to a boil and simmer for 15 minutes.

3 Stir in the zucchini, tomato paste, sugar, and olives. Simmer for 10 minutes.

4 Meanwhile, bring a pan of water to a boil. Arrange the mussels in a steamer or a large strainer and place over the water. Sprinkle with the remaining wine and the orange rind. Cover and steam until the mussels open (discard any that remain closed).

5 Remove the mussels with a draining spoon and arrange on a serving plate. Discard the herbs and spoon the sauce over the mussels. Garnish with chopped parsley and serve with crusty bread.

Oriental Dishes

The Far East's many miles of coastline, rivers, and lakes offer an enormous variety of fresh- and salt-water fish and seafood. Among the most popular are carp, bass,

bream, clams, crab, crawfish, and shrimp. Dishes which include shark's fins, abalone, squid, and edible seaweed are also common. When buying fish and seafood for Oriental cooking, freshness is imperative to flavor, so be sure to buy it and use it as soon as possible, preferably on the same day. Oriental chefs buy live fish whch are kept alive until just before cooking. Favorite cooking methods for fish are steaming and quick poaching in boiling water or broth.

Shrimp & Corn Patties

Chopped (small) shrimp and corn are combined in a light batter, which is dropped in spoonfuls into hot fat to make these tasty patties.

NUTRITIONAL INFORMATION

Calories	250	Sugars	.........1g
Protein	........17g	Fat	..........9g
Carbohydrate	...26g	Saturates	.......2g

35 MINS   20 MINS

SERVES 4

INGREDIENTS

1 cup all-purpose flour

1½ tsp baking powder

2 eggs

about 1 cup cold water

1 garlic clove, very finely chopped

3 scallions, trimmed and very finely chopped

1 cup peeled (small) shrimps, chopped

½ cup canned corn, drained

vegetable oil for frying

salt and pepper

TO GARNISH

scallion brushes (see Cook's Tip, right)

lime slices

1 chili flower, to garnish

 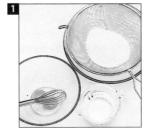 

1 Sift the flour, baking powder and ½ tsp salt into a bowl. Add the eggs and half the water and beat to make a smooth batter, adding extra water to give the consistency of heavy cream. Add the garlic and scallions. Cover and leave for 30 minutes.

2 Stir the (small) shrimps and corn into the batter. Season with pepper.

3 Heat 2–3 tablespoons of oil in a wok. Drop tablespoonfuls of the batter into the wok and cook over a medium heat until bubbles rise and the surface just sets. Flip the patties over and cook the other side until golden brown. Drain on paper towels.

4 Cook the remaining batter in the same way, adding more oil to the wok if required. Garnish and serve at once.

COOK'S TIP

Make a scallion brush by trimming off the tips of the leaves and making several fine cuts from the leaf tips to the top of the bulb. Place in iced water to make the leaves curl.

Shrimp Stir-Fry

A very quick and tasty stir-fry using shrimp and cucumber, cooked with lemongrass, chili and ginger.

NUTRITIONAL INFORMATION

Calories	178	Sugars	.........1g
Protein	........22g	Fat	...........7g
Carbohydrate	....3g	Saturates	.......1g

5 MINS   5 MINS

SERVES 4

I N G R E D I E N T S

½ cucumber

2 tbsp sunflower oil

6 scallions, halved lengthways and cut into 1½ inch lengths

1 stalk lemon grass, sliced thinly

1 garlic clovc, chopped

1 tsp chopped fresh red chili

4½ oz oyster mushrooms

1 tsp chopped gingerroor

12 oz cooked peeled shrimp

2 tsp cornstarch

2 tbsp water

1 tbsp dark soy sauce

½ tsp fish sauce

2 tbsp dry sherry or rice wine

boiled rice, to serve

1 Cut the cucumber into strips about ¼ x 1¾ inches.

2 Heat the sunflower oil in a wok or large skillet.

3 Add the scallions, cucumber, lemongrass, garlic, chili, oyster mushrooms, and ginger to the wok or skillet and stir-fry for 2 minutes.

4 Add the shrimp and stir-fry for a further minute.

5 Mix together the cornstarch, water, soy sauce and fish sauce, until smooth.

6 Stir the cornstarch mixture and sherry or wine into the wok and heat through, stirring, until the sauce has thickened. Serve with rice.

COOK'S TIP

The white part of the lemongrass stem can be thinly sliced and left in the cooked dish. If using the whole stem, remove it before serving. You can buy lemongrass chopped and dried, or preserved in jars, but neither has the fragrance or delicacy of the fresh variety.

Hot & Sweet Shrimp

Uncooked shrimp are speared on skewers, brushed with a sesame oil, lime juice, and cilantro baste and then grilled.

NUTRITIONAL INFORMATION

Calories 239	Sugars 8g	
Protein 28g	Fat 11g	
Carbohydrate 8g	Saturates 2g	

🦐 🦐 🦐

1 HOUR   ⏱ 10 MINS

SERVES 4

INGREDIENTS

wooden skewers soaked in warm water for 20 minutes

2½ cups uncooked shrimp

3 tbsp sesame oil

2 tbsp lime juice

1 tbsp chopped fresh cilantro

SAUCE

4 tbsp light malt vinegar

2 tbsp fish sauce or light soy sauce

2 tbsp water

2 tbsp light muscovado sugar

2 garlic cloves, minced

2 tsp grated fresh gingerroor

1 red chili, seeded and chopped finely

2 tbsp chopped fresh cilantro

salt

1 Peel the shrimp, leaving the tails intact. Remove the black vein that runs along the back of each one, then skewer the shrimp on to the wooden skewers.

2 Mix together the sesame oil, lime juice, and chopped cilantro in a shallow bowl. Lay the skewered shrimp in this mixture. Cover and chill in the refrigerator for 30 minutes, turning once, so that the shrimp absorb the marinade.

3 Meanwhile, make the sauce. Heat the vinegar, fish sauce or soy sauce, water, sugar, and salt to taste until boiling. Remove from the heat and leave to cool.

4 Mix together the minced garlic, grated ginger, red chili, and cilantro in a small serving bowl. Add the cooled vinegar mixture and stir until well combined.

5 Place the shrimp on a foil-lined broiler pan under a preheated broiler for about 6 minutes, turning once and basting often with the marinade, until cooked.

6 Transfer to a warmed serving platter and serve with the dipping sauce.

Shrimp with Vegetables

In this recipe, a light Chinese omelet is shredded and tossed back into the dish before serving.

NUTRITIONAL INFORMATION

Calories 258	Sugars 7g
Protein 21g	Fat 15g
Carbohydrate ...10g	Saturates 3g

 10 MINS   15 MINS

SERVES 4

INGREDIENTS

8 oz zucchini

3 tbsp vegetable oil

2 eggs

2 tbsp cold water

8 oz carrots, grated

1 onion, sliced

1½ cups mung bean sprouts

8 oz peeled shrimp

2 tbsp soy sauce

pinch of Chinese five-spice powder

¼ cup peanuts, chopped

2 tbsp fresh chopped cilantro

1 Finely grate the zucchini.

2 Heat 1 tablespoon of the vegetable oil in a large preheated wok.

3 Beat the eggs with the water and pour the mixture into the wok and cook for 2–3 minutes or until the egg sets.

4 Remove the omelet from the wok and transfer to a clean board. Fold the omelet, cut it into thin strips, and set aside until required.

5 Add the remaining oil to the wok. Add the carrots, onion and zucchini and stir-fry for 5 minutes.

6 Add the bean sprouts and shrimp to the wok and cook for a further 2 minutes, or until the shrimp are heated through.

7 Add the soy sauce, Chinese five-spice powder, and peanuts to the wok, together with the strips of omelet and heat through. Garnish with chopped fresh cilantro and serve.

COOK'S TIP

The water is mixed with the egg in step 3 for a lighter, less rubbery omelet.

Fried Shrimp with Cashews

Cashew nuts are delicious as part of a stir-fry with almost any other ingredient. Use the unsalted variety in cooking.

NUTRITIONAL INFORMATION

Calories 406	Sugar 3g
Protein 31g	Fat 25g
Carbohydrate ...13g	Saturates 4g

 5 MINS   5 MINS

SERVES 4

INGREDIENTS

2 garlic cloves, minced

1 tbsp cornstarch

pinch of superfine sugar

1 lb raw jumbo shrimp

4 tbsp vegetable oil

1 leek, sliced

4½ oz broccoli florets

1 orange bell pepper, seeded and diced

¾ cup unsalted cashew nuts

SAUCE

¾ cup fish stock

1 tbsp cornstarch

dash of chili sauce

2 tsp sesame oil

1 tbsp Chinese rice wine

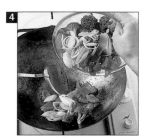

1 Mix together the garlic, cornstarch, and sugar in a bowl.

2 Peel and devein the shrimp. Stir the shrimp into the mixture to coat thoroughly.

3 Heat the vegetable oil in a preheated wok and add the shrimp mixture. Stir-fry over a high heat for 20–30 seconds until the shrimp turn pink. Remove the shrimp from the wok with a draining spoon, drain on absorbent paper towels and set aside until required.

4 Add the leek, broccoli, and bell pepper to the wok and stir-fry for 2 minutes.

5 To make the sauce, place the fish stock, cornstarch, chili sauce to taste, the sesame oil, and Chinese rice wine in a small bowl. Mix well.

6 Add the sauce to the wok, together with the cashew nuts. Return the shrimp to the wok and cook for 1 minute to heat through.

7 Transfer the shrimp stir-fry to a warm serving dish and serve immediately.

Stir-Fried Shrimp

The bell peppers in this dish can be replaced by either snow peas, or broccoli to maintain the attractive pink-green contrast.

NUTRITIONAL INFORMATION

Calories	116	Sugars	.........1g
Protein	........10g	Fat	...........6g
Carbohydrate	....4g	Saturates	.......1g

🍲 5 MINS   🕐 10 MINS

SERVES 4

I N G R E D I E N T S

6 oz raw shrimp, peeled

1 tsp salt

¼ tsp egg white

2 tsp cornstarch paste

1¼ cups vegetable oil

1 scallion, cut into short sections

1-inch piece gingerroot, thinly sliced

1 small green bell pepper, cored, seeded, and cubed

½ tsp sugar

1 tbsp light soy sauce

1 tsp rice wine or dry sherry

a few drops sesame oil

VARIATION

1-2 small green or red hot chilies, sliced, can be added with the green bell pepper to create a more spicy dish. Leave the chilies unseeded for a very hot dish.

1 Mix the shrimp with a pinch of the salt, the egg white and cornstarch paste until well coated.

2 Heat the oil in a preheated wok and stir-fry the shrimp for 30-40 seconds only. Remove and drain on paper towels.

3 Pour off the oil, leaving about 1 tablespoon in the wok. Add the scallion and ginger to flavor the oil for a few seconds, then add the green bell pepper and stir-fry for about 1 minute.

4 Add the remaining salt and the sugar followed by the shrimp. Continue stirring for another minute or so, then add the soy sauce and wine and blend well. Sprinkle with sesame oil and serve immediately.

Shrimp with Ginger

Crispy ginger is a wonderful garnish which offsets the spicy shrimp both visually and in flavor.

NUTRITIONAL INFORMATION

Calories	229	Sugars	.........7g
Protein	........29g	Fat	...........8g
Carbohydrate	...10g	Saturates	.......1g

10 MINS   15 MINS

SERVES 4

I N G R E D I E N T S

2 inch piece gingerroot

oil, for frying

1 onion, diced

8 oz carrots, diced

½ cup frozen English peas

1 cup mung bean sprouts

1 lb peeled colossal shrimp

1 tsp Chinese five-spice powder

1 tbsp tomato paste

1 tbsp soy sauce

1 Using a sharp knife, peel the ginger and slice it into very thin sticks.

2 Heat about 1 inch of oil in a large preheated wok. Add the ginger and stir-fry for 1 minute or until the ginger is crispy. Remove the ginger with a draining spoon and leave to drain on absorbent paper towels.

3 Drain all of the oil from the wok except for about 2 tablespoons. Add the onions and carrots to the wok and stir-fry for 5 minutes. Add the peas and bean sprouts and stir-fry for 2 minutes.

4 Rinse the shrimp under cold running water and pat dry with absorbent paper towels.

5 Combine the five-spice, tomato paste, and soy sauce. Brush the mixture over the shrimp.

6 Add the shrimp to the wok and stir-fry for a further 2 minutes, or until the shrimp are completely cooked through. Transfer the shrimp mixture to a warm serving bowl and top with the reserved crispy ginger. Serve immediately.

VARIATION

Use slices of white fish instead of the shrimp as an alternative, if you wish.

Coconut Shrimp

Fan-tail shrimp make any meal a special occasion, especially when cooked in such a delicious crispy coating.

NUTRITIONAL INFORMATION

Calories . . . . . . .236 Sugars 1g
Protein . . . . .27g Fat 13g
Carbohydrate . . . .3g Saturates 7g

5 MINS   10 MINS

SERVES 4

I N G R E D I E N T S

½ cup shredded coconut

½ cup fresh white bread crumbs

1 tsp Chinese five-spice powder

½ tsp salt

finely grated zest of 1 lime

1 egg white

1 lb fan-tail shrimp

sunflower or corn oil, for frying

lemon wedges, to garnish

soy or chili sauce, to serve

1 Mix together the shredded coconut, white bread crumbs, Chinese five-spice powder, salt, and finely grated lime zest in a bowl.

2 Lightly whisk the egg white in a separate bowl.

3 Rinse the shrimp under cold running water, and pat dry with paper towels.

4 Dip the shrimp into the egg white then into the coconut and breadcrumb mixture, so that they are evenly coated.

5 Heat about 2 inches of sunflower or corn oil in a large preheated wok.

6 Add the shrimp to the wok and stir-fry for about 5 minutes or until golden and crispy.

7 Remove the shrimp with a draining spoon and leave to drain on paper towels.

8 Transfer the coconut shrimp to warm serving dishes and garnish with lemon wedges. Serve immediately with a soy or chili sauce.

COOK'S TIP

Chinese five-spice powder is a mixture of star anise, fennel seeds, cloves, cinnamon bark, and Szechuan pepper. It is very pungent, so should be used sparingly. It will keep indefinitely in an airtight container

Chili Shrimp

Large shrimps are marinated in a chili mixture then stir-fried with cashews. Serve with a fluffy rice and braised vegetables.

NUTRITIONAL INFORMATION

Calories 435   Sugars 2g
Protein . . . . .4.2g   Fat 23
Carbohydrate . . .10g   Saturates 4g

 2¼ HOURS   🕐 5 MINS

SERVES 4

I N G R E D I E N T S

5 tbsp soy sauce

5 tbsp dry sherry

3 dried red chilies, seeded and chopped

2 garlic cloves, minced

2 tsp grated gingerroot

5 tbsp water

1 lb 6 oz shelled jumbo shrimp

1 large bunch scallions, chopped

⅔ cup salted cashew nuts

3 tbsp vegetable oil

2 tsp cornstarch

1 Mix the soy sauce, sherry, chilies, garlic, ginger, and water in a bowl.

2 Add the jumbo shrimp, scallions, and cashews and mix well. Cover tightly and leave to marinate for at least 2 hours, stirring occasionally.

3 Heat the oil in a large wok. Remove the shrimp, scallions, and cashews from the marinade with a draining spoon and add to the wok, reserving the marinade. Stir-fry over a high heat for 1-2 minutes.

4 Mix the reserved marinade with the cornstarch, add to the wok and stir-fry for about 30 seconds, until the marinade forms a slightly thickened shiny glaze over the shrimp mixture. Serve immediately.

COOK'S TIP

For an attractive presentation serve this dish on mixed wild rice and basmati rice. Start cooking the wild rice in boiling water. After 10 minutes, add the basmati rice or other rice and continue boiling until all grains are tender. Drain well and adjust the seasoning.

Sweet & Sour Shrimp

Use raw shrimp if possible. Omit steps 1 and 2 if ready-cooked ones are used.

NUTRITIONAL INFORMATION

Calories 373	Sugars 11g
Protein 13g	Fat 26g
Carbohydrate . . .19g	Saturates 3g

  3¹/₂ HOURS   10 MINS

SERVES 4

I N G R E D I E N T S

6-9 oz peeled raw jumbo shrimp

pinch of salt

1 tsp egg white

1 tsp cornstarch paste

1¼ cups vegetable oil

S A U C E

1 tbsp vegetable oil

½ small green bell pepper, cored, seeded, and thinly sliced

½ small carrot, thinly sliced

4½ oz canned water chestnuts, drained and sliced

½ tsp salt

1 tbsp light soy sauce

2 tbsp sugar

3 tbsp rice or sherry vinegar

1 tsp rice wine or dry sherry

1 tbsp tomato sauce

½ tsp chili sauce

3-4 tbsp stock or water

2 tsp cornstarch paste

a few drops sesame oil

 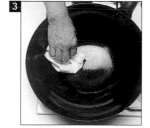 

1 Mix together the shrimp with the salt, egg white and cornstarch paste.

2 Heat the oil in a preheated wok and stir-fry the shrimp for 30-40 seconds only. Remove and drain on paper towels.

3 Pour off the oil and wipe the wok clean with paper towels. To make the sauce, first heat the tablespoon of oil. Add the vegetables and stir-fry for about 1 minute, then add the seasonings with the stock or water and bring to a boil.

4 Add the shrimp and stir until blended well. Thicken the sauce with the cornstarch paste and stir until smooth. Sprinkle with sesame oil and serve hot.

Cantonese Shrimp

This shrimp dish is very simple and is ideal for supper or lunch when time is short.

NUTRITIONAL INFORMATION

Calories 460   Sugar 3g
Protein ....53g   Fat 24
Carbohydrate ....6g   Saturates 5g

10 MINS   20 MINS

SERVES 4

INGREDIENTS

5 tbsp vegetable oil

4 garlic cloves, minced

1½ lb raw shrimp, shelled and deveined

2-inch piece gingerroot, chopped

6 oz lean pork, diced

1 leek, sliced

3 eggs, beaten

shredded leek and red bell pepper
    matchsticks, to garnish

rice, to serve

SAUCE

2 tbsp Chinese rice wine or dry sherry

2 tbsp light soy sauce

2 tsp superfine sugar

⅔ cup fish stock

4½ tsp cornstarch

3 tbsp water

1 Heat 2 tablespoons of the vegetable oil in a preheated wok.

2 Add the garlic to the wok and stir-fry for 30 seconds.

3 Add the shrimp to the wok and stir-fry for 5 minutes, or until they

change color. Remove the shrimp from the wok or skillet with a draining spoon, set aside and keep warm.

4 Add the remaining oil to the wok and heat, swirling the oil around the base of the wok until it is really hot.

5 Add the ginger, diced pork, and leek to the wok and stir-fry over a medium heat for 4-5 minutes, or until the pork is lightly colored and sealed.

6 To make the sauce, add the rice wine or sherry, soy sauce, superfine sugar, and fish stock to the wok and stir to blend.

7 In a small bowl, blend the cornstarch with the water to form a smooth paste and stir it into the wok. Cook, stirring, until the sauce thickens and clears.

8 Return the shrimp to the wok and add the beaten eggs. Cook for 5–6 minutes, gently stirring occasionally, until the eggs set.

9 Transfer to a warm serving dish, garnish with shredded leek and bell pepper matchsticks and serve immediately with rice.

Shrimp with Vegetables

This colorful and delicious dish is cooked with vegetables: vary them according to seasonal availability.

NUTRITIONAL INFORMATION

Calories 298   Sugars 1g
Protein ....13g   Fat 26g
Carbohydrate ....3g   Saturates 3g

 5 MINS   10 MINS

SERVES 4

INGREDIENTS

2 oz snow peas

½ small carrot

2 oz baby-corn-on-the-cobs

2 oz straw mushrooms

6-9 oz raw jumbo shrimp, peeled

1 tsp salt

½ egg white, lightly beaten

1 tsp cornstarch paste

about 1¼ cups vegetable oil

1 scallion, cut into short sections

4 slices gingerroot, pcclcd and finely
    chopped

½ tsp sugar

1 tbsp light soy sauce

1 tsp Chinese rice wine or dry sherry

a few drops sesame oil

lemon slices and chopped fresh chives,
    to garnish

1 Using a sharp knife, top and tail the snow peas; cut the carrot into the same size as the snow peas; halve the baby corn-on-the-cobs and straw mushrooms.

2 Mix the shrimp with a pinch of the salt, the egg white and cornstarch paste until the shrimp are evenly coated.

3 Preheat a wok over a high heat for 2-3 minutes, then add the vegetable oil and heat to medium-hot.

4 Add the shrimp to the wok, stirring to separate them. Remove the shrimp with a draining spoon as soon as the color changes.

5 Pour off the oil, leaving about 1 tablespoon in the wok. Add the snow peas, carrot, corn, mushrooms, and scallions.

6 Add the shrimp together with the ginger, sugar, soy sauce, and wine or sherry, blending well.

7 Sprinkle with the sesame oil and serve hot, garnished with lemon slices, and chopped fresh chives.

Spiced Scallops

Scallops are available both fresh and frozen. Make sure they are completely defrosted before cooking.

10 MINS   10 MINS

SERVES 4

I N G R E D I E N T S

12 large scallops with coral attached, defrosted if frozen, or 12 oz small scallops without coral, defrosted

4 tbsp sunflower oil

4-6 scallions, thinly sliced diagonally

1 garlic clove, minced

1 inch gingerroot, finely chopped

9 oz snow peas

4½ oz button or closed cup mushrooms, sliced

2 tbsp sherry

2 tbsp soy sauce

1 tbsp clear honey

¼ tsp ground allspice

salt and pepper

1 tbsp sesame seeds, toasted

1 Wash and dry the scallops, discarding any black pieces and detach the corals, if using.

2 Slice each scallop into 3-4 pieces and if the corals are large halve them.

3 Heat 2 tablespoons of the sunflower oil in a preheated wok or large,

heavy-bottomed skillet, swirling it around until really hot.

4 Add the scallions, garlic, and ginger to the wok or skillet and stir-fry for about 1 minute.

5 Add the snow peas to the wok and continue to cook for a further 2-3 minutes, stirring continuously. Remove to a bowl and set aside.

6 Add the remaining sunflower oil to the wok and when really hot add the scallops and corals and stir-fry for a couple of minutes.

7 Add the mushrooms and continue to cook for a further minute or so.

8 Add the sherry, soy sauce, honey, and allspice to the wok, with salt and pepper to taste. Mix thoroughly, then return the snow peas mixture to the wok.

9 Season well with salt and pepper and toss together over a high heat for a minute or so until very hot. Serve the scallops and vegetables immediately, sprinkled with sesame seeds.

Seared Scallops

Scallops have a wonderful, subtle flavor which is complemented in this dish by the buttery sauce.

NUTRITIONAL INFORMATION

Calories	272	Sugars	.........0g
Protein	........28g	Fat	..........17g
Carbohydrate	....2g	Saturates	.......8g

  5 MINS   10 MINS

SERVES 4

INGREDIENTS

1 lb fresh scallops, without roe, or the same amount of frozen scallops, defrosted thoroughly

6 scallions

2 tbsp vegetable oil

1 green chili, seeded and sliced

3 tbsp sweet soy sauce

1½ tbsp butter, cubed

1 Rinse the scallops thoroughly under cold running water, drain, and pat the scallops dry with absorbent paper towels.

2 Using a sharp knife, slice each scallop in half horizontally.

COOK'S TIP

If you buy scallops on the shell, slide a knife underneath the membrane to loosen it and cut off the tough muscle that holds the scallop to the shell. Discard the black stomach sac and intestinal vein.

3 Using a sharp knife, trim and slice the scallions.

4 Heat the vegetable oil in a large preheated wok or heavy-bottomed skillet, swirling the oil around the base of the wok until it is really hot.

5 Add the sliced green chili, scallions, and scallops to the wok and stir-fry over a high heat for 4–5 minutes, or until the scallops are just cooked through. If using frozen scallops, be sure not to overcook them as they will easily disintegrate.

6 Add the soy sauce and butter to the scallop stir-fry and heat through until the butter melts.

7 Transfer to warm serving bowls and serve hot.

Scallop Pancakes

Scallops, like most shellfish, require very little cooking, and this original dish is a perfect example of how to use shellfish to its full potential.

NUTRITIONAL INFORMATION

Calories	240	Sugars	.........1g
Protein	........29g	Fat	..........9g
Carbohydrate	....11g	Saturates	.......1g

  5 MINS 🕐 30 MINS

SERVES 4

INGREDIENTS

3½ oz fine green beans

1 red chili

1 lb scallops, without roe

1 egg

3 scallions, sliced

½ cup rice flour

1 tbsp fish sauce

oil, for frying

salt

sweet chili dip, to serve

1 Using a sharp knife, trim the green beans and slice them very thinly.

2 Using a sharp knife, seed and very finely chop the red chili.

3 Bring a small saucepan of lightly salted water to a boil. Add the green beans to the pan and cook for 3–4 minutes or until just soft.

4 Roughly chop the scallops and place them in a large bowl. Add the cooked beans to the scallops.

5 Mix the egg with the scallions, rice flour, fish sauce and chili until well combined. Add to the scallops and mix well.

6 Heat about 1 inch of oil in a large preheated wok. Add a ladleful of the mixture to the wok and cook for 5 minutes until golden and set.

7 Remove the pancake from the wok and leave to drain on absorbent paper towels. Keep warm while cooking the remaining pancake mixture. Serve the pancakes hot with a sweet chili dip.

VARIATION

You could use shrimp or shelled clams instead of the scallops, if you prefer.

Scallops in Ginger Sauce

Scallops are both attractive and delicious. Cooked with ginger and orange, this dish is perfect served with plain rice.

NUTRITIONAL INFORMATION

Calories 216	Sugars 4g
Protein 30g	Fat 8g
Carbohydrate 8g	Saturates 1g

 5 MINS   10 MINS

SERVES 4

I N G R E D I E N T S

2 tbsp vegetable oil

1 lb scallops, cleaned and halved

1-inch piece gingerroot, finely chopped

3 garlic cloves, minced

2 leeks, shredded

¾ cup shelled English peas

4½ oz canned bamboo shoots, drained and rinsed

2 tbsp light soy sauce

2 tbsp unsweetened orange juice

1 tsp superfine sugar

orange zest, to garnish

1 Heat the vegetable oil in a preheated wok or large skillet. Add the scallops and stir-fry for 1–2 minutes. Remove the scallops from the wok with a draining spoon, keep warm and set aside until required.

2 Add the ginger and garlic to the wok and stir-fry for 30 seconds. Stir in the leeks and peas and cook, stirring, for a further 2 minutes.

3 Add the bamboo shoots and return the scallops to the wok. Stir gently to mix without breaking up the scallops.

4 Stir in the soy sauce, orange juice, and superfine sugar and cook for 1–2 minutes.

5 Transfer the stir-fry to a serving dish, garnish with the orange zest and serve immediately.

COOK'S TIP

The edible parts of a scallop are the round white muscle and the orange and white coral or roe. The frilly skirt surrounding the muscle – the gills and mantle – may be used for making shellfish stock. All other parts should be discarded.

Baked Crab with Ginger

In Chinese restaurants, only live crabs are used, but ready-cooked ones can be used at home quite successfully.

NUTRITIONAL INFORMATION

Calories 261   Sugars 0.5g
Protein . . . . .18g   Fat 17g
Carbohydrate . . . .5g   Saturates 2g

3³/₄ HOURS   10 MINS

SERVES 4

INGREDIENTS

1 large or 2 medium crabs, weighing about 1 lb 10 oz in total

2 tbsp Chinese rice wine or dry sherry

1 egg, lightly beaten

1 tbsp cornstarch

3-4 tbsp vegetable oil

1 tbsp finely chopped gingerroot

3-4 scallions, cut into sections

2 tbsp light soy sauce

1 tsp sugar

about ⅓ cup stock or water

½ tsp sesame oil

cilantro leaves, to garnish

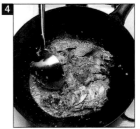

1 Cut the crab in half from the under-belly. Break off the claws and crack them with the back of a cleaver or a large kitchen knife.

2 Discard the legs and crack the shell, breaking it into several pieces. Discard the feathery gills and the stomach sac. Place the crabmeat in a bowl.

3 Mix together the wine or sherry, egg and cornstarch. Pour the mixture over the crab and leave to marinate for 10-15 minutes.

4 Heat the vegetable oil in a preheated wok and stir-fry the crab with the chopped ginger and scallions for 2-3 minutes.

5 Add the soy sauce, sugar, and Chinese stock or water, blend well and bring to a boil. Cover and cook for 3-4 minutes, then remove the lid, sprinkle with sesame oil, and serve, garnished with fresh cilantro leaves.

COOK'S TIP

Crabs are almost always sold ready-cooked. The crab should feel heavy for its size, and when it is shaken, there should be no sound of water inside. A good medium-sized crab should yield about 1 lb meat, enough for 3-4 people.

Crab in Ginger Sauce

In this recipe, the crabs are served in the shell for ease and visual effect and coated in a glossy ginger sauce.

NUTRITIONAL INFORMATION

Calories	125	Sugars	.........2g
Protein	.........8g	Fat	...........8g
Carbohydrate	....5g	Saturates	.......1g

10 MINS   10 MINS

SERVES 4

I N G R E D I E N T S

2 small cooked crabs

2 tbsp vegetable oil

3-inch piece gingerroot,
    grated

2 garlic cloves, thinly sliced

1 green bell pepper, seeded and cut into
    thin strips

6 scallions, cut into
    1-inch lengths

2 tbsp dry sherry

½ tsp sesame oil

⅔ cup fish stock

1 tsp light brown sugar

2 tsp cornstarch

⅔ cup water

1 Rinse the crabs and gently loosen around the shell at the top. Using a sharp knife, cut away the grey tissue and discard. Rinse the crabs again.

2 Twist off the legs and claws from the crabs. Using a pair of crab claw crackers or a cleaver, gently crack the claws to break through the shell to expose the flesh. Remove and discard any loose pieces of shell.

3 Separate the body and discard the inedible lungs and sac. Cut down the center of each crab to separate the body into two pieces and then cut each of these in half again.

4 Heat the oil in a preheated wok. Add the ginger and garlic and stir-fry for 1 minute. Add the crab pieces and stir-fry for a further minute.

5 Stir in the bell pepper, scallions, sherry, sesame oil, stock, and sugar. Bring to a boil, reduce the heat, cover, and simmer for 3–4 minutes.

6 Blend the cornstarch with the water and stir into the wok. Bring to a boil, stirring, until the sauce is thickened and clear. Transfer to a warm serving dish and serve immediately.

VARIATION

If preferred, remove the crabmeat from the shells prior to stir-frying and add to the wok with the bell pepper.

Crabmeat Cakes

Make these tasty crabmeat cakes to serve as a snack or starter, or as an accompaniment to a main meal.

NUTRITIONAL INFORMATION

Calories 262	Sugars 4g
Protein 13g	Fat 17g
Carbohydrate ...14g	Saturates 3g

20 MINS   55 MINS

SERVES 4

INGREDIENTS

generous 1 cup long-grain rice

1 tbsp sesame oil

1 small onion, chopped finely

1 large garlic clove, minced

2 tbsp chopped fresh cilantro

7 oz can of crabmeat, drained

1 tbsp fish sauce or light soy sauce

1 cup coconut milk

2 eggs

4 tbsp vegetable oil

salt and pepper

sliced scallions, to garnish

1 Cook the rice in plenty of boiling, lightly salted water until just tender, about 12 minutes. Rinse with cold water and drain well.

2 Heat the sesame oil in a small skillet and fry the onion and garlic gently for about 5 minutes, until softened and golden brown.

3 Combine the rice, onion, garlic, cilantro, crabmeat, fish sauce or soy sauce, and coconut milk. Season. Beat the eggs and add to the mixture. Divide the mixture between 8 greased ramekin dishes or teacups and place them in a baking

dish or roasting pan with enough warm water to come halfway up their sides. Place in a preheated oven at 180°C for 25 minutes, until set. Leave to cool.

4 Turn the crab cakes out of the ramekin dishes. Heat the oil in a wok or skillet and fry the crab cakes until golden brown. Drain on paper towels, garnish, and serve.

COOK'S TIP

If you want, you can prepare these crab cakes up to the point where they have been baked. Cool them, then cover and chill, ready for frying when needed.

Crab Claws with Chili

Crab claws are frequently used in Chinese cooking, and look sensational. They are perfect with this delicious chili sauce.

NUTRITIONAL INFORMATION

Calories	154	Sugar	.........3g
Protein	........16g	Fat	...........7g
Carbohydrate	....8g	Saturates	.......1g

5 MINS   10 MINS

SERVES 4

INGREDIENTS

1 lb 9 oz crab claws

1 tbsp corn oil

2 cloves garlic, minced

1 tbsp grated gingerroot

3 red chilies, seeded and finely chopped

2 tbsp sweet chili sauce

3 tbsp tomato catsup

1¼ cups cooled fish stock

1 tbsp cornstarch

salt and pepper

1 tbsp fresh chives, snipped

1 Gently crack the crab claws with a nut cracker. This process will allow the flavors of the chili, garlic, and ginger to fully penetrate the crabmeat.

2 Heat the corn oil in a large preheated wok.

3 Add the crab claws to the wok and stir-fry for about 5 minutes.

4 Add the garlic, ginger, and chilies to the wok and stir-fry for 1 minute, tossing the crab claws to coat all over.

5 Mix together the sweet chili sauce, tomato catsup, fish stock, and cornstarch in a small bowl. Add this mixture to the wok and cook, stirring occasionally, until the sauce starts to thicken.

6 Season the mixture in the wok with salt and pepper to taste.

7 Transfer the crab claws and chili sauce to warm serving dishes, garnish with snipped fresh chives and serve.

COOK'S TIP

If crab claws are not easily available, use a whole crab, cut into eight pieces, instead.

Crab with Chinese Cabbage

The delicate flavor of Chinese cabbage and crabmeat are enhanced by the coconut milk in this recipe.

NUTRITIONAL INFORMATION

Calories 109	Sugars 1g	
Protein 11g	Fat 6g	
Carbohydrate 2g	Saturates 1g	

5 MINS   10 MINS

SERVES 4

I N G R E D I E N T S

8 oz shiitake mushrooms

2 tbsp vegetable oil

2 cloves garlic, minced

6 scallions, sliced

1 head Chinese cabbage, shredded

1 tbsp mild curry paste

6 tbsp coconut milk

7 oz can white crabmeat, drained

1 tsp chili flakes

1 Using a sharp knife, cut the mushrooms into slices.

2 Heat the vegetable oil in a large preheated wok or heavy-bottomed skillet.

3 Add the mushrooms and garlic to the wok or skillet and stir-fry for 3 minutes or until the mushrooms have softened.

4 Add the scallions and shredded Chinese cabbage to the wok and stir-fry until the leaves have wilted.

5 Mix together the mild curry paste and coconut milk in a small bowl.

6 Add the curry paste and coconut milk mixture to the wok, together with the crabmeat and chili flakes. Mix together until well combined.

7 Heat the mixture in the wok until the juices start to bubble.

8 Transfer the crab and vegetable stir-fry to warm serving bowls and serve immediately.

COOK'S TIP

Shiitake mushrooms are now readily available in the fresh vegetable section of most large supermarkets.

Fried Squid Flowers

The addition of green bell pepper and black bean sauce to the squid makes a colorful and delicious dish from the Cantonese school.

NUTRITIONAL INFORMATION

Calories ....172 Sugars 1g
Protein ....13g Fat 13g
Carbohydrate ....2g Saturates 1g

 10 MINS   5 MINS

SERVES 4

I N G R E D I E N T S

12-14 oz prepared and cleaned squid (see Cook's Tip, below)

1 medium green bell pepper, cored and seeded

3-4 tbsp vegetable oil

1 garlic clove, finely chopped

¼ tsp finely chopped gingerroot

2 tsp finely chopped scallions

½ tsp salt

2 tbsp minced black bean sauce

1 tsp Chinese rice wine or dry sherry

a few drops sesame oil

boiled rice, to serve

1 If ready-prepared squid is not available, prepare as instructed in the Cook's Tip, below.

2 Open up the squid and, using a meat cleaver or sharp knife, score the inside of the flesh in a criss-cross pattern.

3 Cut the squid into pieces about the size of an oblong postage stamp.

4 Blanch the squid pieces in a bowl of boiling water for a few seconds. Remove and drain; dry well on absorbent paper towels.

5 Cut the bell pepper into small triangular pieces. Heat the oil in a preheated wok or large skillet and stir-fry the bell pepper for about 1 minute.

6 Add the garlic, ginger, scallion, salt, and squid. Continue stirring for another minute.

7 Finally add the black bean sauce and Chinese rice wine or dry sherry, and blend well.

8 Transfer the squid flowers to a serving dish, sprinkle with sesame oil, and serve with boiled rice.

COOK'S TIP

Clean the squid by first cutting off the head. Cut off the tentacles and reserve. Remove the small soft bone at the base of the tentacles and the transparent backbone, as well as the ink bag. Peel off the thin skin, then wash and dry well.

Crispy Fried Squid

Squid tubes are classically used in Chinese cooking and are most attractive when presented as in the following recipe.

NUTRITIONAL INFORMATION

Calories	156	Sugars 0g
Protein	........17g	Fat 6g
Carbohydrate	....7g	Saturates 8g

 10 MINS   10 MINS

SERVES 4

I N G R E D I E N T S

1 lb squid, cleaned

4 tbsp cornstarch

1 tsp salt

1 tsp freshly ground black pepper

1 tsp chili flakes

peanut oil, for frying

dipping sauce, to serve

1 Using a sharp knife, remove the tentacles from the squid and trim. Slice the bodies down one side and open out to give a flat piece.

2 Score the flat pieces with a criss-cross pattern then cut each piece into 4.

3 Mix together the cornstarch, salt, pepper, and chili flakes.

COOK'S TIP

Squid tubes may be purchased frozen if they are not available fresh. They are usually ready-cleaned and are easy to use. Ensure that they are completely defrosted before cooking.

4 Place the salt and pepper mixture in a large polythene bag. Add the squid pieces and shake the bag thoroughly to coat the squid in the flour mixture.

5 Heat about 2 inches of peanut oil in a large preheated wok.

6 Add the squid pieces to the wok and stir-fry, in batches, for about 2 minutes, or until the squid pieces start to curl up. Do not overcook or the squid will become tough.

7 Remove the squid pieces with a slotted spoon, transfer to absorbent paper towels and leave to drain thoroughly.

8 Transfer the fried squid pieces to serving plates and serve immediately with a dipping sauce.

Octopus & Squid with Chili

Try to buy cleaned squid tubes for this dish; if they are not available, see page 211 for directions on preparing squid.

NUTRITIONAL INFORMATION

Calories 319	Sugars 2g
Protein 40g	Fat 13g
Carbohydrate 4g	Saturates 1g

8¹/₂ HOURS   10 MINS

SERVES 6

INGREDIENTS

⅔ cup rice vinegar

¼ cup dry sherry

2 red chilies, chopped

1 tsp sugar

4 tbsp oil

12 baby octopus

12 small squid tubes, cleaned

2 scallions, sliced

1 garlic clove, minced

1 inch piece ginger, grated

4 tbsp sweet chili sauce

salt

1 Combine the vinegar, dry sherry, red chilies, sugar, 2 tbsp of the oil, and a pinch of salt in a large bowl.

2 Wash each octopus under cold running water and drain. Lay each on its side on a chopping board. Find the 'neck' and cut through. The 'beak' of the octopus should be left in the head; if it is not, make a cut nearer the tentacles and check again. Discard the head and beak, and put the tentacles, which should all be in one piece, into the vinegar mixture.

3 Put the squid tubes into the vinegar mixture and turn to coat well. Cover and chill for 8 hours or overnight.

4 Heat the remaining oil in a wok and stir-fry the scallions, garlic, and ginger for 1 minute over a very hot grill. Remove from the heat and add the chili sauce. Set aside.

5 Drain the fish from the marinade. Cut the pointed bottom end off each squid tube, so the tubes are of even width. Open out the squid so that it is flat. Score the squid to create a lattice pattern.

6 Cook the octopus and squid over the hottest part of the grill for 4–5 minutes, turning them constantly. The octopus tentacles will curl up, and are cooked when the flesh is no longer translucent. The squid tubes will curl back on themselves, revealing the lattice cuts.

7 When cooked, toss them into the pan with the chili sauce to coat completely and serve immediately.

Squid with Black Bean Sauce

Squid really is wonderful if quickly cooked as in this recipe, and contrary to popular belief it is not tough and rubbery unless it is overcooked.

NUTRITIONAL INFORMATION

Calories ....180 Sugars 2g
Protein ....19g Fat 7g
Carbohydrate ...10g Saturates 1g

 5 MINS   20 MINS

SERVES 4

INGREDIENTS

1 lb squid rings

2 tbsp all-purpose flour

½ tsp salt

1 green bell pepper

2 tbsp peanut oil

1 red onion, sliced

5¾ oz jar black bean sauce

1 Rinse the squid rings under cold running water and pat dry thoroughly with absorbent paper towels.

2 Place the all-purpose flour and salt in a bowl and mix together. Add the squid rings and toss until they are evenly coated.

3 Using a sharp knife, seed the bell pepper. Slice the bell pepper into thin strips.

4 Heat the peanut oil in a large preheated wok or heavy-bottomed skillet, swirling the oil around the base until it is really hot.

5 Add the bell pepper slices and red onion to the wok or skillet and stir-fry for about 2 minutes, or until the vegetables are just beginning to soften.

6 Add the squid rings to the wok or skillet and cook for a further 5 minutes, or until the squid is cooked through. Be careful not to overcook the squid.

7 Add the black bean sauce to the wok and heat through until the juices are bubbling. Transfer the squid stir-fry to warm serving bowls and serve immediately.

COOK'S TIP

Serve this recipe with fried rice or noodles tossed in soy sauce, if you wish.

Squid with Oyster Sauce

Squid is a delicious fish, which if prepared and cooked correctly, is a quick cooking, attractive and tasty ingredient.

NUTRITIONAL INFORMATION

Calories 320   Sugars 1g
Protein ....18g   Fat 26g
Carbohydrate ....2g   Saturates 3g

 5 MINS   15 MINS

SERVES 4

INGREDIENTS

1 lb squid

⅔ cup vegetable oil

½-inch piece gingerroot, grated

2 oz snow peas

5 tbsp hot fish stock

red bell pepper triangles, to garnish

SAUCE

1 tbsp oyster sauce

1 tbsp light soy sauce

pinch of superfine sugar

1 garlic clove, minced

1 To prepare the squid, cut down the center of the body lengthways. Flatten the squid out, inside uppermost, and score a lattice design deep into the flesh, using a sharp knife.

2 To make the sauce, combine the oyster sauce, soy sauce, sugar, and garlic in a small bowl. Stir to dissolve the sugar and set aside until required.

3 Heat the oil in a preheated wok until almost smoking. Lower the heat slightly, add the squid and stir-fry until they curl up. Remove with a draining spoon and drain thoroughly on paper towels.

4 Pour off all but 2 tablespoons of the oil and return the wok to the heat. Add the ginger and snow peas and stir-fry for 1 minute.

5 Return the squid to the wok and pour in the sauce and hot fish stock. Leave to simmer for 3 minutes until thickened. Transfer to a warm serving dish, garnish with bell pepper triangles and serve immediately.

COOK'S TIP

Take care not to overcook the squid, otherwise it will be rubbery and unappetizing.

Mussels with Lettuce

Mussels require careful preparation but very little cooking. They are available fresh or in vacuum packs when out of season.

NUTRITIONAL INFORMATION

Calories 205   Sugars 0.3g
Protein ....31g   Fat 9g
Carbohydrate ....1g   Saturates 4g

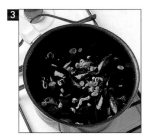

 15 MINS   5 MINS

SERVES 4

INGREDIENTS

2 lb mussels in their shells, scrubbed

2 stalks lemongrass

1 Iceberg lettuce

2 tbsp lemon juice

⅓ cup water

2 tbsp butter

finely grated zest of 1 lemon

2 tbsp oyster sauce

1 Place the scrubbed mussels in a large saucepan.

2 Using a sharp knife, thinly slice the lemongrass and shred the lettuce.

3 Add the lemongrass, lemon juice, and water to the pan of mussels, cover with a tight-fitting lid and cook for 5 minutes or until the mussels have opened. Discard any mussels that do not open.

4 Carefully remove the cooked mussels from their shells, using a fork and set aside until required.

5 Heat the butter in a large preheated wok or skillet. Add the lettuce and finely grated lemon zest to the wok or skillet and stir-fry for 2 minutes, or until the lettuce begins to wilt.

6 Add the oyster sauce to the mixture in the wok and heat through, stirring well until the sauce is thoroughly incorporated in the mixture.

7 Transfer the mixture in the wok to a warm serving dish and serve immediately.

COOK'S TIP

When using fresh mussels, be sure to discard any opened mussels before scrubbing and any unopened mussels after cooking.

Mussels with Lemongrass

Give fresh mussels a Far Eastern flavor by using some Kaffir lime leaves, garlic, and lemongrass in the stock used for steaming them.

NUTRITIONAL INFORMATION

Calories	194	Sugar	.........0g
Protein	........33g	Fat	..........7g
Carbohydrate	....1g	Saturates	.......1g

10 MINS   10 MINS

SERVES 4

I N G R E D I E N T S

1 lb 10 oz live mussels

1 tbsp sesame oil

3 shallots, chopped finely

2 garlic cloves, chopped finely

1 stalk lemongrass

2 Kaffir lime leaves

2 tbsp chopped fresh cilantro

finely grated rind of 1 lime

2 tbsp lime juice

1¼ cups hot vegetable stock

crusty bread, to serve

fresh cilantro, to garnish

1 Using a small sharp knife, scrape the beards off the mussels under cold running water. Scrub them well, discarding any that are damaged or remain open when tapped. Keep rinsing until there is no trace of sand.

2 Heat the sesame oil in a large saucepan and fry the shallots and garlic gently until softened, about 2 minutes.

3 Bruise the lemongrass, using a meat mallet or rolling pin, and add to the pan with the Kaffir lime leaves, cilantro, lime rind and juice, mussels, and stock. Put the lid on the saucepan and cook over a

moderate heat for 3–5 minutes. Shake the pan from time to time.

4 Lift the mussels out into 4 warmed soup plates, discarding any that remain shut. Boil the remaining liquid rapidly to reduce slightly. Remove the lemongrass and lime leaves, then pour the liquid over the mussels.

5 Garnish with cilantro and lime wedges, and serve at once.

COOK'S TIP

Mussels are now farmed, so they should be available from good fishstore throughout the year.

Mussels in Black Bean Sauce

This dish looks so impressive, the combination of colors making it look almost too good to eat!

NUTRITIONAL INFORMATION

Calories ....174 Sugars 4g
Protein ....19g Fat 8g
Carbohydrate ....6g Saturates 1g

 5 MINS   10 MINS

SERVES 4

INGREDIENTS

12 oz leeks

12 oz cooked green-lipped mussels (shelled)

1 tsp cumin seeds

2 tbsp vegetable oil

2 cloves garlic, minced

1 red bell pepper, seeded and sliced

¾ cup canned bamboo shoots, drained

6 oz baby spinach

5¾ oz jar black bean sauce

1 Using a sharp knife, trim the leeks and shred them.

2 Place the cooked green-lipped mussels in a large bowl, sprinkle with the cumin seeds and toss well to coat all over. Set aside until required.

COOK'S TIP

If the green-lipped mussels are not available they can be bought shelled in cans and jars from most large supermarkets.

3 Heat the vegetable oil in a preheated wok, swirling the oil around the base of the wok until it is really hot.

4 Add the shredded leeks, garlic, and sliced red bell pepper to the wok and stir-fry for 5 minutes, or until the vegetables are tender.

5 Add the bamboo shoots, baby spinach leaves, and cooked green-lipped mussels to the wok and stir-fry for about 2 minutes.

6 Pour the black bean sauce over the ingredients in the wok, toss well to coat all the ingredients in the sauce and leave to simmer for a few seconds, stirring occasionally.

7 Transfer the stir-fry to warm serving bowls and serve immediately.

Fish in Szechuan Hot Sauce

This is a classic Szechuan recipe. When served in a restaurant, the fish head and tail are removed before cooking.

NUTRITIONAL INFORMATION

Calories 470   Sugar 3g
Protein . . . . .45g   Fat 29g
Carbohydrate . . . .7g   Saturates 4g

  3³/₄ HOURS   15 MINS

SERVES 4

INGREDIENTS

1 carp, bream, sea bass, trout, grouper, or grey mullet, about 1 lb 10 oz, gutted

1 tbsp light soy sauce

1 tbsp Chinese rice wine or dry sherry

vegetable oil, for deep-frying

flat-leaf parsley or cilatnro sprigs, to garnish

SAUCE

2 garlic cloves, finely chopped

2-3 scallions, finely chopped

1 tsp finely chopped gingerroot

2 tbsp chili bean sauce

1 tbsp tomato paste

2 tsp sugar

1 tbsp rice vinegar

½ cup stock or water

1 tbsp cornstarch paste

½ tsp sesame oil

1 Wash the fish and dry well on absorbent paper towels.

2 Score both sides of the fish to the bone with a sharp knife, making diagonal cuts at intervals of 1 inch.

3 Rub the fish with the soy sauce and rice wine or sherry on both sides. Transfer the fish to a plate, cover with plastic wrap and leave to marinate in the refrigerator for 10-15 minutes.

4 Heat the oil in a preheated wok or large skillet until smoking.

5 Deep-fry the fish in the hot oil for about 3-4 minutes on both sides, or until golden brown.

6 Pour off the oil, leaving about 1 tablespoon in the wok. Push the fish to one side of the wok and add the garlic, white parts of the scallions, ginger, chili bean sauce, tomato paste, sugar, vinegar, and Chinese stock or water.

7 Bring the mixture in the wok to a boil and braise the fish in the sauce for 4-5 minutes, turning it over once.

8 Add the green parts of the scallions and stir in the cornstarch paste to thicken the sauce.

9 Sprinkle with sesame oil and serve immediately, garnished with fresh parsley or cilantro.

Crispy Fish

This is a very hot dish – not for the faint hearted! It may be made without the chili flavorings, if preferred.

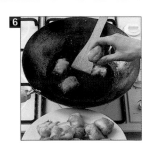

NUTRITIONAL INFORMATION

Calories 281   Sugars 3g
Protein . . . . .25g   Fat 12g
Carbohydrate . . .15g   Saturates 2g

 30 MINS   40 MINS

SERVES 4

INGREDIENTS

1 lb white fish fillets

BATTER

½ cup all-purpose flour

1 egg, separated

1 tbsp peanut oil

4 tbsp milk

vegetable oil, for deep-frying

SAUCE

1 fresh red chili, chopped

2 garlic cloves, minced

pinch of chili powder

3 tbsp tomato paste

1 tbsp rice wine vinegar

2 tbsp dark soy sauce

2 tbsp Chinese rice wine

2 tbsp water

pinch of superfine sugar

1 Cut the fish into 1-inch cubes and set aside.

2 Sift the all-purpose flour into a mixing bowl and make a well in the center. Add the egg yolk and peanut oil to the mixing bowl and gradually stir in the milk, incorporating the flour to form a smooth batter. Leave to stand for about 20 minutes.

3 Whisk the egg white until it forms peaks and fold into the batter until thoroughly incorporated.

4 Heat the vegetable oil in a preheated wok or large skillet. Dip the fish into the batter and fry, in batches, for 8–10 minutes, until cooked through. Remove the fish from the wok with a draining spoon, set aside and keep warm until required.

5 Pour off all but 1 tablespoon of oil from the wok and return to the heat. Add the chili, garlic, chili powder, tomato paste, rice wine vinegar, soy sauce, Chinese rice-wine, water, and sugar and cook, stirring, for 3–4 minutes.

6 Return the fish to the wok and stir gently to coat it in the sauce. Cook for 2–3 minutes, until hot. Transfer to a serving dish and serve immediately.

Fish with Saffron Sauce

White fish cooked in a bamboo steamer over the wok and served with a light creamy saffron sauce with a real bite to it.

NUTRITIONAL INFORMATION

Calories 254	Sugars 0.5g	
Protein 30g	Fat 14g	
Carbohydrate 2g	Saturates 5g	

 5 MINS   30 MINS

SERVES 4

I N G R E D I E N T S

1 lb 6 oz-1 lb 10 oz white fish fillets (cod, haddock, whiting etc)

pinch of Chinese five-spice powder

4 sprigs fresh thyme

large pinch saffron threads

1 cup boiling fish or vegetable stock

2 tbsp sunflower oil

4½ oz button mushrooms, thinly sliced

grated rind of ½ lemon

1 tbsp lemon juice

½ tsp freshly chopped thyme or ¼ tsp dried thyme

½ bunch watercress, chopped

1½ tsp cornstarch

3 tbsp light or heavy cream

salt and pepper

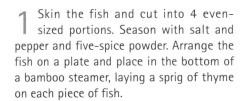

1 Skin the fish and cut into 4 even-sized portions. Season with salt and pepper and five-spice powder. Arrange the fish on a plate and place in the bottom of a bamboo steamer, laying a sprig of thyme on each piece of fish.

2 Stand a low metal trivet in a wok and add water to come almost to the top of it. Bring to a boil, stand the bamboo steamer on the trivet, and cover with the bamboo lid and then the lid of the wok or a piece of foil. Simmer for 20 minutes until the fish is tender, adding more boiling water to the wok if necessary. Meanwhile, soak the saffron threads in the boiling stock.

3 When the fish is tender, remove and keep warm. Empty the wok and wipe dry. Heat the oil in the wok and stir-fry the mushrooms for about 2 minutes. Add the saffron stock, lemon rind and juice and, chopped thyme and bring to a boil. Add the watercress and simmer for 1-2 minutes.

4 Blend the cornstarch with the cream, add a little of the sauce from the wok, then return to the wok and heat gently until thickened. Serve the fish surrounded by the sauce.

Fish with Coconut & Basil

Fish curries are sensational and this is no exception. Red curry and coconut are fantastic flavors with the fried fish.

NUTRITIONAL INFORMATION

Calories	209	Sugars	........10g
Protein	........21g	Fat	...........8g
Carbohydrate	...15g	Saturates	.......1g

 5 MINS 15 MINS

SERVES 4

INGREDIENTS

2 tbsp vegetable oil

1 lb skinless cod fillet

¼ cup seasoned flour

1 clove garlic, minced

2 tbsp red curry paste

1 tbsp fish sauce

1¼ cups coconut milk

6 oz cherry tomatoes, halved

20 fresh basil leaves

fragrant rice, to serve

1 Heat the vegetable oil in a large preheated wok.

2 Using a sharp knife, cut the fish into large cubes, removing any bones with a pair of clean tweezers.

3 Place the seasoned flour in a bowl. Add the cubes of fish and mix until well coated.

4 Add the coated fish to the wok and stir-fry over a high heat for 3–4 minutes, or until the fish just begins to brown at the edges.

5 In a small bowl, mix together the garlic, curry paste, fish sauce, and coconut milk. Pour the mixture over the fish and bring to a boil.

6 Add the tomatoes to the mixture in the wok and leave to simmer for 5 minutes.

7 Roughly chop or tear the fresh basil leaves. Add the basil to the wok, stir carefully to combine, taking care not to break up the cubes of fish.

8 Transfer to serving plates and serve hot with fragrant rice.

COOK'S TIP
Take care not to overcook the dish once the tomatoes are added, otherwise they will break down and the skins will come away.

Fish with Ginger Butter

Whole mackerel or trout are stuffed with herbs, wrapped in foil, baked and then drizzled with a fresh ginger butter.

NUTRITIONAL INFORMATION

Calories ....328 Sugar 0g
Protein ....24g Fat 25g
Carbohydrate ....1g Saturates 13g

10 MINS   30 MINS

SERVES 4

INGREDIENTS

4 x 9 oz whole trout or mackerel, gutted

4 tbsp chopped fresh cilantro

5 garlic cloves, minced

2 tsp grated lemon or lime zest

2 tsp vegetable oil

banana leaves, for wrapping (optional)

6 tbsp butter

1 tbsp grated gingerroot

1 tbsp light soy sauce

salt and pepper

cilantro sprigs and lemon or lime wedges, to garnish

1 Wash and dry the fish. Mix the cilantro with the garlic, lemon or lime zest, and salt and pepper to taste. Spoon into the fish cavities.

2 Brush the fish with a little oil, season well and place each fish on a double thickness sheet of baking parchment or foil and wrap up well to enclose. Alternatively, wrap in banana leaves (see right).

3 Place on a baking sheet and bake in a preheated oven for about 25 minutes or until the flesh will flake easily.

4 Meanwhile, melt the butter in a small pan. Add the ginger and mix well.

5 Stir the light soy sauce into the saucepan.

6 To serve, unwrap the fish packets, drizzle over the ginger butter, and garnish with cilantro and lemon or lime wedges.

COOK'S TIP

For a really authentic touch, wrap the fish in banana leaves, which can be ordered from specialist oriental supermarkets. They are not edible, but impart a delicate flavor to the fish.

Braised Fish Fillets

Any white fish, such as lemon sole or plaice, is ideal for this delicious dish.

NUTRITIONAL INFORMATION

Calories	107	Sugars	2g
Protein	17g	Fat	2g
Carbohydrate	6g	Saturates	0.3g

 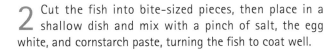

4 HOURS   10 MINS

SERVES 4

INGREDIENTS

3-4 small Chinese dried mushrooms

10½-12 oz fish fillets

1 tsp salt

½ egg white, lightly beaten

1 tsp cornstarch paste

2½ cups vegetable oil

1 tsp finely chopped gingerroot

2 scallions, finely chopped

1 garlic clove, finely chopped

½ small green bell pepper, seeded
and cut into small cubes

½ small carrot, thinly sliced

½ cup canned sliced bamboo shoots, rinsed
and drained

½ tsp sugar

1 tbsp light soy sauce

1 tsp rice wine or dry sherry

1 tbsp chili bean sauce

2-3 tbsp stock or water

a few drops of sesame oil

1 Soak the dried mushrooms in a bowl of warm water for 30 minutes. Drain thoroughly on paper towels, reserving the soaking water for stock or soup. Squeeze the mushrooms to extract all of the moisture, cut off and discard any hard stems and slice thinly.

2 Cut the fish into bite-sized pieces, then place in a shallow dish and mix with a pinch of salt, the egg white, and cornstarch paste, turning the fish to coat well.

3 Heat the oil in a preheated wok. Add the fish pieces to the wok and deep-fry for about 1 minute. Remove the fish pieces with a draining spoon and leave to drain on paper towels.

4 Pour off the excess oil, leaving about 1 tablespoon in the wok. Add the ginger, scallions, and garlic to flavor the oil for a few seconds, then add the bell pepper, carrots, and bamboo shoots and stir-fry for about 1 minute.

5 Add the sugar, soy sauce, wine, chili bean sauce, stock or water, and the remaining salt and bring to a boil. Add the fish pieces, stirring to coat with the sauce, and braise for 1 minute. Sprinkle with sesame oil and serve.

Shrimp Fu-Yong

The classic ingredients of this popular dish are eggs, carrots, and (small) shrimps. Add extra ingredients such as peas or crabmeat, if desired.

NUTRITIONAL INFORMATION

Calories 240	Sugars 1g
Protein 22g	Fat 16g
Carbohydrate 1g	Saturates 3g

5 MINS   10 MINS

SERVES 4

INGREDIENTS

2 tbsp vegetable oil

1 carrot, grated

5 eggs, beaten

8 oz raw (small) shrimp, peeled

1 tbsp light soy sauce

pinch of Chinese five-spice powder

2 scallions, chopped

2 tsp sesame seeds

1 tsp sesame oil

1 Heat the vegetable oil in a preheated wok or skillet, swirling it around until the oil is really hot.

2 Add the grated carrot and stir-fry for 1–2 minutes.

3 Push the carrot to one side of the wok or skillet and add the beaten eggs. Cook, stirring gently, for 1–2 minutes.

4 Stir the shrimp, light soy sauce, and five-spice powder into the mixture in the wok. Stir-fry the mixture for 2–3 minutes, or until the shrimps change color and the mixture is almost dry.

5 Turn the shrimp fu-yong out on to a warm plate and sprinkle the scallions, sesame seeds, and sesame oil on top. Serve immediately.

COOK'S TIP

If only cooked shrimp are available, add them just before the end of cooking, but make sure they are fully incorporated into the fu-yong. They require only heating through. Overcooking will make them chewy and tasteless.

Gingered Angler Fish

This dish is a real treat and is perfect for special occasions. Angler fish has a tender flavor which is ideal with asparagus, chili and ginger.

NUTRITIONAL INFORMATION

Calories 133   Sugars 0g
Protein . . . . .21g   Fat 5g
Carbohydrate . . . .1g   Saturates 1g

   5 MINS   10 MINS

SERVES 4

I N G R E D I E N T S

1 lb angler fish

1 tbsp freshly grated gingerroot

2 tbsp sweet chili sauce

1 tbsp corn oil

1 cup fine asparagus

3 scallions, sliced

1 tsp sesame oil

1 Using a sharp knife, slice the fish into thin flat rounds. Set aside until required.

2 Mix together the freshly grated gingerroot and the sweet chili sauce in a small bowl until thoroughly blended. Brush the ginger and chili sauce mixture over the fish pieces, using a pastry brush.

COOK'S TIP

Angler fish is quite expensive, but it is well worth using as it has a wonderful flavor and texture. At a push you could use cubes of chunky cod fillet instead.

3 Heat the corn oil in a large preheated wok or heavy-bottomed skillet.

4 Add the fish pieces, asparagus and chopped scallions to the wok or skillet and cook for about 5 minutes, stirring gently so the fish pieces do not break up.

5 Remove the wok or skillet from the heat, drizzle the sesame oil over the stir-fry and toss well to combine.

6 Transfer the stir-fried gingered fish to warm serving plates and serve immediately.

Tuna & Vegetable Stir-Fry

Fresh tuna is a dark, meaty fish and is now widely available at fresh fish stores. It lends itself perfectly to the rich flavors in this recipe.

NUTRITIONAL INFORMATION

Calories 245   Sugars 11g
Protein ....30g   Fat 7g
Carbohydrate ...14g   Saturates 1g

10 MINS   10 MINS

SERVES 4

INGREDIENTS

8 oz carrots

1 onion

1¾ cups baby-corn-on-the-cobs

2 tbsp corn oil

2½ cups snow peas

1 lb fresh tuna

2 tbsp fish sauce

1 tbsp jaggery

finely grated zest and juice of 1 orange

2 tbsp sherry

1 tsp cornstarch

rice or noodles, to serve

1 Using a sharp knife, cut the carrots into thin sticks, slice the onion and halve the baby-corn-on-the-cobs.

2 Heat the corn oil in a large preheated wok or skillet.

3 Add the onion, carrots, snow peas, and baby-corn-on-the-cobs to the wok or skillet and stir-fry for 5 minutes.

4 Using a sharp knife, thinly slice the fresh tuna.

5 Add the tuna slices to the wok or skillet and stir-fry for about 2–3 minutes, or until the tuna turns opaque.

6 Mix together the fish sauce, jaggery, orange zest and juice, sherry, and cornstarch.

7 Pour the mixture over the tuna and vegetables and cook for 2 minutes, or until the juices thicken. Serve the stir-fry with rice or noodles.

VARIATION

Try using swordfish steaks instead of the tuna. Swordfish steaks are now widely available and are similar in texture to tuna

Mullet with Ginger

Ginger is used widely in Chinese cooking for its strong, pungent flavor. Although fresh ginger is best, ground ginger may be used instead.

NUTRITIONAL INFORMATION

Calories	195	Sugars	.........6g
Protein	........31g	Fat	...........3g
Carbohydrate	....9g	Saturates	.......0g

 10 MINS   15 MINS

SERVES 4

I N G R E D I E N T S

1 whole mullet, cleaned and scaled

2 scallions, chopped

1 tsp grated gingerroot

½ cup garlic-wine vinegar

½ cup light soy sauce

3 tsp superfine sugar

dash of chili sauce

½ cup fish stock

1 green bell pepper, seeded and
   thinly sliced

1 large tomato, skinned, seeded, and
   cut into thin strips

salt and pepper

sliced tomato, to garnish

1 Rinse the fish inside and out and pat dry with paper towels.

2 Make 3 diagonal slits in the flesh on each side of the fish. Season the fish with salt and pepper inside and out, according to taste.

3 Place the fish on a heatproof plate and scatter the chopped scallions and grated ginger over the top. Cover and steam for 10 minutes, or until the fish is cooked through.

4 Meanwhile, place the garlic-wine vinegar, light soy sauce, superfine sugar, chili sauce, fish stock, bell pepper, and tomato in a saucepan and bring to a boil, stirring occasionally.

5 Cook the sauce over a high heat until the sauce has slightly reduced and thickened.

6 Remove the fish from the steamer and transfer to a warm serving dish. Pour the sauce over the fish, garnish with tomato slices, and serve immediately.

VARIATION

Use fillets of fish for this recipe if preferred, and reduce the cooking time to 5–7 minutes.

Trout with Pineapple

Pineapple is widely used in Chinese cooking. The tartness of fresh pineapple complements fish particularly well.

NUTRITIONAL INFORMATION

Calories	243	Sugars	........4g
Protein	........30g	Fat	...........11g
Carbohydrate	....6g	Saturates	.......2g

 5 MINS   15 MINS

SERVES 4

I N G R E D I E N T S

4 trout fillets, skinned

2 tbsp vegetable oil

2 garlic cloves, cut into slivers

4 slices fresh pineapple, peeled and diced

1 celery stalk, sliced

1 tbsp light soy sauce

¼ cup fresh or unsweetened pineapple juice

⅔ cup fish stock

1 tsp cornstarch

2 tsp water

shredded celery leaves and fresh red chili slices, to garnish

1 Cut the trout fillets into strips. Heat 1 tablespoon of the vegetable oil in a preheated wok until almost smoking. Reduce the heat slightly, add the fish and sauté for 2 minutes. Remove from the wok and set aside.

2 Add the remaining oil to the wok, reduce the heat and add the garlic, diced pineapple, and celery. Stir-fry for 1–2 minutes.

3 Add the soy sauce, pineapple juice, and fish stock to the wok. Bring to a boil and cook, stirring, for 2–3 minutes, or until the sauce has reduced.

4 Blend the cornstarch with the water to form a paste and stir it into the wok. Bring the sauce to a boil and cook, stirring constantly, until the sauce thickens and clears.

5 Return the fish to the wok, and cook, stirring gently, until heated through. Transfer to a warmed serving dish and serve, garnished with shredded celery leaves and red chili slices.

VARIATION

Use canned pineapple instead of fresh pineapple if you wish, choosing slices in unsweetened, natural juice in preference to a syrup.

Sesame Salmon with Cream

Salmon fillet holds its shape when tossed in sesame seeds and stir-fried.
It is served in a creamy sauce of diced zucchini.

NUTRITIONAL INFORMATION

Calories	550	Sugars	.........1g
Protein	........35g	Fat	..........45g
Carbohydrate	....2g	Saturates	......12g

 5 MINS   10 MINS

SERVES 4

I N G R E D I E N T S

1 lb 6 oz–1 lb 10 oz salmon or pink trout
fillets

2 tbsp light soy sauce

3 tbsp sesame seeds

3 tbsp sunflower oil

4 scallions, thinly sliced diagonally

2 large zucchini, diced, or 5-inch piece
cucumber, diced

grated rind of ½ lemon

1 tbsp lemon juice

½ tsp turmeric

6 tbsp fish stock or water

3 tbsp heavy cream or fromage blanc

salt and pepper

curly endive, to garnish

1 Skin the fish and cut into strips about
$1^{1}/_{2}$ x $^{3}/_{4}$ inches. Pat dry on paper
towels. Season lightly, then brush with soy
sauce and sprinkle all over with sesame
seeds.

2 Heat 2 tablespoons of oil in the wok.
Add the pieces of fish and stir-fry for
3-4 minutes until lightly browned all over.
Remove with a slice, drain on paper towels
and keep warm.

3 Heat the remaining oil in the wok and
add the scallions and zucchini or
cucumber and stir-fry for 1-2 minutes. Add
the lemon rind and juice, turmeric, stock,
and seasoning and bring to a boil for 1
minute. Stir in the cream or fromage
blanc.

4 Return the fish pieces to the wok and
toss gently in the sauce until they are
really hot. Garnish and serve.

COOK'S TIP

Lay the fillet skin-side down.
Insert a sharp, flexible knife at
one end between the flesh and
the skin. Hold the skin tightly at
the end and push the knife along,
keeping the knife blade as flat as
possible against the skin.

Stir-Fried Salmon with Leeks

Salmon is marinated in a deliciously rich, sweet sauce, stir-fried, and served on a bed of crispy leeks.

NUTRITIONAL INFORMATION

Calories	360	Sugars	........9g
Protein	........24g	Fat	25
Carbohydrate	....11g	Saturates	.......4g

 35 MINS 15 MINS

SERVES 4

I N G R E D I E N T S

1 lb salmon fillet, skinned

2 tbsp sweet soy sauce

2 tbsp tomato catsup

1 tsp rice wine vinegar

1 tbsp demerara sugar

1 clove garlic, minced

4 tbsp corn oil

1 lb leeks, thinly shredded

finely chopped red chilies,
    to garnish

1 Using a sharp knife, cut the salmon into slices. Place the slices of salmon in a shallow non-metallic dish.

2 Mix together the soy sauce, tomato catsup, rice-wine vinegar, sugar and garlic.

3 Pour the mixture over the salmon, toss well and leave to marinate for about 30 minutes.

4 Meanwhile, heat 3 tablespoons of the corn oil in a large preheated wok.

5 Add the leeks to the wok and stir-fry over a medium-high heat for about 10 minutes, or until the leeks become crispy and tender.

6 Using a draining spoon, carefully remove the leeks from the wok and transfer to warmed serving plates.

7 Add the remaining oil to the wok. Add the salmon and the marinade to the wok and cook for 2 minutes.

8 Remove the salmon from the wok and spoon over the leeks, garnish with finely chopped red chilies and serve immediately.

VARIATION

You can use a fillet of beef instead of the salmon, if you prefer.

Mediterranean Dishes

The Mediterraneans eat everything that comes out of the sea, from the smallest whitebait to the massive tuna fish. Fish markets in southern Europe are fascinating, with a huge variety of fish on display, but as most of the fish comes from the Mediterranean, it is not always easy to find an equivalent elsewhere. However, fresh or frozen imported fish of all kinds is appearing increasingly in fish stores and supermarkets both in the United States and Britain. Make the most of it with these tempting recipes.

Charred Tuna Steaks

Tuna has a firm flesh, which is ideal for grilling, but it can be a little dry unless it is marinated first.

NUTRITIONAL INFORMATION

Calories	153	Sugars	.........1g
Protein	........29g	Fat	...........3g
Carbohydrate	....1g	Saturates	......1g

 2 HOURS   15 MINS

SERVES 4

INGREDIENTS

4 tuna steaks

3 tbsp soy sauce

1 tbsp Worcestershire sauce

1 tsp wholegrain mustard

1 tsp superfine sugar

1 tbsp sunflower oil

green salad, to serve

TO GARNISH

flat-leaf parsley

lemon wedges

1 Place the tuna steaks in a shallow dish.

2 Mix together the soy sauce, Worcestershire sauce, mustard, sugar, and oil in a small bowl.

3 Pour the marinade over the tuna steaks.

4 Gently turn over the tuna steaks, using your fingers or a fork. Make sure that the fish steaks are well coated with the marinade.

5 Cover and place the tuna steaks in the refrigerator. Leave to chill for between 30 minutes and 2 hours.

6 Grill the marinated fish over hot coals for 10–15 minutes, turning once.

7 Baste frequently with any of the marinade that is left in the dish.

8 Garnish with flat-leaf parsley and lemon wedges. Serve with a fresh green salad.

COOK'S TIP

If a marinade contains soy sauce, the marinating time should be limited, usually to 2 hours. If allowed to marinate for too long, the fish will dry out and become tough.

Tuna with Roast Bell Peppers

Fresh tuna will be either a small bonito fish or steaks from a skipjack. The more delicately flavored fish have a paler flesh.

NUTRITIONAL INFORMATION

Calories 428	Sugars 5g	
Protein 60g	Fat 19g	
Carbohydrate 5g	Saturates 3g	

20 MINS 30 MINS

SERVES 4

INGREDIENTS

4 tuna steaks, about 9 oz each

3 tbsp lemon juice

4 cups water

6 tbsp olive oil

2 orange bell peppers

2 red bell peppers

12 black olives

1 tsp balsamic vinegar

salt and pepper

1 Put the tuna steaks into a bowl with the lemon juice and water. Leave for 15 minutes.

2 Drain and brush the steaks all over with olive oil and season well with salt and pepper.

3 Halve, core, and seed the bell peppers. Put them over a hot grill and cook for 12 minutes until they are charred all over. Put them into a plastic bag and seal it.

4 Meanwhile, cook the tuna over a hot grill for 12–15 minutes, turning once.

5 When the bell peppers are cool enough to handle, peel them and cut each piece into 4 strips. Toss them with the remaining olive oil, olives, and balsamic vinegar.

6 Serve the tuna steaks very hot, with the roasted bell pepper salad.

COOK'S TIP

Red, orange, and yellow bell peppers can also be peeled by cooking them in a hot oven for 30 minutes, turning them frequently, or roasting them straight over a naked gas flame, again turning them frequently. In both methods, seed the bell peppers after peeling.

Orange Mackerel

Mackerel can be quite rich, but when it is stuffed with oranges and toasted ground almonds it is tangy and light.

NUTRITIONAL INFORMATION

Calories 623	Sugars 7g
Protein 42g	Fat 47g
Carbohydrate 8g	Saturates 8g

 15 MINS   35 MINS

SERVES 4

I N G R E D I E N T S

2 tbsp oil

4 scallions, chopped

2 oranges

1¾ oz ground almonds

1 tbsp oats

1¾ oz mixed green and black olives, pitted
  and chopped

8 mackerel fillets

salt and pepper

crisp salad, to serve

1 Heat the oil in a skillet. Add the scallions and cook for 2 minutes.

2 Finely grate the rind of the oranges, then, using a sharp knife, cut away the remaining skin and white pith.

3 Using a sharp knife, segment the oranges by cutting down either side of the lines of pith to loosen each segment. Do this over a plate so that you can reserve any juices. Cut each orange segment in half.

4 Lightly toast the almonds, under a preheated broiler, for 2–3 minutes or until golden; watch them carefully as they brown very quickly.

5 Mix the scallions, oranges, ground almonds, oats, and olives together in a bowl and season to taste with salt and pepper.

6 Spoon the orange mixture along the center of each fillet. Roll up each fillet, securing it in place with a toothpick or skewer.

7 Bake in a preheated oven at 375°F for 25 minutes until the fish is tender.

8 Transfer to serving plates and serve warm with a salad.

Sea Bass with Olive Sauce

A favorite fish for chefs, the delicious sea bass is now becoming increasingly common in supermarkets and fish stores for family meals.

10 MINS   30 MINS

SERVES 4

INGREDIENTS

1 lb dried macaroni

1 tbsp olive oil

8 x 4 oz sea bass medallions

SAUCE

2 tbsp butter

4 shallots, chopped

2 tbsp capers

1½ cups pitted green

olives, chopped

4 tbsp balsamic vinegar

1¼ cups fish stock

1¼ cups heavy cream

juice of 1 lemon

salt and pepper

TO GARNISH

lemon slices

shredded leek

shredded carrot

1 To make the sauce, melt the butter in a skillet. Add the shallots and cook over a low heat for 4 minutes. Add the capers and olives and cook for a further 3 minutes.

2 Stir in the balsamic vinegar and fish stock, bring to a boil and reduce by half. Add the cream, stirring, and reduce again by half. Season to taste with salt and pepper and stir in the lemon juice. Remove the pan from the heat, set aside and keep warm.

3 Bring a large pan of lightly salted water to a boil. Add the pasta and olive oil and cook for about 12 minutes, until tender but still firm to the bite.

4 Meanwhile, lightly broil the sea bass medallions for 3–4 minutes on each side, until cooked through, but still moist and delicate.

5 Drain the pasta thoroughly and transfer to large individual serving dishes. Top the pasta with the fish medallions and pour over the olive sauce. Garnish with lemon slices, shredded leek, and shredded carrot and serve immediately.

Trout in Red Wine

This recipe from Trentino is best when the fish are freshly caught, but it is a good way to cook any trout, giving it an interesting flavor.

20 MINS   45 MINS

SERVES 4

INGREDIENTS

4 fresh trout, about 10 oz each

1 cup red or white wine vinegar

1¼ cups red or dry white wine

⅔ cup water

1 carrot, sliced

2–4 bay leaves

thinly pared rind of 1 lemon

1 small onion, sliced very thinly

4 sprigs fresh parsley

4 sprigs fresh thyme

1 tsp black peppercorns

6–8 whole cloves

6 tbsp butter

1 tbsp chopped fresh mixed herbs

salt and pepper

TO GARNISH

sprigs of herbs

lemon slices

1 Gut the trout but leave their heads on. Dry on paper towels and lay the fish head to tail in a shallow container or baking pan large enough to hold them.

2 Bring the wine vinegar to a boil and pour slowly all over the fish. Leave the fish to marinate in the refrigerator for about 20 minutes.

3 Meanwhile, put the wine, water, carrot, bay leaves, lemon rind, onion, herbs, peppercorns, and cloves into a pan with a good pinch of sea salt and heat gently.

4 Drain the fish thoroughly, discarding the vinegar. Place the fish in a fish kettle or large skillet so they touch. When the wine mixture boils, strain gently over the fish so they are about half covered. Cover the pan and simmer very gently for 15 minutes.

5 Carefully remove the fish from the pan, draining off as much of the liquid as possible, and arrange on a serving dish. Keep warm.

6 Boil the cooking liquid until reduced to about 4–6 tbsp. Melt the butter in a pan and strain in the cooking liquor. Season and spoon the sauce over the fish. Garnish and serve.

Broiled Stuffed Sole

A delicious stuffing of sun-dried tomatoes and fresh lemon thyme are used to stuff whole sole.

NUTRITIONAL INFORMATION

Calories 207   Sugars 0.2g
Protein . . . . .24g   Fat 10g
Carbohydrate . . . .8g   Saturates 4g

 25 MINS   20 MINS

SERVES 4

INGREDIENTS

1 tbsp olive oil

2 tbsp butter

1 small onion, finely chopped

1 garlic clove, chopped

3 sun-dried tomatoes, chopped

2 tbsp lemon thyme

1¾ oz bread crumbs

1 tbsp lemon juice

4 small whole sole, gutted and cleaned

salt and pepper

lemon wedges, to garnish

fresh green salad leaves, to serve

1 Heat the oil and butter in a skillet until it just begins to froth.

2 Add the onion and garlic to the skillet and cook, stirring, for 5 minutes until just softened.

3 To make the stuffing, mix the tomatoes, thyme, bread crumbs, and lemon juice in a bowl, and season.

4 Add the stuffing mixture to the pan, and stir to mix.

5 Using a sharp knife, pare the skin from the bone inside the gut hole of the

fish to make a pocket. Spoon the tomato and herb stuffing into the pocket.

6 Cook the fish, under a preheated broiler, for 6 minutes on each side or until golden brown.

7 Transfer the stuffed fish to serving plates and garnish with lemon wedges. Serve immediately with fresh green salad leaves.

COOK'S TIP

Lemon thyme (*Thymus* x *citriodorus*) has a delicate lemon scent and flavor. Ordinary thyme can be used instead, but mix it with 1 teaspoon of lemon rind to add extra flavor.

Sole Fillets in Marsala

A rich wine and cream sauce makes this an excellent dinner party dish. Make the stock the day before to cut down on the preparation time.

NUTRITIONAL INFORMATION

Calories	474	Sugars	.........3g
Protein	........47g	Fat	..........28g
Carbohydrate	....3g	Saturates	......14g

1¼ HOURS   1½ HOURS

SERVES 4

INGREDIENTS

1 tbsp peppercorns, lightly crushed

8 sole fillets

⅓ cup Marsala

⅔ cup heavy cream

STOCK

2½ cups water

bones and skin from the sole fillets

1 onion, peeled and halved

1 carrot, peeled and halved

3 fresh bay leaves

SAUCE

1 tbsp olive oil

1 tbsp butter

4 shallots, finely chopped

3½ oz baby button mushrooms, wiped and halved

1 To make the stock, place the water, fish bones and skin, onion, carrot, and bay leaves in a large saucepan and bring to a boil.

2 Reduce the heat and leave the mixture to simmer for 1 hour or until the stock has reduced to about ⅔ cup. Drain the stock through a fine strainer, discarding the bones and vegetables, and set aside.

3 To make the sauce, heat the oil and butter in a skillet. Add the shallots and cook, stirring, for 2–3 minutes or until just softened.

4 Add the mushrooms to the skillet and cook, stirring, for a further 2–3 minutes or until they are just beginning to brown.

5 Add the peppercorns and sole fillets to the skillet in batches. Fry the sole fillets for 3–4 minutes on each side or until golden brown. Remove the fish with

a draining spoon, set aside and keep warm while you cook the remainder.

6 When all the fillets have been cooked and removed from the pan, pour the wine and stock into the pan and leave to simmer for 3 minutes. Increase the heat and boil the mixture in the pan for about 5 minutes or until the sauce has reduced and thickened.

7 Pour in the cream and heat through. Pour the sauce over the fish and serve with the cooked vegetables of your choice.

Salt Cod Fritters

These tasty little fried fish cakes make an excellent snack or main course. Prepare in advance as the salt cod needs to be soaked overnight.

NUTRITIONAL INFORMATION

Calories ....142 Sugars 2g
Protein ....10g Fat 5g
Carbohydrate ...14g Saturates 1g

30 MINS   45 MINS

SERVES 6

INGREDIENTS

3½ oz self-rising flour

1 egg, beaten

⅔ cup milk

9 oz salt cod, soaked overnight

1 small red onion, finely chopped

1 small fennel bulb, finely chopped

1 red chili, finely chopped

2 tbsp oil

TO SERVE

crisp salad and chili relish, or cooked rice
  and fresh vegetables

1 Sift the flour into a large bowl. Make a well in the center of the flour and add the egg.

2 Using a wooden spoon, gradually draw in the flour, slowly adding the milk, and mix to form a smooth batter. Leave to stand for 10 minutes.

3 Drain the salt cod and rinse it under cold running water. Drain again thoroughly.

4 Remove and discard the skin and any bones from the fish, then mash the flesh with a fork.

5 Place the fish in a large bowl and combine with the onion, fennel, and chili. Add the mixture to the batter and blend together.

6 Heat the oil in a large skillet and, taking about 1 tablespoon of the mixture at a time, spoon it into the hot oil. Cook the fritters, in batches, for 3–4 minutes on each side until golden and slightly puffed. Keep warm while cooking the remaining mixture.

7 Serve with salad and a chili relish for a light meal or with vegetables and rice.

COOK'S TIP

If you prefer larger fritters, use 2 tablespoons per fritter and cook for slightly longer.

Celery & Salt Cod Casserole

Salt cod is dried and salted in order to preserve it. It has an unusual flavor, which goes particularly well with celery in this dish.

NUTRITIONAL INFORMATION

Calories 173	Sugars 3g	
Protein 14g	Fat 12g	
Carbohydrate 3g	Saturates 1g	

25 MINS   25 MINS

SERVES 4

I N G R E D I E N T S

9 oz salt cod, soaked overnight

1 tbsp oil

4 shallots, finely chopped

2 garlic cloves, chopped

3 celery stalks, chopped

1 x 14 oz can tomatoes, chopped

⅔ cup fish stock

1¾ oz pine nuts

2 tbsp roughly chopped tarragon

2 tbsp capers

crusty bread or mashed potato, to serve

1 Drain the salt cod, rinse it under plenty of running water and drain again thoroughly. Remove and discard any skin and bones. Pat the fish dry with paper towels and cut it into chunks.

2 Heat the oil in a large skillet. Add the shallots and garlic and cook for 2–3 minutes. Add the celery and cook for a further 2 minutes, then add the tomatoes and stock.

3 Bring the mixture to a boil, reduce the heat, and leave to simmer for about 5 minutes.

4 Add the fish and cook for 10 minutes or until tender.

5 Meanwhile, place the pine nuts on a baking sheet. Place under a preheated broiler and toast for 2–3 minutes or until golden.

6 Stir the tarragon, capers, and pine nuts into the fish casserole and heat gently to warm through.

7 Transfer to serving plates and serve with lots of fresh crusty bread or mashed potato.

COOK'S TIP

Salt cod is a useful ingredient to keep in the storecupboard and, once soaked, can be used in the same way as any other fish. It does, however, have a stronger, salty flavor than normal. It can be found in fish stores, larger supermarkets and delicatessens.

Italian Cod

Cod roasted with herbs and topped with a lemon and rosemary crust is a delicious main course.

10 MINS   35 MINS

SERVES 4

INGREDIENTS

2 tbsp butter

1¾ oz whole-wheat bread crumbs

1 oz chopped walnuts

grated rind and juice of 2 lemons

2 sprigs rosemary, stalks removed

2 tbsp chopped parsley

4 cod fillets, each about 5½ oz

1 garlic clove, crushed

3 tbsp walnut oil

1 small red chili, diced

salad leaves, to serve

VARIATION

If preferred, the walnuts may be omitted from the crust. In addition, extra virgin olive oil can be used instead of walnut oil, if you prefer.

1 Melt the butter in a large saucepan, stirring.

2 Remove the pan from the heat and add the bread crumbs, walnuts, the rind and juice of 1 lemon, half of the rosemary, and half of the parsley.

3 Press the breadcrumb mixture over the top of the cod fillets. Place the cod fillets in a foil-lined roasting pan.

4 Bake in a preheated oven at 400°F for 25–30 minutes.

5 Mix the garlic, the remaining lemon rind and juice, rosemary, parsley, and chili in a bowl. Beat in the walnut oil and mix to combine. Drizzle the dressing over the cod steaks as soon as they are cooked.

6 Transfer to serving plates and serve immediately.

Smoked Haddock Casserole

This quick, easy, and inexpensive dish would be ideal for a mid-week family supper.

NUTRITIONAL INFORMATION

Calories ....525 Sugars 8g
Protein ....41g Fat 18g
Carbohydrate ...53g Saturates 10g

20 MINS   45 MINS

SERVES 4

INGREDIENTS

2 tbsp butter, plus extra for greasing

1 lb smoked haddock fillets,
    cut into 4 slices

2½ cups milk

¼ cup all purpose flour

pinch of freshly grated nutmeg

3 tbsp heavy cream

1 tbsp chopped fresh parsley

2 eggs, hard cooked and mashed to a pulp

4 cups dried fusilli

1 tbsp lemon juice

salt and pepper

boiled new potatoes and beet, to serve

1 Thoroughly grease a casserole with butter. Put the haddock in the casserole and pour over the milk. Bake in a preheated oven at 400°F for about 15 minutes. Carefully pour the cooking liquid into a pitcher without breaking up the fish.

2 Melt the butter in a saucepan and stir in the flour. Gradually whisk in the reserved cooking liquid. Season to taste with salt, pepper, and nutmeg. Stir in the cream, parsley, and mashed egg and cook, stirring constantly, for 2 minutes.

3 Meanwhile, bring a large saucepan of lightly salted water to a boil. Add the fusilli and lemon juice and cook for 8–10 minutes until tender, but still firm to the bite.

4 Drain the pasta and spoon or tip it over the fish. Top with the egg sauce and return the casserole to the oven for 10 minutes.

5 Serve the casserole with boiled new potatoes and beet.

VARIATION

You can use any type of dried pasta for this casserole. Try penne, conchiglie, or rigatoni.

Sardinian Red Mullet

Red mullet has a beautiful pink skin, which is enhanced in this dish by being cooked in red wine and orange juice.

NUTRITIONAL INFORMATION

Calories	287	Sugars	........15g
Protein	........31g	Fat	...........9g
Carbohydrate	...15g	Saturates	.......1g

2¹/₂ HOURS   25 MINS

SERVES 4

INGREDIENTS

1¾ oz golden raisins

⅔ cup red wine

2 tbsp olive oil

2 medium onions, sliced

1 zucchini, cut into 2 inch sticks

2 oranges

2 tsp coriander seeds, lightly crushed

4 red mullet, boned and filleted

1¾ oz can anchovy fillets, drained

2 tbsp chopped, fresh oregano

1 Place the golden raisins in a bowl. Pour over the red wine and leave to soak for about 10 minutes.

COOK'S TIP

Red mullet is usually available all year round – frozen, if not fresh – from your fish store or supermarket. If you cannot get hold of it try using telapia. This dish can also be served warm, if you prefer.

2 Heat the oil in a large skillet. Add the onions and sauté for 2 minutes.

3 Add the zucchini to the pan and fry for a further 3 minutes or until tender.

4 Using a citrus zester, pare long, thin strips from one of the oranges. Using a sharp knife, remove the skin from both of the oranges, then segment the oranges by slicing between the lines of pith.

5 Add the orange zest to the skillet with the coriander seeds, red wine, golden raisins, red mullet, and anchovies to the pan and leave to simmer for 10–15 minutes or until the fish is cooked through.

6 Stir in the oregano, set aside and leave to cool. Place the mixture in a large bowl and leave to chill, covered, in the refrigerator for at least 2 hours to allow the flavors to mingle. Transfer to serving plates and serve.

Baked Red Snapper

You can substitute other whole fish for the snapper, or use cutlets of cod or halibut.

NUTRITIONAL INFORMATION

Calories	.519	Sugars	.12g
Protein	.61g	Fat	.23g
Carbohydrate	.18g	Saturates	.3g

20 MINS   50 MINS

SERVES 4

INGREDIENTS

1 red snapper, about 2 lb 12 oz, cleaned

juice of 2 limes, or 1 lemon

4-5 sprigs of thyme or parsley

3 tbsp olive oil

1 large onion, chopped

2 garlic cloves, finely chopped

1 x 15 oz can chopped tomatoes

2 tbsp tomato paste

2 tbsp red wine vinegar

5 tbsp low-fat yogurt

2 tbsp chopped parsley

2 tsp dried oregano

6 tbsp dry bread crumbs

¼ cup low-fat cheese, crumbled

salt and pepper

SALAD

1 small lettuce, thickly sliced

10-12 young spinach leaves, torn

½ small cucumber, sliced and quartered

4 scallions, thickly sliced

3 tbsp chopped parsley

2 tbsp olive oil

2 tbsp plain low-fat yogurt

1 tbsp red wine vinegar

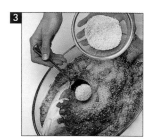

1 Sprinkle the lime or lemon juice inside and over the fish and season. Place the herbs inside the fish.

2 Heat the oil in a pan and fry the onion until translucent. Stir in the garlic and cook for 1 minute, then add the chopped tomatoes, tomato paste, and vinegar. Simmer, uncovered, for 5 minutes. Allow the sauce to cool, then stir in the yogurt, parsley, and oregano.

3 Pour half of the sauce into an ovenproof dish just large enough for the fish. Add the fish and then pour the remainder of the sauce over it, and sprinkle with bread crumbs. Bake uncovered for 30-35 minutes. Sprinkle the cheese over the fish and serve with lime wedges and dill sprigs.

4 Arrange the salad ingredients in a bowl. Whisk the oil, yogurt, and vinegar and pour over the salad.

Marinated Fish

Marinating fish, for even a short period, adds a subtle flavor to the flesh and makes even simply broiled or fried fish delicious.

NUTRITIONAL INFORMATION

Calories	361	Sugars	. . . . .0g
Protein	. . . . .26g	Fat	. . . . .29g
Carbohydrate	. . . .0g	Saturates	. . . . . . .5g

45 MINS   15 MINS

SERVES 4

I N G R E D I E N T S

4 whole mackerel, cleaned and gutted

4 tbsp chopped marjoram

2 tbsp extra virgin olive oil

finely grated rind and juice of 1 lime

2 garlic cloves, minced

salt and pepper

1 Under gently running water, scrape the mackerel with the blunt side of a knife to remove any scales.

2 Using a sharp knife, make a slit in the stomach of the fish and cut horizontally along until the knife will go no further very easily. Gut the fish and rinse under water. You may prefer to remove the heads before cooking, but it is not necessary.

3 Using a sharp knife, cut 4–5 diagonal slashes on each side of the fish. Place the fish in a shallow, non-metallic dish.

4 To make the marinade, mix together the marjoram, olive oil, lime rind and juice, garlic, and salt and pepper in a bowl.

5 Pour the mixture over the fish. Leave to marinate in the refrigerator for about 30 minutes.

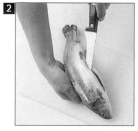  

6 Cook the mackerel, under a preheated broiler, for 5–6 minutes on each side, brushing occasionally with the reserved marinade, until golden.

7 Transfer the fish to serving plates. Pour over any remaining marinade before serving.

COOK'S TIP

If the lime is too hard to squeeze, microwave on high power for 30 seconds to release the juice. This dish is also excellent cooked on the grill.

Squid & Macaroni Stew

This scrumptious seafood dish is quick and easy to make, yet deliciously satisfying to eat.

NUTRITIONAL INFORMATION

Calories 292	Sugars 3g
Protein 13g	Fat 14g
Carbohydrate ...24g	Saturates 2g

15 MINS   35 MINS

SERVES 6

I N G R E D I E N T S

2 cups dried short-cut macaroni or other
   small pasta shapes

7 tbsp olive oil

2 onions, sliced

12 oz prepared squid, cut into
   1½ inch strips

1 cup fish stock

⅝ cup red wine

12 oz tomatoes, skinned and thinly sliced

2 tbsp tomato paste

1 tsp dried oregano

2 bay leaves

2 tbsp chopped fresh parsley

salt and pepper

crusty bread, to serve

1 Bring a large saucepan of lightly salted water to a boil. Add the pasta and 1 tablespoon of the olive oil and cook for 3 minutes. Drain, return to the pan, cover, and keep warm.

2 Heat the remaining oil in a pan over a medium heat. Add the onions and fry until they are translucent. Add the squid and stock and simmer for 5 minutes. Pour in the wine and add the tomatoes, tomato paste, oregano, and bay leaves. Bring the sauce to a boil, season to taste, and cook for 5 minutes.

3 Stir the pasta into the pan, cover and simmer for about 10 minutes, or until the squid and macaroni are tender and the sauce has thickened. If the sauce remains too liquid, uncover the pan and continue cooking for a few minutes longer.

4 Remove and discard the bay leaves. Reserve a little parsley and stir the remainder into the pan. Transfer to a warm serving dish and sprinkle over the remaining parsley. Serve with crusty bread to soak up the sauce.

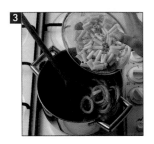

COOK'S TIP

To prepare squid, peel off the skin, then cut off the head and tentacles. Discard the transparent flat oval bone from the body. Remove the sac of black ink, then turn the body sac inside out. Wash in cold water. Cut off the tentacles; discard the rest. Rinse.

Stuffed Squid

Whole squid are stuffed with a mixture of fresh herbs and sun-dried tomatoes and then cooked in a wine sauce.

NUTRITIONAL INFORMATION

Calories 276   Sugars 1g
Protein . . . . .23g   Fat 8g
Carbohydrate . . .20g   Saturates 1g

25 MINS   35 MINS

SERVES 4

I N G R E D I E N T S

8 squid, cleaned and gutted but left whole
   (ask your fish store to do this)

6 canned anchovies, chopped

2 garlic cloves, chopped

2 tbsp rosemary, stalks removed and
   leaves chopped

2 sun-dried tomatoes, chopped

5½ oz bread crumbs

1 tbsp olive oil

1 onion, finely chopped

¾ cup white wine

¾ cup fish stock

cooked rice, to serve

1 Remove the tentacles from the body of the squid and chop the flesh finely.

2 Grind the anchovies, garlic, rosemary, and tomatoes to a paste in a mortar and pestle.

3 Add the bread crumbs and the chopped squid tentacles and mix. If the mixture is too dry to form a thick paste at this point, add 1 teaspoon of water.

4 Spoon the paste into the body sacs of the squid then tie a length of cotton around the end of each sac to fasten

them. Do not overfill the sacs, because they will expand during cooking.

5 Heat the oil in a skillet. Add the onion and cook, stirring, for 3–4 minutes or until golden.

6 Add the stuffed squid to the pan and cook for 3–4 minutes or until brown all over.

7 Add the wine and stock and bring to a boil. Reduce the heat, cover and then leave to simmer for 15 minutes.

8 Remove the lid and cook for a further 5 minutes or until the squid is tender and the juices reduced. Serve with plenty of cooked rice.

Squid Casserole

Squid is often served fried in Italy, but here it is casseroled with tomatoes and bell peppers to give a rich sauce.

NUTRITIONAL INFORMATION

Calories 281	Sugars 8g
Protein 31g	Fat 10g
Carbohydrate 9g	Saturates 1g

 25 MINS   1½ HOURS

SERVES 4

INGREDIENTS

2 lb whole squid, cleaned or

   1 lb 10 oz squid rings, defrosted if frozen

3 tbsp olive oil

1 large onion, sliced thinly

2 garlic cloves, minced

1 red bell pepper, cored, seeded and sliced

1–2 sprigs fresh rosemary

⅔ cup dry white wine and 1 cup water, or

   1½ cups water or fish stock

14 oz can chopped tomatoes

2 tbsp tomato paste

1 tsp paprika

salt and pepper

fresh sprigs of rosemary or parsley,

to garnish

1 Cut the squid pouch into ½ inch slices; cut the tentacles into lengths of about 2 inches. If using frozen squid rings, make sure they are fully defrosted and well drained.

2 Heat the oil in a flameproof casserole and fry the onion and garlic gently until soft. Add the squid, increase the heat, and continue to cook for about 10 minutes until sealed and beginning to color lightly. Add the red bell pepper, rosemary, wine (if using), and water or stock and bring up to a boil. Cover and simmer gently for 45 minutes.

3 Discard the sprigs of rosemary (but don't take out any leaves that have come off). Add the tomatoes, tomato paste, seasonings, and paprika. Continue to simmer gently for 45–60 minutes, or cover the casserole tightly and cook in a moderate oven, 350°F, for 45–60 minutes until tender.

4 Give the sauce a good stir, season, and serve with fresh, crusty bread.

Pan-Fried Shrimp

A luxurious dish which makes an impressive starter or light meal.
Shrimp and garlic are a winning combination.

NUTRITIONAL INFORMATION

Calories .... .455   Sugars 0g
Protein .... .6g   Fat .... .37g
Carbohydrate ... .0g   Saturates ...... .18g

 10 MINS   5 MINS

SERVES 4

I N G R E D I E N T S

4 garlic cloves

20–24 unshelled large raw shrimp

8 tbsp butter

4 tbsp olive oil

6 tbsp brandy

salt and pepper

2 tbsp chopped fresh parsley

TO SERVE

lemon wedges

ciabatta bread

1 Using a sharp knife, peel and slice the garlic.

2 Wash the shrimp and pat dry using paper towels.

3 Melt the butter with the oil in a large skillet, add the garlic and shrimp, and fry over a high heat, stirring, for 3–4 minutes until the shrimp are pink.

4 Sprinkle with brandy and season with salt and pepper to taste. Sprinkle with parsley and serve immediately with lemon wedges and ciabatta bread, if liked.

Mussel Casserole

Mussels are not difficult to cook, just a little messy to eat. Serve this dish with a finger bowl to help keep things clean!

NUTRITIONAL INFORMATION

Calories 299	Sugars 3g	
Protein 33g	Fat 7g	
Carbohydrate 3g	Saturates 1g	

 25 MINS   25 MINS

SERVES 4

INGREDIENTS

2 lb mussels

⅔ cup white wine

1 tbsp oil

1 onion, finely chopped

3 garlic cloves, chopped

1 red chili, finely chopped

3½ oz sieved tomatoes

1 tbsp chopped marjoram

toast or crusty bread, to serve

1 Scrub the mussels to remove any mud or sand.

2 Remove the beards from the mussels by pulling away the hairy bit between the two shells. Rinse the mussels in a bowl of clean water. Discard any mussels that do not close when they are tapped – they are dead and should not be eaten.

3 Place the mussels in a large saucepan. Pour in the wine and cook for 5 minutes, shaking the pan occasionally until the shells open. Remove and discard any mussels that do not open.

4 Remove the mussels from the saucepan. Strain the cooking liquid through a fine strainer set over a bowl, reserving the liquid.

5 Heat the oil in a large skillet. Add the onion, garlic, and chili and cook for 4–5 minutes or until just softened.

6 Add the reserved cooking liquid to the pan and cook for 5 minutes or until reduced, stirring.

7 Stir in the sieved tomatoes, marjoram, and mussels and cook until hot, about 3 minutes.

8 Transfer to serving bowls and serve with toast or plenty of crusty bread to mop up the juices.

COOK'S TIP

Finger bowls are individual bowls of warm water with a slice of lemon floating in them. They are used to clean your fingers at the end of a meal.

Mussels with Tomato Sauce

This recipe for Mediterranean-style baked mussels, topped with a fresh tomato sauce and bread crumbs, has been adapted for the microwave.

NUTRITIONAL INFORMATION

Calories . . . . . . .254 Sugars 1g
Protein . . . . .37g Fat 10g
Carbohydrate . . . .4g Saturates 3g

20 MINS   15 MINS

SERVES 4

INGREDIENTS

½ small onion, chopped

1 garlic clove, minced

1 tbsp olive oil

3 tomatoes

1 tbsp chopped fresh parsley

2 lb live mussels

1 tbsp freshly grated Parmesan cheese

1 tbsp fresh white bread crumbs

salt and pepper

chopped fresh parsley, to garnish

1 Place the onion, garlic, and oil in a bowl. Cover and cook on HIGH power for 3 minutes.

2 Cut a cross in the base of each tomato and place them in a small bowl. Pour on boiling water and leave for about 45 seconds. Drain and then plunge into cold water. The skins will slide off easily. Chop the tomatoes, removing any hard cores.

3 Add the tomatoes to the onion mixture, cover, and cook on HIGH power for 3 minutes. Stir in the parsley and season to taste.

4 Scrub the mussels well in several changes of cold water. Remove the beards and discard any open mussels and those which do not close when tapped sharply with the back of a knife.

5 Place the mussels in a large bowl. Add enough boiling water to cover them. Cover and cook on HIGH power for 2 minutes, stirring halfway through, until the mussels open. Drain well and remove the empty half of each shell. Arrange the mussels in 1 layer on a plate.

6 Spoon the tomato sauce over each mussel. Mix the Parmesan cheese with the bread crumbs and sprinkle on top.

Cook, uncovered, on HIGH power for 2 minutes. Garnish with parsley and serve.

COOK'S TIP

Dry out the bread crumbs in the microwave for an extra crunchy topping. Spread them on a plate and cook on HIGH power for 2 minutes, stirring once. Leave to stand, uncovered.

Index